THOMAS BURKE RESTLESS REVOLUTIONARY

John Sayle Watterson

University Press
of America™

TO DIXIE

TABLE OF CONTENTS

INTRODUCTION

The unusual career of Thomas Burke stems in part from the distinct character of the American Revolution. "Politics" during that formative period attained a dignity and urgency that has rarely been surpassed. The officeholder was not simply a politician, but an advocate who first argued for colonial rights against Great Britain and then became a public architect combining theory and experience to reconstruct the system. When British control collapsed in 1775 and 1776, old patterns momentarily disintegrated. Men who might never have stood for election were drafted into the constitutional conventions and assemblies. A few like Burke rode this wave into the center of national politics. The tempo of ideas and trends accelerated, as if in the path of a tempest; political careers that might ordinarily have spanned a generation were compressed into the relatively brief period of national crisis. The new credo of republicanism released political energies that could be sublimely creative as well as blindly destructive, and in the rapid onrush of events be dissolved in the turmoil that accompanies such upheaval.

Burke's meteoric ascent would not have occurred in quieter times, nor would his fortunes have collapsed so rapidly once established. During his seven years of public service, he was always located in the eye of the storm, especially as a member of Congress and later as Governor of North Carolina during the British campaign in the South. As a self-styled expert on republican institutions and advocate for his state, Burke formulated the doctrine of states' rights before his contemporaries had observed any discrepancies in the newly created national establishment. His most noteworthy contribution was the proposal of a states' rights amendment to the Articles of Confederation. As a result, he qualifies as a major figure in the drama of states' rights, its first advocate after independence and originator of one of its most celebrated principles. Despite significant changes in wording, the basis of his proposal survives today in the Tenth Amendment of the Bill of Rights.

Of course, Burke was involved in a life and death struggle, and as such he responded to the shifting priorities of that experience. After his states' rights phase, he was drawn toward opposing views of the needs of the states and the United States. At the end of his career, he would adopt a drastically altered view of the Revolution and his part in it. In these varying roles, Burke's career provides a fresh perspective, one not drawn from the usual vantage points. An immigrant to America, dead before the age of forty, he participated in neither of the touchstones of the Revolutionary era, the Declaration of Independence or the Constitutional Convention of 1787. Yet, Burke may be more representative of Revolutionary politics than many who did, for his career was wholly a product of that peculiar experience and the extraordinary events that it produced.

The two centers of Burke's political activity were the Revolutionary conventions of North Carolina and the Congress at Philadelphia. The events of his budding career in Orange County, North Carolina, his early affiliations, and public attitudes shed light both on Burke himself and on the complex web of North Carolina politics, which has been so often misunderstood. In turn, the political milieu of national politics, in which Burke served from 1777 to 1781, has frequently been ignored by historians in favor of prewar protest, independence, the Constitution, and military affairs. Yet, while Burke was in Congress, most of the central concepts that would be contested in the 1780's and even afterward, had been set forth by the delegates in Congress, including Burke in his advocacy of states' rights. Despite the financial quagmire, administrative inefficiency, and a functionally weak form of government, the national government survived and gave a measure of direction to the war effort. The experience of those perpetual crises provided the key to restructuring the system after the war was over.

In my research, I relied primarily on two
collections of manuscripts: the Thomas Burke
Papers, 1763-1789, in the Southern Historical
Collection at the University of North Carolina
at Chapel Hill and the Thomas Burke Papers, 1763-
1852, in the State Department of Archives and History at Raleigh. These two collections, which
have been brought together in a single microfilmed
collection, provide a basis for understanding
Burke's public as well as personal life. The bulk
of these papers pertain to his career in Congress
and term as Governor. Certain aspects of his life,
such as his early years in Virginia and his relationship with his wife, appear infrequently. In
addition to these materials, I found useful items
in the *Colonial* and *State Records of North Carolina* as well as in the *Virginia Gazettes*. My research also led me to repositories in North Carolina, Virginia, Pennsylvania, and Michigan, as
well as the Library of Congress. In these loca-
tions, I found relatively few items, but some of
them proved unexpectedly useful. I was fortunate
that the Burke Papers formerly in the possession
of the Johnston family of Marion, Alabama, came
to light while I was working on Burke and helped
to round out my picture of him. The inventory of
Burke's will in the Orange County Records at the
State Department of Archives and History gave me
an insight into his intellectual life through the
listing of books in his possession at his death.
In addition, I had a search conducted by the Genealogical Section at Dublin Castle, which did indicate that Burke came from an Anglo-Irish Protestant rather than Roman Catholic background.

I have always dreamed of finding a portrait
of Thomas Burke. The closest I came were des-
criptions in letters as well as family items be-
longing to G. Burke Johnston of Blacksburg, Virginia, among them Burke's seal. The reactions of
friends and adversaries give a vivid picture of
his personality, one of force, intelligence, and
replete with contradictions. I have not attempted
to psychoanalyze Burke--the materials are insuffi-
cient--but to understand him in terms of his own
political experiences and the Revolutionary milieu.
I do not claim that he was unique in his ideas or

always in his responses to situations, but I know of no individual of his generation to whom life or his career can be closely compared.

This biography of Thomas Burke was first undertaken as a Ph.D. dissertation at Northwestern University. My wife Dixie has been closely associated with its creation. Her editing and suggestions have been invaluable. I would also like to acknowledge the support of my major adviser at Northwestern, Clarence Ver Steeg, and the encouragement of my colleagues in the Department of History at The University of South Dakota. I wish also to thank Professor G. Burke Johnston and Mary Tabb Johnston of Blacksburg, Virginia for their helpfulness in making their Burke materials available to me.

It is my hope that this biography will give to Burke the recognition and attention that his brief but influential and poignant life deserves.

ABOUT THE AUTHOR

John Sayle Watterson was born in Cleveland,
Ohio, and graduated from University School. He
received his B.A. from the University of Virginia,
his M.A. from Western Reserve University and Ph.D.
from Northwestern University. Since 1970, he
has taught at the University of South Dakota, where
he is currently an Associate Professor of History.
He and his wife, Dixie, have twin daughters, Martha
Sayle and Emily Burke.

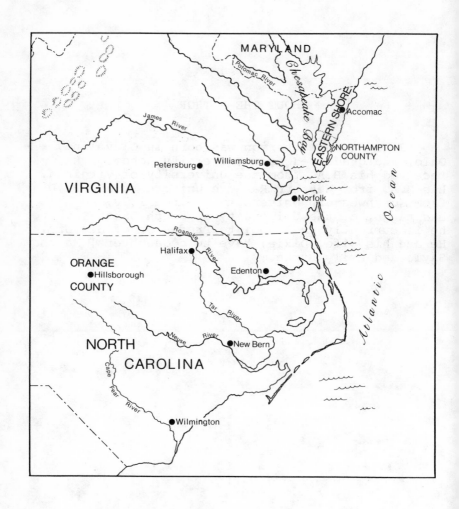

"HYMN TO SPRING"

In the eighteenth century, the pace of immi-
gration into the American colonies had dramatically
risen. Many of those disembarking in America had
come from the far corners of the British Isles,
including Scotland and Ireland. While a majority
were from poor, rural backgrounds, a few were drawn
from the educated or well-to-do, and would step
into careers as merchants, lawyers, or doctors.
Later, some of these newcomers were even involved
in the American Revolution.

One such immigrant was Thomas Burke. Unlike
his American-born contemporaries, Burke qualified
as a citizen of the empire, who had glimpsed more
than one facet of the British system and had been
exposed to ideas and experiences on two continents.
Yet, his commitment to the rights of Englishmen,
to the interests of the new nation, and to the creed
of republicanism was as strongly anchored as if he
had been born in Virginia or North Carolina.
Burke's political insights, which led him to anticipate such issues as states' rights and nationalism, originated in several layers of experience,
including that of representing North Carolina in
Congress. If he had begun life in Norfolk or
Hillsborough, however, it is unlikely that he
would have been as sensitive to the discrepancies
in the new American system of government. His
flight from Ireland, though obscure in its details,
was the beginning of his Revolutionary career.

Thomas Burke was born in 1744 or 1745 in Ireland. Though his ancestors had once lived in Con-
naught province, he grew up in Dublin where his
family was probably affiliated with the Protestant
Church of Ireland. If the Burkes had once been
wealthy landed gentry, as he later intimated, this
was no longer the case, and the prospects of his
immediate family were far from satisfactory. In
later years, Burke practically never mentioned his
parents, Ulick and Letitia, but with his Uncle,
Sir Fielding Ould, he obviously felt a strong bond.
Sir Fielding had distinguished himself as a physi-

cian, the same profession that Burke himself would
at first embrace. When he afterwards wrote his
uncle from Virginia, Burke's obvious, almost im-
modest attempts to impress him indicate that Fielding Ould had once held a significant place in his
life. In a different sense, this was also true
of his cousin, Miss Sidney Shaw, who became for
him the girl he had left behind. Writing to her
years afterward from Virginia, his memory of her
was still strong, and he once again was the adolescent brimming with his own youthful accomplishments and nostalgia for his native Ireland.[1]

Burke put his childhood behind him when he
left home around the age of fifteen. His departure brought a total break both physically and
spiritually with his Irish past. He once crypti-
cally commented that he had been given a choice
between "Domestick [sic] Indolent Dependence or
an Enterprising Peregrination."[2] Probably his
migration to the colonies was precipitated by a
quarrel with his family. Seven years later, it
still rankled in his memory as he indignantly
referred to being persecuted, abandoned, and
denied justice--and recalled "his melancholy
enmity" that he had held so long afterwards.[3]
Whatever happened, Burke felt that it was he,
free of "vices" and "levity," who had been
wronged.[4] This feeling of having been mistreated
and the resulting vulnerability stayed with him
throughout his life. The deep wound--or what it
symbolized--never entirely healed. When his de-
fenses dropped or when he felt himself unjustly
criticized, he would again react with the hatred
and anguish of a boy of fourteen. This was a dis-
cordant note in what otherwise was a bright and
highly capable individual; it often seemed
strangely at odds with his commitment to order
and rationality.

"Tom" Burke, as his friends in Dublin called
him, probably left Ireland in 1759 or 1760. When
he emerged in America, he was living on the Eastern Shore of Virginia, that portion of Virginia
separated from the Mainland by the Chesapeake
Bay. The records of Northampton County indicate
that he was established there by 1760 and that in

2

November of 1761, he and a companion were charged with gambling on county court day.[5] In 1763 and perhaps earlier, he was practicing medicine and thereafter would be referred to as "Dr. Burke." In Ireland, he had received a formal education, and throughout his life he would remain an avid reader of serious works.[6] Even with his education, Burke's medicine was largely self-taught. In his letter to Sir Fielding Ould, he boasted of a familiarity with Newtonian principles and their application to medicine. He assured his uncle that he had worked very hard at his profession and had acquired a proficiency equal or superior to most he encountered. In view of his later achievements in the law and politics, he was probably not greatly exaggerating.[7]

The physician in eighteenth century Virginia, however, was poorly paid for his labors and forever plagued with unpaid bills. Having mastered the technical skills, Burke was dissatisfied with the returns from his medical practice. In about 1765 and 1766, he began to prepare himself for the law, a career that promised more rewards, plunging into this new endeavor with characteristic energy and aplomb. As he explained it, he had in his "earliest years acquired an Art of methodizing my Thoughts and Reasonings and this made every Species of study easy to me..."[8] According to Burke, he easily passed his licensing examinations to the plaudits of the examiners.[9] Medicine was now relegated to occasional visits with patients in extreme distress, while his new profession consumed most of his time. His practice involved periodic appearances before the county court of Northampton as well as efforts to cultivate contacts with the merchants, whose patronage was necessary for success in the law. If such efforts were successful, he could hope to overcome the limitations of being a propertyless immigrant and begin to accumulate a fortune of his own.[10]

As Burke brashly testified, it was his capacity and perseverance that made it possible to establish himself in a new country and move from one profession into another. Yet he also made up for his lack of connections with a palpable charm

3

and capacity for friendship.[11] On the Eastern
Shore, he was held in high esteem by several young
men with whom he shared his knowledge and insights.
Women were fascinated by Burke as well, perhaps
because of a charm derived from his versatile intelligence and perhaps his unusual looks. Someone who later recorded a meeting with Burke described him as being of "Middle Stature, thin Vis-
age, Much Mark'd with Small Pox," in addition to
being blind in his right eye.[12]

Despite fond memories of Sidney Shaw, Burke
soon found new romantic interests. Indeed, he may
have entertained long-range hopes for Elizabeth
Harmanson, a young girl scarcely in her teens.
Burke must have glimpsed some unusual intelligence
or curiosity in Betsy, for he was soon writing to
her of authors like John Locke and Dean Swift.
He emphasized that a woman who was preoccupied
with domesticity often let her mind remain in an
undeveloped state. The ideal woman, he counseled,
should place cultivation of the mind above "house-
wifery."[13] As a model of what women might aspire
to, he called her attention to the writings of
Lady Mary Worley Montagu, whose letters from the
Near East had described the strange pagan customs
of the Turks. Betsy's mentor sent her his copy
of the letters and called her attention to the
despotic customs of the Turkish "Bassaws" who
cruelly and tyrannically ruled their households
like their kingdoms. As a student of the Enlightenment, Burke viewed the Turkish harem with
a mixture of fascination and contempt, especially
the tyranny of the male and the arbitrary grati-
fication of his passions. Yet, he reminded Betsy
that even in Turkey, women of "Beauty and Spirit"
when thrown with men of refinement could command
their respect and affection.[14]

Throughout Burke's earliest poems and his
letters to Betsy Harmanson, there is the recur-
ring theme of freedom coupled with the possibility of tyranny. Probably his early encounter with
parental tyranny made him receptive to the ideal
of freedom. But, it was the political opposition
to the Stamp Act that aroused him to the defense
of liberty and condemnation of British politics

4

as tyrannical. In a letter to Sir Fielding Ould, Burke proclaimed himself "a passionate lover of Liberty and Hater of Tyranny."[15] His arguments differed little from those of his fellow Americans. Liberty meant that laws should be based upon the consent of the political community which in turn should govern the disposition of their property. For Burke personally, liberty and property would be inseparably linked as well. It was his rebellion against the restraints of his family that had enabled him to escape "Domestick Indolent Dependence" and actively pursue his fortune.[16]

The campaign against the Stamp Act and its aftermath also provided him with his first taste of glory. In Northampton County, opposition had been fierce, and the County Court had gone so far as to declare it unconstitutional. News of the repeal of the Stamp Act had been greeted with great rejoicing and a celebration was planned. Burke had secretly written a poem for the occasion, which he intended to read anonymously. Reluctant to expose his private scribblings--lest he be branded with the "idle Character of a Rhimer"-- Burke showed it to a friend with the intention that he should read it.[17] The result was quite the opposite, but perhaps not that far from what the poet had hoped or even intended. The poem instead was passed from hand to hand, and the author's identity loudly acclaimed. Far from being frowned upon, he was instantly a celebrity. He was even persuaded to let the poem appear in print. Buoyant with success, he confided to his uncle that "universal Approbation re-echoed from every corner, the Author was looked upon as a Prodigy of Genious [sic]."[18] Eager to impress his uncle, he included some excerpts from the poem in his letter.

> Triumph *America*! Thy patriot Voice
> Has made the Greatest of Mankind rejoice
> Immortal *Pitt*, an ever glorious Name
> Far, far unequall'd in the Rolls of Fame?
> What Breast (for Virtue is by all approv'd
> and Freedom ev'n by *Asia's* Slaves belov'd),
> What Breast but glow with Gratitude to Thee;

Boast of Mankind, great Prop of Liberty!
Would 'twere in Pity to Mankind decreed
That still a *Pitt* should be to a *Pitt*
   succeed;
When proud Oppression would subvert the Laws,
That still a *Camden* should defend the Cause,
Nor let's forget the gallant Barre's Merit,
His *Tully's* Periods and his *Cato's* Spirit,
His too an honest, independent Heart,
Where Fear nor Fraud nor Avarice have
   Part.[19]

Burke who had been cautiously writing his
poems in shorthand now burst into public view,
joining the brigade of poets whose political satires filled the pages of the two newspapers.
In part, the poetry was an outgrowth of politics,
especially during the anxious decade of the 1760's.
Aside from the Stamp Act, there were local scandals
and debates that competed for public attention in
Virginia. It became known, for example, that the
late Treasurer and Speaker of the House of Bur-
gesses, John Robinson, had embezzled public funds
and had used them for loans to his hard-pressed
friends. Soon after the Robinson scandal was pub-
licized, a murder took place in Williamsburg, involving a prominent member of the gentry, Colonel
John Chiswell, who stabbed to death a Scottish
merchant following a drunken argument. Because
of his influential connections, which had included the late Speaker Robinson, he was released
on bail after a routine inquest. These episodes
only stoked the fires of political controversy,
some of which spilled over into the essays and
poems that appeared in the two gazettes.[20]

The poems often contained references to the
leading political figures mixed indiscriminately
with literary and classical allusions, and Burke's
were no exception: in his first political satire,
"An Address to the Goddess Dullness," he compared
the eloquence of the political figures and poets
that he admired to the dullness produced by some
of the poets whom he disliked. In another poem,
he launched a caustic attack on Landon Carter,
the province's chief landholder, who was also a
political figure and one of the poets involved

in the fray. Building upon classical mythology,
Burke showed his contempt for the aristocratic
grandee by having the goddess Diana turn "Carter
to an Ass."[21]

Such clever lines earned him a widening reputation and made him fair game for the other poets.
Though the poems were published anonymously or
under pseudonyms, some showed that they knew his
identity by referring to details of his appearance.
Said one: "Burke's eye, in double sense, is single, Enabling truth with wit to mingle..." others
who were less favorable wrote tiresome satires using references to his physical appearance and his
Irish background.[22] On January 22, 1767, one of
Burke's poems was featured by Rind's *Virginia
Gazette*, while his competitor Alexander Purdie
was running a satire on poetry supposedly coming
from "A------k" off the pen of "D----- B----."[23]
Within a few months, however, the poets began to
lose interest and the battle ceased.

Nevertheless, Burke's literary output continued for a time afterwards. Obviously, he had
enjoyed the contest and the notoriety that he
had gained. He even abandoned the usual pretense
at anonymity in an essay attacking the custom of
duelling. It was an odd cause for him to champion, since his sensitivity to public criticism
would later tempt him to defend his honor by combat.[24] Even more jarring was the poem which he
published anonymously in September of 1768 protesting the riots that had recently taken place
in Norfolk against innoculation for smallpox.
The victims whom he lavishly praised were the
wives of the merchants with whom he would soon be
associated in Norfolk and their enemies, the rioters, would become his adversaries. Although written in the popular mode, this imitation of the
epic poem was one of his worst efforts, laden
with melodrama and mawkish sentimentality, lengthy
and repetitive.[24]

Relentless hear the sickening virgin's moan;
Relentless see the mother's keen distress;
Whose trembling infants to their bosom press;

7

While furious fevers scorch their tender
   frames;
and fire each nerve with pestilential
   flames....[25]

Perhaps Burke, at best a mediocre rhymster,
was taking his literary reputation too seriously
and as a result inviting ridicule. One critic
with icy derision observed that Burke had "given
the *nerves the smallpox, made the clouds gape,*
heat Jove's *arm red hot,* and had made a Lady at
the same time, like the silver moon and the *blaz-
ing* sun; and then *changed* her into an Angel to
make her expostulate in a midnight bed and in a
desert wood."[26] Burke's response, comparing his
techniques to those of Homer, only brought more
savage attacks. After this Burke retired from
battle, allowing his muse to lay silent until
awakened by the onrush of the American Revolution.

By the time his critics lost interest, Burke
had left the scene of his literary debut, moving
from the Eastern shore to Norfolk in 1769. Despite his close friends and contacts, he probably
never intended to remain in Northampton.[27] Burke
already knew merchants, probably some from Norfolk,
and a seaport would provide more opportunities,
especially Norfolk which was a smaller version
of Dublin or Philadelphia. Norfolk served as a
trading center for North Carolina as well as Virginia, and its wharves were crowded with ships
from Great Britain and the West Indies. Much of
its commercial life was dominated by the English
and Scots merchants, who would shortly become his
chief patrons. The climate of money-making was
reflected in the opulent houses with elegant inter-
iors as well as in the crowded dockets of the
courts where estates were settled and lawsuits
initiated. Around the merchant elite spun a galaxy of enterprise and activity--slaves and sailors,
skilled workmen, and young lawyers like himself
who gained their entry into the law by collecting
debts. With its population of nearly five thousand, Norfolk was larger than any other southern
town expect Charles Town, South Carolina, and very
close to that.[28]

This rapid growth had created social tensions, especially with the influx of English and Scots merchants. Political dissension had been brought to the surface by the Stamp Act and the great debate over the limits of English authority. The anti-innoculation riots of 1768 reflected these political animosities, and the instigators of the rioting had earlier been opponents of the Stamp Act. Their hostility to innoculation was rooted in a deep hatred of the influential merchants who had taken the British side during the Stamp Act protest. It was difficult to live in Norfolk and to avoid taking sides, as Burke with his excitable temperament soon discovered.[29]

Ironically, the same young lawyer who had loudly championed the American cause was now identified with the merchant or loyalist factions, who were supporting his law practice. There is no sign that these new friends caused him any embarrassment. In 1769, the issue of loyalists had not reached the immutable stage that it would in 1775 and 1776, so that attitudes toward the mother country did not automatically determine who was a friend or a business associate. Yet, his letters during this period bear no mention of the dispute with Great Britain--despite the Townshend Acts and the tests of strength in Boston. Absorbed in his legal business, he seems to have lost interest in the larger political discussion.

Instead, Burke with his penchant for controversy was drawn into the maelstrom of local politics, particularly into a conflict with the Sergeant of the Borough, Joseph Calvert. The Sergeant had gained a reputation for harrassing the merchants of Norfolk with whom Burke was becoming associated. During the innoculation episode in August, which had inspired Burke's epic poem, Calvert had been responsible for inciting the mob to violence. Among his activities, Burke devoted his legal talents to freeing a merchant, Lewis Hansford, who had been summarily imprisoned by Joseph Calvert.[30] These efforts included an attempt to start an action of false imprisonment and civil suits against Calvert for

holding Hansford and other political prisoners
without a formal court appearance. Burke even
wrote George Wythe, the lawyer and legal philosopher, now a member of the General Court of Virginia, apprising him of what had happened and seeking
to remove the case from the local "Hustings Court"
of Norfolk to a new venue.[31] Given Burke's temperament, especially his contentiousness and
quickness to anger, such actions only served to
embroil him personally. Despite his recent essay
on duelling, he soon found himself challenged to
fight by Calvert's brother, who had "the Ignorant
Confidence to Expect me to become the challen-
ger."[32] Burke was especially antagonized by the
"abusive Language" which had perhaps been designed
to provoke him into combat.[33] He left the door
open to a contest, and Calvert responded by printing a notice that if he met Burke on the Princess
Anne Road he would expect satisfaction. The young
attorney laconically informed Calvert that he would
be on the Princess Anne Road on the first of August accompanied by a single companion. After be-
littling Calvert for insisting on a written reply
to his challenge, he sarcastically ended with the
cryptic finale that "Mr. Burke's Thumb is Sprained
and therefore cannot Finish---" as if he had suddenly become incapacitated.[34]

        After this orgy of insults, a fight did take
place, though its results are unknown. Burke's
friend John Tazewell wrote him not long afterwards
from Williamsburg deploring the violence and commenting that the accounts of both Burke and Calvert were remarkably alike. Tazewell queried
Burke if reconciliation might take place between
them and gently rebuked his contentious friend for
his involvement. "When I hear of any fresh Broil
in Norfolk," he observed, "it is very far from
being an Object of Myrth to me, especially when
you happen to be concerned in it, short as life
is it is subject to enough of unavoidable Ills...
but when to these private quarrels and animosities
are added, [it is] likely to end only with life..."[35]

        At length, the political prisoners including
Hansford were freed by order of the Governor in
Council, and Burke returned with relief to his

own law practice, which had been stymied by the protracted squabbles. Soon afterward, Burke received an appointment as notary public, a commission that he had long sought and for which there had been much time and effort expended. A friend in London had handled the formalities of application there, and it had required more than a year to secure the witnesses, certificates, and commissions signed and countersigned on both sides of the Atlantic. However, the expense of the notarial commission and the loss of income due to the political unrest had undermined Burke's dreams of financial independence. On Christmas Eve, he completed a letter to a friend in Northampton asking him for a loan of one hundred pounds to compensate for the slow-moving law practice that "has yet brought me in but very little money."[36]

His concern with finances was heightened by his intention of being married, for soon afterwards Burke purchased a license to wed Mary Freeman. His wife-to-be, "Polly", was possibly quite young. If her own calculations later in life were correct, she was no more than fourteen or fifteen when she married Burke in March of 1770.[37] In courtship as in politics, Burke's involvement was complete. A copy of a letter in which he proposed marriage shows him hovering between ardor and conceit, aware of the polite conventions of awaiting a lady's consent and yet chafing at the delays and the chance that other suitors might intervene. He explained to Polly that he was forming plans that depended upon her decision. If she gave her consent, he could quickly procure a house, furniture, and the other necessities. The poet and romantic of the Eastern Shore was being displaced by the aggressive lawyer of Norfolk. The demands of his law practice crowded into his proposal as he related that he would have to leave for the Eastern Shore for a difficult business trip. After his return, he would throw himself at her feet to be given "my Sentence either of Happiness or Misery from your lovely Lips."[38] Acknowledging that his life had previously revolved around a lively circle and that he had been fully exposed to feminine

11

charms, he confessed that he had never experienced "the new guest" now dwelling within his heart. He was not, he observed, unemotional--"one of those persons who are...blest with the unfeeling property of Trees and Flint," nor was he dishonest--"I heartily despise every Species of Falsehood."[39]

His overtures succeeded. Thomas Burke and Mary Freeman were married on March 28, 1770. In the absence of a personal correspondence, it is very difficult to evaluate their relationship. During his later career in Congress, Thomas and Polly lived apart for five or six months at a time. At Philadelphia, he often acted like the gay bachelor of the Eastern Shore, actively charming the women that he met. With his extremes of temperament, Burke might have proved difficult to live with; yet there are indications that Polly herself was temperamental. Besides occasional glimpses of his obstinacy, the final episode of Burke's tragic illness without his wife and the apparent failure of Polly's second marriage suggest that she was not well suited to married life.[40]

Whether it was his marriage or simply a better situation for practicing law, his prospects began to improve. From the court records of Norfolk County, it appears that starting in 1770 his caseload began to increase until by 1772 he was very busy with court appearances. Burke was largely involved in commercial law, and much of his work in court consisted of collecting or settling debts. His clients included not only local businessmen, but often merchants in far-off places like Baltimore, Philadelphia, or New York. It was not unusual for him to prosecute five or six lawsuits on court day in addition to others that were settled outside of court. He also served as an agent or correspondent for his distant clients, such as his friend John Ingram in London, helping them to balance their accounts and performing personal services.[41]

In Norfolk, Burke was exposed to cases that tested his commitment to political liberty. One

12

such case involved a seaman named Mosely who was
suing the captain of his ship for assault and
battery, an encounter which had resulted from an
attempt by the captain to administer discipline.
Burke's interpretation of events was deeply col-
ored by his strong identification with the interests of the captain and the shipowners that he
represented. It was imperative, he argued, to
keep order aboard ship. Unless the shipmasters
"wantonly" or "Cruelly abuse their People," the
benefit of the doubt should be in their favor.[42]
What was his theoretical basis? The young attorney argued that the property interests of the
shipowners and investors would rest upon the captain's orders.[43] As a result it would be better
to overlook his misdeeds than to prosecute him
for what Burke considered justifiable use of violence.[44] Burke wrote to John Blair in Williamsburg seeking to remove Mosely's lawsuit to the
General Court. As a Scotsman, the captain was
fearful of his chances in the borough court of
Norfolk, where hostility to the Scots merchants
had been so marked.

Burke's position on personal liberty had
subtly shifted as a result of his new circumstances. In 1766, when he wrote "Triumph America"
upon repeal of the Stamp Act, he affirmed his belief in political liberty and by implication to
personal rights as well. In his earlier "Hymn
to Spring by a Physician," he had rejoiced in the
atmosphere of personal freedom and the absence of
feudal tyranny such as that found in Europe. Even
with regard to the slave, Burke had also been
capable of mild idealism. In "Hymn to Spring,"
slavery is depicted as a curse and a "crime," and
yet the impact is softened by the reflection that
even the slave should be grateful for the climate
of ease and plenty in which he labored. In America, the poet contended, "Benevolence" and "reason"
were predominant, so that peace-loving servants
obeyed their beloved masters.[45]

In fact, since coming to Norfolk, Burke himself had become a small slaveowner. In January
of 1771, he purchased for fifty pounds a Negro
boy named York and not long afterwards a male

13

slave, America. Having taken advantage of his
dealings with estates that included slaves, he
quickly found that he had no use for the fourteen
year old York and was soon trying to sell him.
Although he continued to keep a personal servant,
it was not until he settled in North Carolina
that he began to acquire slaves on a larger scale.
When he died in 1783, his estate included fifteen
slaves.[46]

If Burke's outlook had shifted, it is not
surprising in view of his new commerical and propertied affiliations. It indicated that the former immigrant had been absorbed into the society
of Norfolk and culture of Virginia. Even Burke's
oscillation between human and property rights was
echoed by other Virginians during the Revolutionary era. While property rights dominated the controversy with Great Britain, there was a later
thrust toward equality and personal liberty. His
slaveholding acquaintance from Albemarle, Thomas
Jefferson, would write the classic statement of
liberty and equality. Yet, there was never agreement as to whether human or property rights should
have priority--or how the confusing shadings of
legal status should be integrated into the corpus
of Revolutionary principles. Moreover, Burke himself was forced at times to place humanity before
the rigors of the law, especially on one occasion
when he was faced with starting proceedings against
a blacksmith who owed money to one of his clients,
a Baltimore merchant. "I found myself so touched
with Compassion," he wrote to his client, "for a
poor man with a large family and nothing but his
labor to Support them that I could not refuse his
request [to stay the proceedings]."[47]

As Burke's practice increased, he also found
himself dealing with cases that were technically
more intricate and far-reaching. Living in a
small society, this inevitably brought him into
contact with the Virginia legal fraternity and
those who were its great and near-great. In addition to George Wythe, he communicated with Edmund
Pendelton, Richard Bland, and Robert Carter Nicholas who were lawyers as well as political figures.
In 1770, he began a correspondence with one of

14

Wythe's former students--a young lawyer from Albemarle County by the name of Thomas Jefferson.[48]

The letters pertained chiefly to one case
related to the estate of Colonel Robert Tucker
and raised questions that had a peculiar link to
the problem of the colonists' status within the
British Empire. Tucker, like many planters, had
incurred numerous debts that at his death were
far greater than the assets in his estate. Most
of the creditors, including Burke's clients,
lived in the colonies, but there was one important exception. A debt of 7500 was owed to
Robert Hunt, an English merchant, who claimed
priority over the American creditors. In part,
his claim was based on the fact that one of the
debts was a bill of exchange that might be viewed
as having precedence.

However, the bulk of the estate consisted of
lands, and the question arose as to whether British creditors would be considered as eligible
for first consideration in the case of real estate.
How the case was resolved also depended on whether
the courts chose to apply statutes of Parliament
to a colonial situation and whether those laws were
applied to the Americans in the same way as to the
English.[49] Burke complained to Jefferson that if
the British creditor, Hunt, were given a preference, nothing would remain to satisfy the American
debts. He pointed out that the General Court in
Williamsburg had already made the disturbing ruling that British creditors had a special--if not
prior--claim on the real estate of Americans.
"Real estate," he declared to Jefferson, "can be
no exclusive fund for British debts."[50] Suppose
a debtor had no lands, he speculated; would anyone
seriously contend that his personal property should
be subject first to British creditors?

The Norfolk attorney was demonstrating a
sure grasp of the complex and unorthodox questions
posed by a case of conflicting jurisdictions.
Jefferson's response to his commentary is not recorded, but it is highly unlikely that in 1770
either of them as lawyers would have looked at
the case in political or patriotic terms, espe-

15

cially before a decision was handed down. In any
case, their interchange lasted only a year and
almost completely concerned legal matters. There
is no indication that they met to confer on Tucker's case, but Burke did write to Jefferson in
August of 1771 expressing regret that they had
not been able to get together while Jefferson had
been in Williamsburg. Soon afterwards, their paths
diverged and passed only briefly at a distance
during the Revolution. Curiously each of them
would become a Revolutionary governor, and for both
Burke and Jefferson the British invasion of the
South would result in serious damage to their
public reputations.[51]

Unlike Jefferson, Burke's Revolutionary career was not to take root in Virginia. His restless temperament was again leading him toward
still another change of location. Despite his
recent success in Norfolk, the former immigrant
was surveying a more ideal site for his maturing
ambitions. In September of 1771, he had informed
Jefferson that he was leaving on a long journey
that would take him to North Carolina. For the
ambitious lawyer, travel even to an adjacent colony was not uncommon, and Burke's papers contain
several receipts for ferries taking him to and
from Norfolk. Soon afterwards, however, in December of 1771 Thomas Burke was issued a license to
practice law in that province by its Governor,
Josiah Martin.[52]

His decision to relocate in North Carolina
is not surprising. Since its trade had been historically linked with Norfolk, there were two
routes by land that provided easy access, and
Burke already had connections in Halifax and Hillsborough. The Virginia newspapers carried advertisements for land in the relatively unsettled
western piedmont which Burke was now eyeing. For
Burke, the miasmic climate of Norfolk had proved
unwholesome, and the fall of 1771 had been particularly debilitating. Commenting on an outbreak
that had affected all Virginia, he summed up the
situation: "to no Place I believe has the Fall
proved more fatal than to our Borough. Yet I am
persuaded the Disorder in kind differed nothing

16

from what is common and its greater Degree of
Symptoms [in Norfolk] is owing to some of our
local Circumstances..."[53]

In the spring of 1772, he again travelled to
North Carolina, spending over two weeks at Hillsborough where he purchased 591 acres of land.
The area that Burke chose was undergoing a drama-
tic process of population. A continuous stream
of Scotch-Irish and Germans had taken advantage
of the cheap, unoccupied land, so that the county
by 1770 had nearly fourteen thousand people.
Paralleling this flow was a trickle of more substantial migrants drawn from Virginia and eastern
North Carolina. They were attracted not only by
the cheap land in Orange County but also by the
town of Hillsborough. Located on the route to
Salisbury, it served as a commercial entrepot
for western trade. In addition, it was the meeting place for the county court of Orange and the
Superior Court for the Hillsborough District
which would assure Burke a busy law practice.
Three of the town's forty buildings were taverns,
and the activity during court sessions belied the
small size of the town.[54]

Though recent in origin, Hillsborough had
been the center of an insurrection by small farmers calling themselves the Regulators. As
victims of systematic extortion and denied justice in the courts, the wronged farmers had taken
matters into their own hands. The legal officials, in particular the hated Edmund Fanning,
were driven from town, and the Regulators conducted mock trials of those most loathsome to
them. The disturbances, which began in 1768,
had culminated in 1771 with the defeat of a Regulator army at the Battle of Alamance. Now the
area was free of turbulence, so much in fact that
Governor Martin transferred his court there in
the summer of 1772. For Burke, it was fairly
certain that he could avoid the political head-
aches that had plagued him during his first months
in Norfolk.[55]

The prevalence of smaller farms and land
prices cheaper than in Virginia meant that an

ambitious man could more easily secure a place
among the local gentry. For Burke, despite the
financial strain, the ownership of land represented a triumph over his own past. As he told
a contact in Ireland, he had settled on "a little
Country seat," and he named it Tyaquin after the
Burke ancestral estates in Ireland. Land in the
eighteenth century was the hallmark of status
and source of political power. If on a limited
scale, Burke had joined the landed elite, and in
the years that followed, he continued to acquire
land, even though he could often ill afford it.[56]

In the summer of 1772, the Burkes moved to
Tyaquin and after several months the Doctor was
well satisfied with his move. In the short time
since leaving Norfolk, he had "regained a vigorous and happy state of health," in a climate that
he described as "Remarkably moderate and healthy."[57]
In addition, his practice brought him into contact
with the legal elite of North Carolina, many of
whom became his political associates during the
Revolution. In November, Burke mentioned the name
of Samuel Johnston in a vehement remark over a
debt he was trying to collect: "I have made dili-
gent inquiry regarding _____, and learn from Mr.
Sam Johnston that he [the debtor] is a Sob and
worth nothing."[58] Soon afterward, Burke corresponded with Johnston's son-in-law, James Iredell,
the future Supreme Court justice, and Iredell
wrote in turn that he was "much obliged, Sir, by
this Instance of your Confidence in me who is
entirely a Stranger to you, but who has a very
pleasing knowledge of your character."[59]

While his first year was a success in most
respects, it was marred by two unexpected events.
In July of 1773, while he was in Norfolk, a freak
and violent hail storm destroyed his wheat crop.
With this loss, he had little use for his slaves
and debated whether to sell three hands or to
keep them in hopes of growing tobacco the following year.[60]

The other episode concerned his brother Redmond. In 1769, Burke had received a letter from
Ireland that was directed to him--at Boston. Im-

18

pressed by his success, though confused as to his location, the family was sending his brother Redmond to join him. The letter informed him that Redmond would soon arrive in Boston.[61]

When Redmond reached Boston, he was penniless and without the contacts that he expected; his temporary solution was to join the British regiments that were occupying Boston as a result of the recent agitation. After learning of his brother's predicament, Burke immediately sought his release. From his friends in Norfolk, he was supplied with the name of a merchant in Boston, Nathaniel Coffin, who might supply assistance. He called upon the Boston merchant to obtain Redmond's release, outfit him, lend him money, and send him to Norfolk, where Burke was then living. In turn, the attorney assured him that he would be fully reimbursed for his expenses. As it turned out, the task of securing his release was far more difficult and drawn out than anticipated. According to Burke, his brother had so impressed the British commander, General Gage, with his appearance and talents, that the General was unwilling to part with him. Finally Coffin in desperation recommended an appeal to the Secretary of War in London if all else failed. At length, their attempts to free him succeeded, and Redmond went to live with his brother and sister-in-law in Norfolk. When the Burke household moved to North Carolina, Redmond accompanied them, and Thomas set out to obtain him a post with the provincial government. There is no indication exactly how old Redmond was and nothing personal about him until Burke's fateful communication of March 3, 1773.[62]

On that day, Burke relayed the news of a bombshell that had exploded in the Burke household. While he was away in New Bern, Redmond tried to seduce Polly Burke. According to Thomas, his brother had come into Polly's bedroom late at night "stript to his Shirt" and had tried to get into bed with her.[63] She was warned of his presence by a young girl who slept in the same room, and so she was able to escape what Burke felt would have been "forcible Violation"--in modern terms, rape.[64]

Redmond then substituted persuasion for force. He tried to convince Polly that her husband was jealous and "treasured up several little Incidents that were the result merely of good humoured Chat between her and me and attempted to pervert them into Symptoms of the Strongest Suspicion." Falling short, he phantasized other incidents--and again failed--"Mrs. Burke had too strong a Conviction of the Contrary. She well knew my Opinion of her Honor and delicacy as well as her affection for me, would not admit of the slightest Suspicion to her Prejudice."[65]

Undeterred, Redmond then switched tactics and tried to undermine her morals. He directed her attention to the sexual habits of the English ruling classes and proposed "what he called an Amour."[66] Failing in this, Redmond began to back off and sought to cover his tracks. In Burke's angry words, Redmond used "the vilest methods" to intimidate her into silence, threatening to reveal fictitious misdeeds and to use them to ruin her reputation.[67] Instead, taking these charges that Redmond had unwisely set to paper, Polly had a friend question her on each of them, which she proceeded to deny. Finally aware that his gambit had failed, Redmond became contrite and begged her not to tell his brother. He pleaded with her to punish him herself and invited her to shoot him with a loaded pistol. Burke did not describe what happened on his return or the confrontation with Redmond if there was one.[68]

Thomas Burke had been absent in New Bern, the provincial capital, ironically to seek Governor Martin's assistance on his brother's behalf. Undoubtedly he had treated Redmond as a member of the family and introduced him to all of his new friends, for one of his first concerns was to prevent his neighbors from giving assistance to his brother. He even wrote the Governor asking him to disregard his recent requests. He was angry enough to have sought revenge, but wisely restrained himself. "When I listen to revenge," he fumed, "I am tempted to take one of a different kind--but after I withdrew my Protection and

20

Countenance...he becomes very contemptible..."[69]
Redmond now disappeared from his life.[70]

The tenuous ties to the past, which Redmond had undermined, may have affected Burke's outlook in subtle ways. Although now a southerner, a slaveholder, and at times an advocate of American rights, he often differed from his native born and North Carolina contemporaries. Despite agreement in principle, he would respond with uncommon awareness and intensity to Revolutionary situations. In his energy, his devotion to republican ideals, his grasp of contradictions, and even in his periodic shifts, Burke stood apart, as he did in his unpredictable emotions. The frequent change of location and profession, the exposure to varying cultures and ideas, had resulted in both a political and personal sensitivity. Yet, it was particularly his clarity of thought and ideal that would draw him to the forefront of the Revolutionary movement. His recent arrival in North Carolina and late entry into politics seemed to endow him with more determination and purposefulness. In the changing political milieu of 1775 and 1776, what might otherwise have blocked or slowed his progress would work to his immediate advantage.

IN THE PROVINCE OF LA MANCHA

When Burke arrived in North Carolina, the controversies between England and the colonies had abated, and the resulting calm seemed to signal a return to relative harmony. Yet, the major outbreaks such as the Stamp Act controversy had been preceded by smaller, more localized disputes and even now these differences persisted. In 1773, for example, an issue involving the courts flared up, when Governor Josiah Martin insisted that judicial legislation could not go into effect until it got approval in London. As a result, a temporary bill was necessary, and the two chambers of the Assembly could not reach agreement. In the end, the British government vetoed the original bill, and the Assembly then refused to appropriate money for the criminal courts that the Governor was attempting to establish. When the former statutes expired in December of 1773, North Carolina was left without a court system.[1]

While this struggle raged, the Governor had been eyeing the Clerk of Pleas office. The importance of the office stemmed from the power of its occupant to appoint clerks for the local or county courts. Formerly, the clerks or their henchmen had often belonged to the Assembly and had opposed the royal authority. Now, as the Crown prepared to abolish the office, it was held by a member of the Council, Samuel Strudwick, who was a loyal friend of Governor Martin. The Governor perceived Strudwick's potential usefulness and was concerned that his powers might be lost to the Crown.[2] Strudwick's "inflexible integrity," as Martin saw it, would both prevent corruption and allow the government to reward its supporters in the Assembly. He was also worried, however, that the Assembly meant to emasculate the powers of the Clerk and convert them to its own use.[3]

In the spring of 1774, the related issues of the courts and the Clerk began to attract attention. With the Assembly ready to meet, it was certain that there would be controversy, and in

23

anticipation, Strudwick was trying to recruit support, and he requested Burke to help him retain the power of appointment. A substantial landowner in Orange County, Strudwick may have employed Burke's legal services and could have promised him the office of county clerk. Whatever the circumstances, Burke refused to support Strudwick's claim, calling it "a flagrant Usurpation," an obvious reference to Strudwick's other position on the Governor's Council. Despite the dilemma posed by their friendship, Burke nonetheless felt that he had a private obligation to oppose such an unlawful action. Since it was a matter of conscience, Burke asked that his refusal remain unpublicized, preferring to avoid, as he put it, "the Eclat of Patriotism."[4]

The lines of division in the courts controversy carried over into the protest against the Coercive or Intolerable Acts, the punitive legislation enacted in response to the Boston Tea Party. As one pro-British friend of Burke pointed out, support of the Governor would represent a commitment to British prerogative. The Governor and Strudwick were obligated to support the Crown "by every constitutional, Legal and honorable method within their power..."[5] Clearly, Burke had at last descended on the American or patriot side of the controversy. As it turned out, he never had to take a public stand, for in March of 1774 Governor Martin reluctantly consented to the re-establishment of the criminal court system for a term of one year. Afterwards, larger issues overshadowed the court question; as a result it was never resolved. Within a year, Thomas Burke was caught up in revolutionary politics, while his loyal friends like Strudwick were becoming enemies of the body politic.[6]

While in Norfolk, Burke's contacts had been with English and Scots merchants, and in his pursuit of business, the question of American rights had disappeared from his correspondence. Despite his merchant affiliations in the Norfolk political milieu, there is no indication that he was sympathetic with British authority. Not only had he defended American rights during the Stamp Act con-

24

troversy, but he also had come to America from
Ireland, a land that had been treated with contempt by England far longer than the American
colonies. Somewhat earlier, he had received a
letter from his Irish friend on the Eastern Shore
of Virginia, AEdanus Burke, who recounted to him
the inhumanities practiced on the Irish by the
English under Cromwell.[7]

Whatever the effect of being Irish, Thomas
Burke was also reacting as one would expect of
an ambitious young man of moderate means who had
no official ties with the royal administration.
Having given a firm demonstration of loyalty to
the re-emerging Revolutionary movement, he would
be swept by the rapid flow of events into political activism and away from those of his friends
who could not go along. Already the Coercive
Acts, especially the closing of Boston as a port,
were generating both local and general resistance,
including the first Continental Congress which met
in September of 1774. In North Carolina, meetings
held in many of the cities and counties condemned
the acts of Parliament and called for a provincial
congress to meet in August. Some groups, without
waiting for either a provincial or continental
congress, initiated their own boycotts of commerce
with Great Britain. The local bases for political
action were now in existence.[8]

While Thomas Burke did not attend the first
provincial Congress at New Bern, he could not help
but be aware of its deliberations. While affirming their loyalty to George III, the delegates
vigorously indicted Parliament for invasion of
their rights. Following up the local measures,
they called for a boycott of British goods and
provided for a network of county committees of
safety for the purpose of enforcement. These
measures were viewed as more than temporary expedients and were the beginnings of the new republican system of government that would claim his
services. Plans were formulated for another con-
gress--one which Burke would attend--and three
delegates were appointed to represent North Carolina at the first Continental Congress in Philadelphia.[9]

Soon afterwards, the impact of the measures were being felt, especially by incipient loyalists like Burke's merchant friend, Andrew Miller, who encountered frustrating restrictions and obstacles to his business operations. In December of 1775, the committee of Halifax County summoned Miller to sign the boycott or Association as it was now called. When he refused, the committee agreed upon no further contacts with him and advised the local people to do the same. Miller complained to Burke that since failing to sign the Association, he had received only one of the letters sent to him from Great Britain. Although professing a wish for the colonies to be free, he disapproved of the methods being used to accomplish it. The leaders of the resistance, "enterprising Geniuses in the Land," were in his opinion "of the Quixote kind."[10] Would not the British Secretary of State be astounded, he asked, to find "in the list of Colonies La Mancha...."[11]

As the Revolution closed in on him, Miller was increasingly alienated by the course of events, and he expressed deep misgivings in his letters to Burke. He felt that the military preparations of the Virginians in March of 1775 would only widen the breach and make reconciliation impossible. The British would repeal much of their unpopular legislation, he contended, if they were approached through the assemblies rather than the illegally constituted congresses. Furthermore, North Carolina could not succeed against British military power nor survive without their maritime cooperation. It was his advice to the Quixotes of the colonies to submit to taxation, at least until their manufacturing was developed.[12]

Unhappily for Miller, his friend, Dr. Burke, was already taking up residence in the province of La Mancha. In March, Miller had declined Burke's invitation to accompany him to New Bern for the second provincial congress. He sensed that a person in his predicament "would not be an agreeable companion in a Meeting of Delegates."[13] This appraisal was not inaccurate; the uncompromising positions which he found so distasteful were again much in evidence. As for

Burke, he did not turn his back on friends such
as Miller; after the war when Miller, who had fled
to the West Indies, wished to return to North Carolina, he felt confident enough of Burke's friendship to ask for his help. Though Thomas Burke
took a different path, he still had much in common with his old merchant friends. While a delegate to the Congress in Philadelphia, he would find
congenial company with the business elite of the
new republic. In time, he would even become dis-
enchanted, like Miller, with the tendencies of
the revolutionary movement.

At the second congress, however, Burke was
a newcomer to politics and his meteoric revolutionary career was just beginning. He was one of the
few delegates who was not already sitting in the
legislature. Most of the delegates would be closely associated with him during the Revolutionary
War years; some like Samuel Johnston, Cornelius
Harnett, and Richard Caswell had been in the forefront of North Carolina politics. This group included William Hooper and Joseph Hewes who had
served as delegates to the first Continental Congress. Others such as Allen and Willie Jones of
Halifax were, like himself, relatively new to
politics and would make their careers in conjunc-
tion with the American Revolution. Though fierce-
ly antagonistic to Parliament and royal authority,
the leaders of the emerging movement were men of
impeccable social and political credentials.
Most of them were large landholders or wealthy
merchants from eastern North Carolina; however
radical in their opposition to the British, they
were essentially conservative in their social outlook.

The pattern of the second North Carolina congress was similar to the one in 1774. The resolutions included harsh criticism of British policies
and practical measures to implement the resistance
movement. Provisions were drawn up for encouraging manufactures and agriculture, so that the boycott would not undermine the economy. One expedient was to offer bounties to those who would undertake the production of essential materials; later
Burke himself would join in an unsuccessful venture
to start a gun works in Hillsborough. Moreover,

the delegates at the second congress subscribed
to the Association drawn up by the First Continental Congress, thereby linking themselves to
the larger cause of intercolonial protest. The
three representatives to the First Congress in
Philadelphia were reelected to serve in the
Second Congress which was to meet in May of
1775.[14]

Governor Josiah Martin who had publicly
warned against holding the illegal convention
did not take it lightly, demanding that the dis-
sidents stop the proceedings. Not only did the
members of the lower house blatantly refuse, but
they proceeded to admit Burke and the other delegates who were not members of the House and then
to meet as a revolutionary congress. When Martin protested to the Assembly, the membership
replied with a bold statement of principle.
Speaking now as members of the Assembly rather
than the illegal congress, they grandly declared
their devotion to George III and protested that
their measures, taken to preserve the British
Constitution, exhibited a solemn allegiance
rather than a lack of loyalty. As long as many
colonists continued to hope for reconcilation,
charges of disloyalty were serious allegations
and had to be rebutted. This was especially true
since the colonies regarded themselves as connected to Britain through the Crown rather than
Parliament. In the eighteenth century constitutional monarchy, direct criticism of the King
was usually avoided; the constitutional fiction
persisted that he could do no wrong, but was
betrayed by his ministers of state. Therefore,
it was considered as proper to criticize the
King's perfidious ministers--"wicked and design-
ing men" in the words of the Assembly.[15]

On April 7, 1775, as the congress adjourned,
the Assembly was belatedly dissolved by Governor
Martin. The Governor's action signaled the end
of not only the assembly but the colonial politics
as well. Although an election was scheduled for
June, the authority of the Governor and the system to which he belonged was greatly diminished.
As if symbolic of the rapid changes taking place,
the principal architect of the earlier opposition,

John Harvey, who was Speaker of the House, died
the following month after a fall from his horse.
The style of politics which he had practiced was
undergoing a rapid metamorphosis. Selective acts
of resistance and statements of opposition were
giving way to wholesale, armed retaliation.

The news of Lexington and Concord was the
catalyst for his change. A letter to Burke on
May 9 reported "some very shocking accounts from
Boston," relating that the regulars and the "Bos-
tonians" had clashed and included some exaggerated estimates of British casualties.[16] In North
Carolina, as in other colonies, carefully edited
accounts rushed by express from Massachusetts had
the same electrifying effect. The stories of
enemy atrocities channeled the initial waves of
shock into fear and hatred of the British. After
years of resisting provocations from the mother
country, no one questioned the "war guilt" of
the British. With elaborate preparations under-
way, the news produced more than simply verbal
outrage. The activities of the second Continental Congress, which in June agreed to support
an army, were typical of what was taking place
in the conventions and congresses held throughout the colonies that summer. As John Adams observed, "the battles of Lexington and on the 19th
changed the Instruments of Warfare from the Penn
[sic] to the Sword."[17]

In the hostile climate of opinion that followed the outbreak of warfare, the royal governors
found themselves in impossible positions, and
Josiah Martin of North Carolina was no exception.
Apprehensive over the formation of military units,
he removed the ornamental cannons from the grounds
of the Governor's palace at New Bern. This action
further irritated the militants who were also
spreading rumors that Martin was intriguing to
create unrest among the slaves. Fearing violence,
the Governor put his family aboard a ship for New
York and on May 31 fled to Fort Johnston on the
southern coast of North Carolina. Soon he was reporting that turmoil had reached a state of rebellion and was convinced that stern punishment was
necessary for what he somewhat arrogantly termed
England's "most unnatural children." The people

were now openly talking about "hostility toward Britain in the language of *Aliens* and *avowed Enemies*..."[18]

Indeed, the port of Boston was already under siege by hordes of minute men who had congregated there after Lexington and Concord. The Continental Congress, or at least some of its members, were maneuvering the colonies through the portals of rebellion. Both Governor Martin as well as the commander of the British military in Boston, General Thomas Gage, realized that an army of pacification would be necessary to suppress the mushrooming rebellion. In this twilight of British colonialism, men like Thomas Burke who had been subjects of the Crown since birth found themselves cut adrift from their traditional political moorings. Although they held tenaciously to their self-image as loyal subjects of George III, they were becoming divorced from their former allegiances and forms of government. In the province of "La Mancha," as Andrew Miller described it, the perception of the American political consciousness would subtly alter. What were previously mere abstractions would become the building blocks for constructing the republican political system. Despite the fact that Burke and his confederates acted to preserve what they viewed as their rights and prerogatives, they would now be forced to re-examine their ideals in terms of actual experiments, something that few had ever had the opportunity to do. Inevitably, their eloquent expressions of opposition, when translated into a working republican model, led to disagreements and unexpected threats to their local system of government.

The collapse of royal government left colonial North Carolina in limbo, suspended between what remained of the old colonial system and the newly emerging republicanism. Aside from the local committees, there was no longer a system for governing the province. In South Carolina, a convention was already in progress, filling the vacuum that had been created by the turmoil after the news of Lexington and Concord, and it was not long before North Carolina followed the example

30

of its neighbor. On July 10, 1775, Samuel Johnston, acting in place of the late Speaker, John
Harvey, issued a call for a congress to meet the
next month in Burke's hometown of Hillsborough.

The Third Congress was greatly expanded both
in numbers and in the scope and length of its deliberations. With this, Burke's role grew in proportion, perhaps because the convention was held
so close to home or more likely because the enlarged operations opened the way for relatively
unknown men of ability and energy. In any case,
the extent of his activity, especially on committees, was truly impressive. At the start of
the convention, he was placed on a committee to
prepare a loyalty test for the members of the congress; then, he was one of those appointed to
deal with people in North Carolina who had religious or political scruples that kept them from
identifying with the revolutionary cause. His
co-workers on these committees were men like
Richard Caswell and William Hooper, whose reputations and political experience far exceeded
his own.[19]

The threat of war meant that the delegates
had to undertake far more than the earlier congress which had chiefly produced statements of
protest. After the battles of Lexington and
Concord, it was necessary to consider the creation of an army and the manufacture of military
supplies, from "Bristol steel" and pig iron to
salt and sulphur. An issue of currency and a
two shilling tax were instituted, the first in
a dreary sequence of financial measures that would
result in inadequate revenue and rampant inflation. Faced with practical questions, the congress was developing like so many other assemblies
throughout the colonies into an all-purpose governmental agency, though it still resembled the
legislative assembly out of which it had sprung.[20]

In 1775 and 1776, with the need for a temporary blueprint of government, the experiment in
making a republican constitution began. At the
Hillsborough Congress, a committee for civil government was charged with this responsibility, and

Burke was one of its members. The result reflected the uncertainty as to how far the resistance would proceed and the urgent need for military organization: committees of safety were provided for in the various military districts of North Carolina to act as the eyes and ears for the congress and to report to a provincial congress that would act as executive between sessions of the congress. As for the congress itself, it was placed on a permanent basis with the provision for annual sessions to be elected each fall.[21]

The great changes evident in the electoral system reflected an as yet unarticulated commitment to political representation. Less restrictive rules for voting than under the colonial regime were put into effect, allowing landowners and householders to take part in elections. In counties like Orange, where land titles were often disputed, it was agreed that a man could vote even without clear title to his land. This indicates that the eastern politicians, previously reluctant to meet the demands of the people in the interior, were trying hard to accommodate them in order to attract support.

With such awareness of public opinion, the delegates were also anxious to justify themselves by putting their thoughts and principles into writing. A committee was appointed to prepare an address for the people of North Carolina, one which would be comprehensible to "the meanest Capacity."[22] Perhaps because of his efforts on forming a preliminary constitution, Thomas Burke was later added to the committee and given the responsibility of preparing a draft. Burke's product far exceeded the committee's instructions, being a full-scale inquiry into the assumptions governing civil society. This may explain why his draft was not accepted. Such a comprehensive statement might have been unsuited to the narrower purposes of the convention.[23]

In his statement, he set forth a doctrine of equality that demonstrated his familiarity with the Enlightenment philosophers and was reminiscent of Thomas Jefferson in the Declaration of

Independence. He contended that "the Almighty Great of Heaven and Earth" had endowed men universally with "Souls, Bodies, Senses, Desires, and means of Satisfying them, and thereby made all men Equal."[24] Like Jefferson, he linked equality with the desire for happiness.

> ...and (God) thereby made all men equal--
> as well in the Desire of Happiness, as
> in the power of Imagining and Chusing
> [sic] the most likely means of obtain-
> ing it--and having made choice of the
> means, gave to each man equal Powers of
> acting--agreeable to that choice--and
> this Truth cannot be denied.[25]

Burke added that no one could be kept from making his own choice except by force or by consent to limitations. The idea of equality, like that of consent, was a basic element of political thought with which he was familiar. For example, Burke owned a copy of Adam Ferguson's *Essay on the History of Civil Society*, in which equality was emphasized as the original condition of man. The Scottish philosopher argued that whoever forgets this truth of original equality degenerates into a slave and should not be trusted with the rights of his fellow men.[26] Burke also believed in John Locke's doctrine of a civil contract that had originated with "our Forefathers so Long (ago) that no membor Remains..."[27] Although mankind had long since emerged from a state of nature, Burke pointed out that American society had begun more recently, and the origins of such a contract could be traced to the charters of "new contracts" by which the first settlers had been guaranteed the English constitutional heritage. When the government acted contrary to this contract, as expressed in the laws, it meant that "every person acting under Such Command may be resisted without danger of Penalties or Punishment."[28] The design of the British ministries to deprive Americans of their basic freedoms under the civil contract had driven them to resist.

Although this philosophy was commonly held, Burke was stating his own convictions as well.

33

He was converting political theory and his own
ideas into a systematic image of man and man's
role in the political process. Throughout his
treatise, he referred to the rights guaranteeing
justice and the role of magistrates in ensuring
those rights. This phase of Burke's Revolutionary career would witness a surge of idealism that
was at odds with his recent attachment to property rights. Even though Burke could not accept a
doctrine of pure equality, he believed that men
in aggregate had enough sagacity to choose a
government. Their souls, senses, and desires
could be trusted at the level of political deliberation in which constitutional choices were
being made.[29]

In the early phase of constitution-making
and enthusiasm for American rights, ardent Revolutionaries were often caught up in an atmosphere
of heady optimism and idealism. Burke's emphasis
in this draft was on the rights of mankind rather
than on the need to guarantee property rights.
Yet, property and political rights were interrelated in the ideology of Thomas Burke and his contemporaries, creating an elastic factor in the
republican philosophy of the Revolution. Human
and property rights were not always congruent, and
the point at which the two separated was instru-
mental in determining the outlook of a given individual. Though property rights pervade Burke's
draft, he apparently assumed that man automatically would protect what his labor produced.
Later in his political career, when he had spent
his energies and fortune on what seemed to be an
empty purpose, he would drastically incline toward
the need for authority to guarantee property.

In his draft, he assumed that the good of
the individual was inherent in the choice of a
majority, such as that at the Hillsborough convention. This as yet imprecise view of the political
body took for granted that all men were happy in
a state of society that protected their lives,
limbs, and "produce of their Ingenuity and Industry."[30] Even at the congress in Hillsborough,
however, some of the cautious delegates were already questioning what was being forced upon them

by the unsettled state of society. Samuel Johnston, instinctively conservative in his response
to change, feared that the rapid course of events
would preclude future reconciliation with Great
Britain. An even more conservative friend accused the extremists, especially those of New England, with a "fixed design...to throw off every
connection with Great Britain and act for the
future as totally independent."[31] With some
delegates frightened by the prospect of independence and others impatient with British intransi-
gence, it was difficult in that summer of 1775
to create a consensus.

By spring, the chances for reconciliation
which Johnston had seen dissipating had almost
vanished. Although Burke had drafted his statement from the perspective of a loyal British subject, continuous warfare between British and American arms had radically altered the climate of opinion. In February of 1776, a delegate from North
Carolina in the Continental Congress mentioned
the possibility of separation from Great Britain,
and requested that copies of Thomas Paine's *Common Sense* be despatched to North Carolina. When
it was proposed in Congress to seek alliances with
foreign powers, the delegates wrote to the Provincial Congress asking advice. This motion, if
passed, would be equivalent to leaving the British empire.[32]

As the fourth Congress convened at Halifax
in April, 1776, the delegates returning from
Philadelphia were surprised to find North Carolina
more anxious for independence than Virginia. Recent events had undermined the idea that American
resistance would result in reconciliation with
the mother country or even that this was desirable. On February 27, the military arm of the
movement had met and repelled a force of loyalists from the interior at the Battle of Moore's
Creek Bridge near Wilmington. Burke's former
hometown of Norfolk, the entrepot for the North
Carolina tidewater, was burned after an attack
by a British squadron, and it was widely believed
that the British forces had wantonly started the
fires and would now move southward to threaten
Wilmington.

Besides, confidence in British good will
and in George III had also disappeared, especially
after Paine's assault on the monarchy in *Common
Sense*. On April 8, a committee which included
Thomas Burke was instructed to consider the current state of the conflict and what steps might
be taken to frustrate the enemy. When the committee reported four days later, it recommended
a vote for independence, and on April 12, Congress
authorized the North Carolina delegates to vote
for independence in the Continental Congress.
The aftermath of this decision, framing constitutions at both the state and national level, would
involve Burke in the most significant activity of
his political career.[33]

   The work of the provincial congress, however,
was just beginning. Most of each working day was
consumed by the requirements of both the regular
session and the additional time spent on committee
assignments. A friend who lodged with Burke gave
an account of their busy schedule. Before break-
fast, it was necessary to prepare for the business
of the day. Afterwards, they went to Congress remaining there from nine in the morning until three
in the afternoon when it was finally time for dinner. There was not a moment for relaxation after
dinner; from four until nine in the evening, they
would attend as many as four committee sessions.
Then supper, and "this generally brings us to 12
at night."[34]

   As in the Hillsborough congress, Thomas Burke
was given a critical role in almost every area of
business. He served on committees to pay the
militia, to prevent desertion of slaves, to supply
and finance the war, and to draw up commissions
for privateers. He also headed the powerful committee of Secrecy, Intelligence, and Observation
where he was entrusted with unusual powers.[35]
His committee was given authority comparable to
the quasi-judicial powers of twentieth-century
investigatory committees. It was empowered to
compel the attendance of witnesses, examine suspects, subpoena essential papers, and even to
withhold restricted information from the congress.
With civil and military business interrelated, the
scope of its powers was almost unlimited.[36]

The role that earned Burke the most attention and perhaps criticism was as chairman of the committee to frame a permanent constitution. The single-minded blend of a probing intelligence and articulate devotion to an emerging republican credo made Thomas Burke an irresistible force in the proceedings. William Hooper, the delegate to the Continental Congress, wrote that "Nash and Burke are framing a Constitution for this Colony to preserve it from total Anarchy."[37] The conservative Hooper, whose extremism was confined to hard-line resistance toward Great Britain, reported that the two framers differed "very materially in their ideas from Mr. [Samuel] Johnston, [John] Penn or myself."[38] In his cautious view, the urgent military concerns incapacitated the human mind for formulating acceptable systems of government, though he did not elaborate his differences with Burke and Nash.

Although Hooper and Johnston opposed British authority, they were instinctively cautious when it came to abrupt changes in the political or social structure. Their commitment to preserving the *status quo* filled them with suspicion of violent or injudicious actions. Johnston's brother-in-law, James Iredell, reported that "*wise* and *unwise* heads" were at work in making a constitution.[39] Yet, Samuel Johnston was like Burke preoccupied with the problem of constructing a republican system that was free from Tyranny. Johnston, however, harbored a growing distrust of the delegates who were shaping the future of North Carolina. Faced with the question of how to limit the power of the legislature, Johnston favored annual elections, and in this sense showed more trust of the voters than of the men they would elect. By December of 1776, he was congratulating himself on avoiding membership in the fifth congress, where gentlemen like himself were "suspected and born down *per ignoble Vulgus* a set of men without reading, experience, or principle to govern them."[40] If he included Burke in this category, Johnston carefully disguised his feelings. Even though he objected to the constitution, he had nothing unfavorable to say about Burke.

Burke has sometimes been portrayed as a democrat struggling against the aristocratic old guard.
If he were an extremist, even in terms of 1776,
he showed little sign of it either then or in his
later career in the Continental Congress. Like
Johnston and others reacting to British tyranny,
he was seeking a means to restrain and limit the
powers of government, and in this respect he differed only in degree. Though at times he endorsed
broader qualifications for voting, this was only
one of his preoccupations and distinctly secondary
to his fear of despotism. Thomas Jones, a friend
of Johnston, who served with him on the constitutional committee, reported that he and Burke had
"frequent communion with each other on politics,
defense of the country, &c."[41] Nowhere in his
correspondence does Jones indicate disapproval
of anything Thomas Burke espoused.

Little is known of what transpired within
the constitutional committee, and it is only possible to infer the prevailing sentiments from external scraps of evidence. One indication is John
Adams' *Thoughts on Government*, which was turned
over to Burke by William Hooper who had just returned from Philadelphia. Responding to Hooper's
request, Adams had put down the principles and
practical ideas that should govern the new state
constitutions. His recommendations included bicameralism and rotation in office, both of which
the committee endorsed for North Carolina. In
particular, Adams insisted that a representative
assembly "should be in miniature an exact portrait
of the people at large." Despite the weight of
Adams' essay and the committee's recommendations,
the congress could not agree on the constitution,
so further deliberations were postponed until
the December session of the congress.[42]

Burke had been appointed Paymaster of the
Hillsborough district, so that his public life did
not cease after the congress adjourned. Writing
to General Charles Lee, he confessed that he had
hoped to volunteer for military service under Lee,
but that the demands of his private life prevented
him from doing so. Instead, he entered a partner-
ship with a neighbor for the purpose of setting up

the gun works in Hillsborough, hoping no doubt to apply the thousand dollar bounty promised by Congress. Beset by problems with the machinery, the factory did not work out as planned and finally was abandoned during the war.[43]

The prospect of a British attack, so alarming in early spring, receded by June, when most of the enemy pulled up anchor at Wilmington and sailed on to South Carolina. Burke naively suggested to General Lee that the British should have persisted in their design against North Carolina, since it would have proved less damaging than to South Carolina or Georgia. The members of the provincial council did not share his rash chauvinism, complaining to the delegates in the Continental Congress of shortages in arms and ammunition. North Carolina was faced with not only the threat of British incursions and a possible blockade by the British Navy, but with the Loyalists and Indians as well in early 1776. Fortunately for the new provisional government, the British expedition to Charleston ended in defeat, and rather than attacking North Carolina, the British armada returned to New York. As a result, an expedition could be sent against the Cherokees, and the South was guaranteed an interlude of relative calm before the British onslaught in 1780.[44]

The vexing problem of establishing a formal system of government was given a sense of immediacy by the decision for independence. As they prepared for the Fifth Congress in October, some North Carolinians were disturbed by the experiment taking place in Pennsylvania. William Hooper was bitterly critical of the unicameral legislature and broad franchise calling it a "motley mixture of limited monarchy and execrable democracy--a Beast without a head."[45] He complained to Samuel Johnston that taverns and dram shops were the tribunals to which the laws were to be submitted for approval. Like many of his fellow republicans, Thomas Burke believed strongly that a bicameral system should prevail. Burke left no doubt on this point in reacting to Benjamin Franklin's proposal for national union in 1775, a plan which had been flatly rejected by the third provincial congress.

Franklin's scheme, like the Pennsylvania
document, had provided for a single legislative
house, and in defense of his scheme, Franklin had
likened the conventional two-house system to a
wagon with two horses at each end drawing it in
opposite directions. A year later, in 1776, Burke
observed that Franklin's metaphor was inappropri-
ate and instead suggested the idea of four horses
attached to the front of the wagon as more practical. The two teams of horses could assist each
other in pulling the wagon uphill, the hindmost
horses would counteract the dangerous effect of
the uneven ground and restrain the forces of the
ones in front. If the Pennsylvania plan represented the *avant garde* of radicalism in 1776,
Thomas Burke was somewhere in the rear, more in
keeping with a moderate republicanism that would
be the Revolutionary credo.[46]

In North Carolina, the experiment in republican forms was soon to be tested in the elections
for the fifth Congress. Since a less restrictive
franchise had been instituted, both freeholders
and householders were allowed to cast ballots,
and this meant that in Orange County small farmers
could participate in large numbers. There was
more at stake anyway in this election, since the
delegates who were elected would determine the
fundamental law of the new state. From the turbulence of the elections as well as the Orange County
instructions, there was apparently an unusual interest in politics.

The elections held on October 13 were unexpectedly chaotic. So many people crowded into the
county court house on that election day that the
clerks were unable to register all of their names.
Despite attempts to calm the crowd, bedlam reigned,
and several times the election was first stopped
and then resumed. An hour and a half before sun-
set, the candidates and the clerks had to withdraw
from the uproar. No one in authority was present
to supervise the proceedings from then until sun-
set, when the poll closed. Those who later petitioned the Congress for redress estimated that
not one fourth of the voters had a chance to be
canvassed.

The results were unprecedented: Burke and
all but one of his fellow delegates from the last
convention were defeated, and only one of the new
delegates had served previously. Most of the new
men were farmers who resided in remote areas of
the county, far removed from the courthouse in
Hillsborough through which politics were controlled.
Those who had represented Orange in former congresses had been for the most part large landholders or successful lawyers like Francis Nash, Thomas
Hart, John Williams, and Nathaniel Rochester, all
of whom were friends or associates of Burke. Under the new electoral system, by which the common
landholder was enfranchised, the voters who flood-
ed the polls probably came from more distant points
in the county and voted for candidates from their
own environs. As a result of the early influx,
it was impossible for others to give their votes,
and the poll had to be closed prematurely.[47]

Dissatisfaction and cries for a new election
quickly surfaced. One of the unsuccessful candidates, Colonel John Butler, a large landholder and
commanding officer of the county militia, addressed
the troop muster, insisting that the matter was
their concern rather than his own. Some of the
disgruntled voters did draw up a petition which
was rejected at first by the election committee
of the fifth congress.[48]

The October elections of 1776 have been viewed
as a concerted campaign of radicals who believed
in democracy against conservatives who were fighting desperately to maintain the *status quo*. That
Samuel Johnston, a disgruntled conservative, was
not included in the Provincial Committee of Safety
nor selected as a delegate to the Fifth Congress,
has suggested a struggle to defeat the entrenched
old guard. Yet, it is curious that Thomas Burke,
often regarded as "radical" or "populistic" in his
ideology, was defeated for re-election. If the
modern categories of radical and conservative are
set aside, it appears that Johnston and his friends
with their commitment to the existing social hier-
archy privately feared that the rapid changes were
undermining the position of gentlemen in politics
and society at large. Johnston often complained

41

about the rude newcomers in the conventions whose influence and presence were painfully evident. Johnston's brother-in-law, James Iredell, who welcomed Burke in 1772, is thought to have written a bitter tract, "Creed of a Rioter," a caricature of the "rioter" who regarded gentlemen and their interests with disdain.[49]

Johnston and Iredell had reason for uneasiness. Several of their friends, who had resisted the local committees, had been subjected to violence and abuse. As the social and political relationships of pre-Revolutionary North Carolina were momentarily unhinged, the eastern oligarchy was no longer in a position to dominate the rest of the state. The interior regions gained proportionately greater influence. Although few of the new delegates were low-born or levellers--most were substantial landholders or lawyers--the older leaders commanded less prestige and respect, especially with the new liberalized voting requirements and more equal representation. Without an executive, there was no way of counteracting the impact of these changes on the revolutionary congresses. In keeping with his contempt for the western regions, Johnston was horrified when one of their delegates proposed a religious test for membership in the new General Assembly. Johnston was grateful that he had avoided being a member of the Fifth Congress in which these evils seemed so obtrusive.[50]

Yet, Johnston was remarkably tolerant of men whom he knew or respected, even if their views differed from his own. Willie Jones of Halifax, for example, has often been pictured as Johnston's adversary in the October elections of 1776, although there is no indication that Johnston regarded him with contempt or animosity. The two worked amicably together on several occasions during the Revolution, and it was not until 1787 and afterwards, when they were in opposing factions, that they became bitter opponents. With respect to Thomas Burke, Johnston was always cordial, although he never disguised his disagreement with some of Burke's views. In 1777, when the convention phase was safely past, Johnston in a letter to Burke

42

referred to the North Carolina constitution as "your plan" and was politely critical of it.[51]

Why did Johnston not regard Burke with the contempt that he reserved for other political figures who came from the interior of the state? Johnston's friendliness toward Burke may have stemmed from a trust based upon the fact that he was neither outrageous nor radical. Burke himself belonged to a political oligarchy in Orange County that differed little from the rest of the state, and his political ideals had much in common with the other revolutionists, including Johnston. His republicanism was more typical than his "radicalism," which had narrow limits. If Thomas Burke had been the radical that some historians have claimed, it is doubtful that the Fifth Congress would have dared to elect and re-elect him to the Continental Congress.

Since Burke was associated with the local oligarchy in Orange, his defeat was related to the political climate of which Johnston so strenuously complained. The prospect of having an inexperienced cadre at this all-important congress undoubtedly disturbed Burke, especially since their disputed election did not necessarily reflect the choice of the Orange County voters. As a result, instructions in Thomas Burke's handwriting were drawn up to guide the new delegates in their deliberations. The practice of instructing delegates was scarcely unprecedented, since Burke undoubtedly knew that it had been used as recently as 1773 in Orange County. Caught up in the atmosphere of a republican idealism, Burke's instructions of 1776 reflected his concern with the origins of power and limitations that would prevent its misuse.[52]

In the instructions to the Delegates of Orange County, all power is divided into two categories, original and derived. The original or superior power was described as the will of the people at large, so that those entrusted with the derived or inferior power of governing were bound to respect what obligations and limitations that had been placed upon them by the electorate. After

43

defining the nature of power, the Instructions
dealt with the specific principles and practices
that were to be embodied in the new constitution.
The emphasis on structural safeguards to protect against the misuse of power reflected Burke's
republican concern with the need to prevent any
kind of tyranny.

Specifically, the provisions included principles familiar to a later generation as separation of powers, bicameral assemblies, election by
ballot, and a popularly approved constitution.
In addition, the instructions emphasized that natural rights such as the freedom of religion should
be guaranteed. One article re-affirmed the new
voting qualifications whereby all property holders
were permitted to vote. Another echoed the provision of the constitutional committee by calling
for a weak executive who was elected annually and
would be eligible for only three annual terms.
One can see in these expressions of practical republicanism both the ideas of Burke's committees
and of the previous spring and perhaps also the
shadow of John Adams and his *Thoughts on Government*.[53]

When the Fifth Congress met, the constitution
that they framed only partly caught the spirit
expressed in the Instructions. In place of the
existing franchise, the congress substituted requirements even more restrictive than under the
colonial regime. Perhaps the delegates were conscious of creating a permanent rather than a provisional system or perhaps a reaction had set in
after the turbulence of the fall elections. In
particular, the property restrictions for both
voting for and serving in the state senate indicate that the congress was trying to preserve the
ideal of an aristocratic upper chamber. William
Hooper, the conservative delegate to the Continental Congress, had recently commented that the
upper house should be reserved for men of a higher
status, thereby making it "a refinement of the
first choice of the people at large, selected
for their Wisdom, remarkable Integrity, or that
weight which arises from property..."[54] Yet, in
keeping with this principle, the lower house was

made somewhat more democratic, though it was still
necessary to own one hundred acres in order to be
elected. This meant that men like Burke and Hooper
and their counterparts among the eastern elite
would control the new General Assembly.[55]

Always nervous about change, Hooper's friend
Samuel Johnston was concerned that the delegates
would unwisely permit the election of county justices, opening the door to local dislocation. He
need not have worried, however, for the existing
system of hegemony by the "courthouse rings" was
in the end perpetuated by the Fifth Congress.
The county justices were to be appointed by the
governor with the advice of the assembly, and the
justices would in turn select the sheriffs who
supervised the local elections. If anything, the
legislative branch arm was stronger than it had
been previously, and few perceived, as Burke would
in the Continental Congress, that the legislators
could also be tyrannical and corrupt. Despite
such continuities with the past, the new constitution did sweep away the outworn remnants of the
old system, including the landholding practices
of entail and primogeniture and imprisonment for
debt. Although the changes were far from revolutionary, the process was only beginning, and the
pressures of six years of war culminating in an
enemy invasion would shake the social foundations
of the state and would result at least temporarily
in a chaotic political climate, where few restraints
remained.[56]

Burke was not present while the constitution
was being prepared, but he did reappear before the
final draft was ratified. Having at first sanctioned the results of the October election, the
congress later reversed itself calling for another
election. To prevent the earlier disturbances,
the polls in Orange County were to remain open
for as long as three days with the voting carefully supervised. On December 10, a new election
was held which resulted in the defeat of all but
one of the October delegates, and in their stead
was substituted a delegation that included Burke,
his friend Nathaniel Rochester, and Colonel John
Butler who had publicly protested the results of

the earlier election. Except for one survivor of the previous contest, the December delegates were men of substance more closely associated with the town of Hillsborough. The fluke of the October elections had been rectified.[57]

Out of Congress until December 16, Thomas Burke was probably unable to influence the final version of the constitution, since it was formally ratified two days after he was seated. His feelings about the October election, however, were soon aired before the delegates. Burke moved unsuccessfully to specify the methods and the number of days for polling the voters in future elections. His other suggestions to the congress were now consistently accepted, especially those designed to implement the new system, indicating that if his prestige were diminished by the October election, it was now restored with interest. After electing Richard Caswell as Governor, the delegates on December 20 chose Doctor Thomas Burke as a delegate to the Continental Congress in Philadelphia.[58]

Burke's apparent belief in a less exclusive electoral system did not discredit him with the conservative fifth congress. In fact, he had a great deal in common with the conservative leaders of the Revolutionary movement. His position on voting may have reflected the character of Orange County, where there were few large landholders. In the years that followed, Burke's "populism" was notably quiescent, and only once did he show any concern for establishing a broader electoral system. That came in a roll call held in November of 1777, while Burke was attending the General Assembly between terms in Congress. He was one of those who unsuccessfully supported a bill to enable householders to vote for members of the state senate. Yet, Burke never advocated an unrestricted system for state elections.[59]

Was Burke a "radical" or "conservative" in terms of the Revolutionary politics of 1776? Operating at the local, state, and finally the national level, Burke's location on the ideological spectrum varied according to where he served

46

and with whom he was associated. In Hillsborough, he was leagued with a conservative oligarchy that maintained a monopoly on officeholding. Even so, no candidate could afford to overlook the ordinary voter, and at times of stress, such as in October of 1776, the flow of local politics was temporarily disturbed. Years later, in 1783, William Hooper, recently moved to Hillsborough, was defeated for election to the assembly because he was said to have commented that the votes of "mechanics" could be purchased with a dram. As an associate of the gentlemen who called the political shots, Burke could scarcely have started out by challenging the local system.[60]

At the state level, in contrast, he displayed less caution than some conservative easterners, and at the national level, he was noteworthy by his independent devotion to republican principles, especially to the state sovereignty of North Carolina. Even as a single-minded republican, his anxiety with the uses of power did not by itself distinguish him from others who had been involved in the struggle against British tyranny. Burke subscribed to the popular ideals of the free and proper exercise of power, balanced government, consent of the governed, fear of executive tyranny, bicameralism and so on. Yet, he was more aware of the implications of these ideals, whether at the hands of the British or as he soon would discern, at the hands of his own Continental Congress. His role in the North Carolina constitutional debate had sharpened his awareness and given him a commitment that he would now energetically defend. In the Continental Congress, during the next phase of his career, Thomas Burke acted as a sentinel of the system that he had helped to construct.

SENTINEL OF STATE SOVEREIGNTY

The Continental Congress in which Burke took his seat was far different than the institution which had first emerged in September of 1774. Earlier it was a gathering of resistance leaders from each of the colonies; their formal activities were limited to joint statements of opposition and a boycott of British goods. The system of committees transposed from the colonial legislatures served well for the terminal projects initiated in the Congress, and that which could not be transacted in regular sessions was accomplished in informal politics practiced outside the chamber and committee rooms. Accordingly, the instigators of revolutionary protest in the various colonies were given an opportunity to get acquainted and to synchronize their thinking. They would view with greater confidence the prospect of future confrontations with England.

By May of 1775, when the second Congress convened, the recent battles of Lexington and Concord had altered the context of opposition. Now the attention of Congress was automatically shifted to military questions which required the Congress to assume a heavy legislative and administrative burden. At first, it attempted to force new wine into old bottles, retaining the committee system of organization, but the loads placed on the delegates far exceeded their quantum of time and knowledge. A delegate might be called upon for service on as many as thirty committees during a year, to develop a different expertise for each and to make time from an already crowded schedule. The defective structure of administration was apparent to the critical and schematic minds of men like Robert Morris and Samuel Chase, and as a result, in December of 1776, a committee was appointed to prepare a plan for placing executive affairs in the hands of men from outside of Congress. The Congress, however, never really solved its dilemma. The problem of organization, no matter what was attempted, kept falling back in its lap.

Although overloaded with business, the Continental Congress in 1777 still exuded much of its initial zeal. The continued presence of Robert Morris, James Wilson, Samuel and John Adams, and Richard Henry Lee gave the proceedings a luster that was lacking in the years that followed. The members of Congress represented a galaxy of high literacy, political experience, professionalism, and cosmopolitanism. A majority had received formal academic training, and a few such as Richard Henry Lee had been able to study abroad. Most had practiced law and served a political apprenticeship in the provincial legislatures. Springing primarily from centrally located towns, they felt the early impact of British economic measures and learned to express vigorous opposition. They were the gate-keepers of the Revolutionary establishment. The concerted opposition of the thirteen independent states was testimony to the delegates' capacities for leadership and political coordination.[1]

However, the Congress had begun to suffer from the turnover of members and absenteeism. John Adams complained in February that he had "the melancholly [*sic*] Prospect before me of a Congress continually changing, untill [*sic*] very few Faces remain, that I saw in the First Congress."[2] Those who had left, he explained, had either died, resigned, or were serving at home in the state governments. William Hooper also expressed concern over the increasing absenteeism. He estimated in January that only twenty-two members were in attendance. As a result, delegates lacked the overall experience and knowledge to deal with more specialized questions like finance and military supply. Hooper linked this deficiency with the rapid execution of business in Congress, observing that the "suddenness of decision may be truly attributed to ignorance of the subject."[3]

Frequently, the sessions of Congress, despite the devotion of the delegates, were studies in futility. The assembly seemed helpless before the centrifugal forces that threatened to undermine the war effort. In September and October

of 1776, when Washington's army faced the expira-
tion of enlistments, Congress lengthily debated
the creation of a new military establishment.
Finally, panicked by the British advance into
New Jersey, the delegates in December prematurely
and indecorously fled from Philadelphia to Baltimore. Fortunately, the timely victories at Trent-
on and Princeton in late December renewed the flow
of enlistments sufficiently to stave off the threat
of disintegration.

Inside the Congress, as Burke related to Governor Caswell, the eastern areas were suspected of
combining to profit from the war effort. The
southern delegates were convinced that higher
interest rates on government loans would only result in lining the pockets of the northern financial interests. Burke himself was concerned that
states like Pennsylvania, Maryland, and New Jersey, whose limits were already established, would
try to dispossess those with western land claims.
He advised the state authorities not to permit
any agreements respecting North Carolina's boundaries.[4]

After arriving in Baltimore and taking his
seat on February 5, 1777, Burke immediately made
a record of what occurred in Congress and sent
these abstracts to Governor Caswell. He himself
quickly joined in the debates. Two days after
his first appearance, he was speaking on a motion
which would have required all the states except
Virginia and Massachusetts to send fuller delegations to Congress. Others who were opposed
had pointed out that many states could neither
afford more money nor manpower to increase their
delegations, and Burke as the only delegate from
North Carolina lost no time in justifying his
state's predicament. With uncharacteristic humility, he remarked that the few days that he had
spent in Congress had shown that the demands of
his work exceeded his abilities and experience.
Yet this was not the fault of North Carolina; it
was not expected that delegates separated from
their families and means of support could serve
indefinitely, and there were insufficient resources in the state for supporting a larger

51

delegation. As a result, Burke charged that his
state was being affronted, a charge that was vigorously denied by the sponsors of the motion.
Congress backed off from requiring extra delegates,
although it later established a minimum of two
members in the draft of the Articles of Confederation.[5]

Burke continued his vigilance on the subsequent question of whether to increase interest
rates to six percent. Its advocates argued that
higher interest rates for continental securities
were the only means to rectify the economy, especially the problem of rising prices. If the financial incentives were enhanced, they added, it
would attract the surplus funds of merchants and
financiers, and certainly it was preferable to
further issues of currency. After listening to
the debate, he confessed to the delegates that
he had been unable to get much information. Despite his lack of financial experience, he was
doubtful that further loans could be attracted
in North Carolina, where farmers and gentlemen
might speculate but would reserve their working
capital for the purchase of goods. This distrust
of the northern financial community which Thomas
Burke and other southerners expressed in 1777
would persist throughout the Revolution and into
the period of the new republic. In Burke's case,
however, he became more friendly with the Philadelphia financiers later in the war when the
South was in desperate need of financial support
and the Congress virtually bankrupt.[6]

While these questions were being discussed,
Congress was called upon to give its opinion concerning a conference of the New England states
which had taken place in December of 1776 at the
invitation of Rhode Island. As a result of British military activities, Rhode Island and her
neighbors feared the onset of a full-scale invasion. Describing the debate as "long and inter-
esting...," Burke refused nonetheless to commit
himself to any statement of what his state could
not do.[7] In fact, he contended that North Carolina could do anything "which she had not pre-
cluded herself from by plain and express declaration."[8]

After hearing these arguments, Congress approved the New England conference and proposed that the other states conduct similar regional meetings. In the discussion over how the states would be grouped, Burke encountered a rebuff, as Virginia refused to be linked with North Carolina, insisting instead on Maryland. The North Carolina delegate rose to complain that his state would be excluded from making regulations which might affect her interests, since her markets were chiefly in Virginia. The people of North Carolina, he added, had too much common sense to make regulations that might in the future prevent her from acting against the possible discriminations of Virginia. Richard Henry Lee privately confided to him that he need not worry since Virginia could not enforce regulations that affected other states. Burke responded that he thought it arrogant on the part of Virginia to presume itself the arbiter of North Carolina's affairs and to envision making policies without her consent that would undoubtedly have some impact.[9]

Burke viewed the relationship of the states in a different light than did many of the other delegates. While the shadow of the British experience still darkened many minds, he insisted that the states were independent both from the English and from each other. Burke contended that the duties of the states were determined by the principles of international law, or the "Law of Nations." The states were associated for the purpose of resisting Great Britain. Aside from their voluntary commitments, they stood toward each other as independent nations. But, like independent nations elsewhere, they had to pay the price of autonomy, which meant that they were vulnerable to external threats from their neighbors. Burke's intention was to prevent usurpation of his state's sovereignty, and in so doing, he assiduously cited the "Law of Nations" to define the obligations and prerogatives of statehood.[10]

Burke had even more reason for concern over the debates on February 25, which struck him as threatening to the sovereignty of North Carolina.

The issue was the apprehension of deserters; it had been recommended in a committee report that the states pass laws empowering local officials to seize anyone suspected of desertion. The resolution that passed Congress, however, authorized local committees of inspection and observation to apprehend deserters and convey them directly to the continental army. After the vote, Burke demanded that his dissent be entered in the journals of Congress. After listening to his strong objections, the delegates decided to reconsider the resolution. The debate that followed pitted Burke against James Wilson of Pennsylvania, a strong advocate of national authority.[11]

Wilson contended that any topic relating to national authority was a proper area for congressional action. Since the army was the child of Congress, it too was subject to that body's resolutions, which included the apprehending of military deserters. He further claimed that if army officers could capture deserters, then Congress could also appoint civil magistrates to hear evidence and pass verdicts. According to Wilson, soldiers were not subject to the laws of the states, but rather to continental military regulations. Assignment of officers to enforce those laws was no different than appointing commissaries or other military functionaries.[12]

Burke's reply emphasized that Congress was usurping powers that were not intended for its use. By such actions, it could nullify the constitutions and laws of the states. This would result in separate jurisdiction insulated from state control which might act contrary to the will of the states. Such a condition would violate the ideal of government by consent and might lead to a worse type of tyranny. It threatened to violate "all the Rights of the Citizen's personal freedom."[13] Here, Burke was returning to the principles expressed in the Orange County Instructions. Sovereignty rested in the hands of the people at large, who were the source of all political power. Since that power was delegated to the state assembly, only the representatives

of the people acting in compliance with the state
constitution could deal with questions of the
people's rights. Why resist the unconscionable
use of power by the British, Burke asked, if only
to re-enact it through the very institutions established to resist the original acts of tyranny?[14]

Rather than stop with general observations,
Burke relentlessly pursued Wilson's arguments
into all of their murky corridors. If every officer could detain deserters, he inquired, could
any soldier "call whom he pleased a deserter and
Imprison and punish him as such?"[15] In legal
proceedings, such as the capture and return of
deserters, a power to judge was also present.
If Congress could delegate this authority, it
would be tantamount to allowing military officers
to exercise "Magisterial Discretion and subject
the citizens to that discretion."[16] At least,
the committees of inspection, to which Congress
had earlier recommended the problem of desertion,
derived powers from the authority of the people.
Permitting army officers to exercise these powers
could only lead to unmitigated abuses.[17]

Stunned by Burke's forcefulness, Wilson confessed that he had sketched the issue imprecisely,
but he re-emphasized the practical problem that
would result if deserters were only apprehended
in the state where they had enlisted. His view
was endorsed by Richard Henry Lee who advised that
the question should not be defined too precisely.
After all, the newspapers frequently advertised
for deserters, and this activity was not regarded
as the exercise of magisterial power. John Adams
confessed that he had overlooked the ramifications
which Burke had raised and that the Articles of
War would probably have to be enacted into state
laws; still he believed that the Army officers had
recognized this potential encroachment on state
powers, or they would have pushed the prosecution
of deserters more vigorously.[18]

Burke was disturbed by these arguments, particularly by the attempt of Wilson and Richard
Henry Lee to justify the application of illegal

powers by an appeal to necessity. Necessity was
merely an excuse, he urged, which made actions appear inevitable to those who were sitting in judgment of them. This attitude had often been applied
to legalize unjustifiable impositions like ship
money, royal dispensations, and the recent exactions of Great Britain on America. Burke doubted
that relying on the state would compromise the
enforcement of laws against deserters; it would
simply mean that a fair trial could be given prior
to punishment. Publishing rewards for bringing
suspects before tribunals, as Lee had suggested,
was far different than empowering temporary state
residents both to apprehend and try them. Burke
re-emphasized the necessity of consent. Certainly soldiers had agreed to subject themselves to
martial law, but it was the duty of the state to
decide whether a given individual had actually committed himself to military authority by his own
consent. Otherwise, the deserter would be judged
by his accusers, which was contrary to the canons
of jurisprudence.[19]

Burke's literalism was unanticipated. Although the rights of men had pervaded the anti-
British rhetoric, the rights of Americans with
respect to their own government had been taken
for granted. So absorbing was the project of
constructing a military machine that little time
remained for constitutional speculations. Richard Henry Lee, who later grasped the mantle of
states' rights and wrote tracts opposing the Constitution, was in 1777 devoted to strengthening the
national government. The so-called radicals had
spearheaded intercolonial cooperation against
British usurpations and were not attuned to conflicts between the states and the embryonic
national government. Moreover, Richard Henry
Lee, John Adams, and James Wilson represented
states whose size guaranteed a secure position
in any confederation. Lacking commerce and unity,
militarily insecure, wedged between Virginia and
South Carolina, the state of North Carolina was
in a marginal position which rendered it more
sensitive to potential threats or slights from
its neighbors. Burke, who closely identified with
his state's interests, grasped and fashioned these

56

incongruities into a statement of political principle.

On the following day, February 26, Burke was
again the gadfly of the congressional session.
That morning, it was resolved to adjourn the Congress from Baltimore back to Philadelphia. The
delegates from the distant South resisted the motion. They urged that it would be pointless to
put aside so much essential business with little
prospect of reconvening for several weeks. After
all, the weather was poor, and some of the delegates were encumbered with obligations at home.
Had not General Washington recently informed them
that the enemy might be contemplating an attack
on Philadelphia and that he lacked the force to
stop them? The Board of War, which was lacking
laborers and wagons, felt that business might be
conducted more expeditiously at Philadelphia, yet
others observed that the effort of moving to Philadelphia would cause that and all other business
to grind to a standstill. When a peevish argument
arose on this point, Burke invoked a rule in the
constitution of Congress to have further debate
postponed for a day.[20]

Far from calming the proceedings, Burke's
motion unleashed a torrent of controversy. Although the rules permitted a single state to postpone debate, the eastern delegates (in particular
John Adams, John Witherspoon, and James Wilson)
strenuously objected to its unilateral application.
Since the rule was untested, they wished to refer
it to Congress for interpretation. Perhaps chas-
tened by Burke's earlier criticisms, Richard Henry
Lee did not as usual back the eastern stance. Instead, he pointed to the inconsistency of voting
on a privilege which was reserved to the states
in the original rules of Congress. Although the
members might dislike the rule, they should first
allow the state to invoke it and afterwards consider amending it. His brother, Francis Lightfoot Lee, pursued this argument. He recalled to
Congress that the rule was originally designed
to prevent majorities in the House from taking
precipitate action, and if the rule itself were
made contingent on majorities, then a majority

could always block its application. Another southern delegate "thought it a very extraordinary kind
of proposition to submit to a Majority whether
that Majority should be checked by a Power absolutely reserved for that purpose."[21]

Burke took the floor again to state his position with greater precision. He would not allow
himself to be part of any debate regarding a proposition plainly set forth in the constitution of
Congress. Since the rules governing Congress had
been adopted by common consent, dispensation could
only be by the same means. If a majority could
arbitrarily oppose the rules, no state could be
secure. What would happen if a majority voted
that three or four or five states could institute
their own rules of procedure? It was obvious to
Burke that a few delegates might arrogate to themselves the whole authority of Congress. This would
be tantamount to "an arbitrary tyrannical discretion."[22] The gentlemen were mistaken if they
thought for a minute that Burke would tamely submit to an invasion of his state's rights. If
they persisted in their attempts, he would no
longer consider the Congress an agency "which
ought to be trusted with the Liberties of their
Fellow Citizens and he [Burke] would shape his
conduct accordingly."[23] In short, the delegate
from North Carolina threatened to withdraw if
the question were put. Convinced of Burke's earn-
estness, the eastern delegates waived their opposition, and he was able to exercise his right.[24]

Since the question of whether to adjourn
could be delayed for only one day, it reappeared
in the next day's debate. Burke was already irritated because the Congress had refused to permit
the debates to be entered in the Journals. Since
his testimony would be unavailable if "impeached,"
he would have to speak in a manner which they would
remember. After all, the members might be called
upon one day as witnesses. Following this inci-
sive aside, Burke proceeded to a more general
assault on Congress, using the issue of adjournment as his lever. He observed with regret that
"a predetermined Majority was as much a *ratio
ultima* in Congress as in the British Parliament."[25]

After his experience of the previous day, he had
no tender regard for the personal safety of the
delegates. To the contrary, he argued with ill-
disguised rancor that if all of them were killed
or captured, "public Business wou[ld] suffer no
other injury except the delay until other members
could be chosen [sic]."[26] Now that Burke felt on
equal terms with the other members, he deprecated
their importance as he did his own. He assured
the delegates that his own state had better men
than himself, and he was certain also that "every
state had as good as any in Congress."[27] If it
were simply a matter of the danger which might
result from moving Congress to Philadelphia, he
would not hesitate to acquiesce. He would vote
against adjournment, however, because it was
unwise to halt public business when there was
little chance of resumption for several weeks
or even longer.

Thomas Burke was puzzled and disillusioned
by the reckless atmosphere of congressional politics. In an era of self-analysis, he was extremely conscious of the manner in which men be-
haved. Like the philosopher Mandeville, he attributed individual and institutional behavior to
the self-interest of men interacting in society.
Yet it was difficult to detect unmistakable signs
of self-interest among the members of Congress.
Like himself, many delegates were depriving themselves of the benefits of family and profession
and were serving "under many Insurmountable Difficulties and Inconveniences."[28] Nevertheless, he
was disturbed by their recent attempt to dispense
with the rules. What could induce men with no
apparent motive to enlarge the scope of their power? In a letter to Richard Caswell, he avowed
his belief that "the Root of the Evil is deep
in human Nature."[29] Although its growth could
be partially arrested, the evil could never be
completely extirpated. To prevent abuses of
power, men would have to be restrained by "something which they cannot remove when they please."[30]
Only institutional safeguards and unrelenting
vigilance could defend the community from this
mechanistic version of original sin.

Here, the Newtonian in Burke was striving to reduce human nature to the predictable laws of the universe. To establish a connection, it was necessary to find an empirical means of verifying this hunger for power, something that he had failed to observe in his previous experience with the delegates. In an attempt to reconcile this discrepancy, he was forced to entertain a rational view of this irrational behavior. In his view, man's moral nature could not control the opposing forces within him. Burke was separating power from the human will that exercised it and treating it as an objective entity. Man was a victim of the mechanical universe of which he had so recently become aware. Just as the universe was moved by forces like gravity, man was animated by forces which drove him to irrational actions.

> What could Induce Individuals blest with peaceable domestic affluence to forego all the enjoyment of a pleasing home, to neglect their private affairs, and at the expence [*sic*] of all their time and some part of their private fortunes, to attend public Business under many Insurmountable Difficulties and Inconveniences? What but a generous Zeal for the Public? And what can Induce such men to Endeavour at increasing the Power with which they are Invested, when their Tenure of it must be neither pleasure or profit? *This is a Question I believe cannot be answered but by a plain declaration that Power of all kinds has an Irresistible propensity to increase a desire for itself. It gives the Passion of ambition a Velocity which Increases in its progress, and this is a passion which grows in proportion as it is gratified.*[31]

Burke was verging towards a less optimistic view of man. Like the Lockean conception of society, the rationalistic view of man included a latent pessimism. Although the universe was rational, perhaps man was not. And if man was

60

invested by forces beyond his control, it might become necessary to restrain him with institutional safeguards. Since the American Congress was so disregardful of basic freedoms, would not others be even more so? The original sin of abusing political power was present in all men. What would happen when the habit of political obedience was more firmly ingrained in the common man? Would they not lose sight of the original principles that gave rise to government? Burke concluded that the "more experience I acquire, the stronger is my Conviction that *unlimited power can not be safely Trusted to any man or set of men on Earth.*"[32]

The political image of man in society which Thomas Burke held in 1776 was the product of the colonial experience and the attempts to reassemble the civil contract after the tyrannic acts of the British had dissolved it. The nature of Revolutionary thought was attributed to the British; reconstructing government on the pure principles of consent and due process would extirpate the evils. If the corruption of executive government could be removed, or if the beguiled supporters of Great Britain in America could be dissuaded from their erroneous ways, then government and society could be reconstituted on a more benevolent basis. Now, the experience of laboring in the vineyards of the new order was beginning to temper that initial ardor. Burke was, as others soon would, turning inward and applying the indelible impressions of tyranny to his own cause. Already, the experience of continental service was proving to be a catalyst to new forms of Revolutionary thought.

An occasion to interject his concerns arose unexpectedly in April of 1777 when Congress resumed consideration of the Articles of Confederation. An earlier version of the Articles had been drafted in July of 1775 by Benjamin Franklin. Congress was then, however, operating under the polite fiction that they were loyal subjects of Great Britain, and as a result Franklin's Articles were rejected. In June of 1776, the moment seemed more opportune, and a committee under John Dickinson

61

was appointed to draw up a national constitution. The draft of the Articles drawn up by Dickinson was introduced on July 12, 1776, and since then its progress had been slow. Most of the delegates were divided over the provisions for state representation in Congress, taxation, and control of western lands. After being scrutinized by Congress in July and August, the Articles were recommitted. A second set of Articles was drafted which incorporated many of the suggested alterations but soon afterwards the lengthy debates on the Confederation had to be put aside.[33]

Burke had been first exposed to plans for Confederation in 1775, when Franklin's proposal came before the North Carolina provincial Congress. As a veteran of the lengthy constitutional deliberations in his own state, Thomas Burke was now a wary analyst of political systems. On April 29, he informed Governor Caswell that the Confederation was being considered every second day in Congress and pointedly stated that he would agree to the provisions only on the "clearest conviction and most uncontroverted principles."[34]

Burke's opportunity came when the delegates were considering Article III of Dickinson's revised draft which attempted to distinguish the powers of the states from those given to the Confederation. Dickinson had confined the exclusive power of the states to regulation of their internal police. Beyond that, the states retained only those powers which did not conflict with the Articles of Confederation, while the delineation between the two sectors of government was suspiciously murky. The presumption in favor of national authority struck Burke as incongruous and rekindled in him the specter of future Congresses usurping the powers of the states. In his view, this emphasis "was not what the states expected."[35] As a result, he proposed an amendment to Article III which reserved to the states all powers that were not expressly granted to the United States and further proclaimed their sovereignty, freedom and independence..."[36]

When he first introduced his resolution, it
was "so little understood" that it was some time
before it was seconded.[37] As before, he faced
the combined opposition of James Wilson and Richard Henry Lee. By the time a roll call was taken,
however, Burke had made his case, and eleven
states voted in favor of it, while only Lee and
Whipple of New Hampshire were opposed. The result was that Article II of the final draft pro-
foundly differed from Article III that John Dickinson had drafted.[38]

> ART. III. [Dickinson Draft] Each Colony
> shall retain and enjoy as much of its
> present Laws, Rights and Customs, as it
> may think fit, and reserves to itself
> the sole and exclusive Regulation and
> Government of its internal police, in
> all matters that shall not interfere
> with the Articles of this Confederation.[39]

> ART. II. [Burke's amendment] Each State
> retains its sovereignty, freedom and
> independence, and every other power,
> jurisdiction, and right, which is not
> by this confederation expressly dele-
> gated to the United States, in Congress
> assembled.[40]

Although Burke's amendment has sometimes been
ascribed to states' rights radicalism, it is more
likely the result of his own respect for the state
system and his fear of political despotism. Frequently the political anatomy of 1776 and 1777
has been confused with that of the late 1780's.
Some advocates of central authority like James
Wilson did maintain the same stance with respect
to the Constitution that they struck toward the
Articles. Others like Richard Henry Lee, who
were sirens of nationalism in 1777, later repented
and became bulwarks of state sovereignty. It is
well to remember that Dickinson's draft of the
Articles contained many of the weaknesses that
its critics later described. These included the
requirement of unanimous consent in order to amend,
the lack of taxing power, and an executive that
was virtually non-existent.[41] In his proposal to

revamp Congress several weeks later, Burke would
demonstrate that he was not opposed to having an
effective national government, but merely disturbed by the extent and vagueness of its powers.

In the long run, the amendment to the Articles was to be the most important contribution
of Burke's brief career. In 1791, eight years
after he died, a modified version of his states'
rights provision was incorporated into the Bill
of Rights. Omitting the term "expressly," the
Tenth Amendment guarantees that "the powers not
delegated to the United States by the Constitution, nor prohibited to it by the States, are reserved to the States respectively, or to the
people."[42] Despite the significant change in
language, the basic principle of the earlier version was retained, though in less forceful terms.
While indicative of Burke's early political thought,
it also stands as a reminder of a philosophy that
was frequently evident in the Revolutionary era.
Thomas Burke had made his own unique application
of those ideas. As the sentinel of state sovereignty, he had devised a safeguard for the budding
system and had helped to clarify the always complex relationship between the central government
and its constituent parts.

Much time would be spent scrutinizing the
Articles before Congress finally approved them.
Despite the states' rights amendment, Burke was
never reconciled to the product of those deliberations. He could not accept a system which granted
vital powers to the central government and denied
others to the states. His objections would be
elaborated in a lengthy critique, "Notes on the
Articles of Confederation," which he placed before the North Carolina Assembly in late 1777.
In it, he found fault with nearly all the articles passed after his proposal. He objected, for
example, to the privileges and immunities clause,
giving all citizens of one state the same rights
in other states--a provision that was later included in the Constitution.[43]

As one might expect, Burke resented almost
all limitations on the powers of the states. It

64

was unfair, he argued, to keep the states from
taxing imports and exports. He felt that the
states should be allowed to negotiate agreements
with each other and with foreign governments.
He plausibly maintained that any limitations would
economically impair the state or keep it from best
pursuing its interests. His critique also encom-
passed the lesser powers granted solely to the
national government--the power to determine the
metallic content of coins or to fix weights and
measures.[44]

Nor could he agree with the exclusive control of Indian affairs by the Confederation nor
the monopoly on the construction of naval vessels.
Why should the responsibility for the navy in
peacetime belong only to the national government?
Such a narrow policy would keep the nation from
building a powerful navy. He argued that the
quality of emulation in states as in private individuals would make it possible to supply the United
States with a formidable navy. Perhaps he was
thinking of the ships that North Carolina had already acquired for its own defense.[45]

Burke was even reluctant to grant certain
powers to the central government at all. These
included both borrowing and issuing currency at
will. Such an approach would give Congress the
power over all property and would contradict the
ideals of the North Carolina constitution. As a
good republican, Burke believed any form of taxation should take place only with the direct consent of the voters. He further disagreed with the
plan to grant judicial powers to the Confederation.
What worried him most was the fear that a faction
in Congress would nominate judges who were biased
toward certain states and who would abuse their
powers. As of 1777 and 1778, he was unwilling to
make the leap of faith in support of national
powers, in part because of his states' rights
ideal and also because his experiences in Congress
seemed to confirm his own distrust of power.[46]

In the end, Burke's objections had only a
fleeting impact. When the General Assembly met
in December of 1777, he placed his "Notes" before

a joint committee of both houses. These were accompanied by a statement reiterating his opposition to stationing continental troops within the states. He even urged North Carolina to state its determination not to be bound by anything contrary to the instructions given to its members, a position reminiscent of later doctrines of nullification. The Assembly at first heeded his warnings and only ratified a part of the Articles. In March of 1778, however, the legislature reversed itself and fully endorsed the Confederation.[47]

Even in North Carolina, Thomas Burke's position on states' rights was somewhat unique. Cornelius Harnett, the garrulous delegate from Cape Fear, wrote Burke from Philadelphia in late 1777: "The child Congress has been big with, these two years past, is at last brought forth--(Confederation)." He added: "I fear it will by the several Legislatures be thought a little deformed--you will think it a Monster."[48] Harnett characterized it as "the best Confederacy that could be formed especially when we consider the number of states, their different Interests, Customs, etc., etc."[49] He also regarded it as "the most difficult piece of Business that ever was undertaken by any public Body."[50] Burke was not nearly as convinced of the capacities of Congress for wisdom. He saw only a document that had been carelessly prepared, without any application of the basic axioms of free and just government, as if Congress in their haste had forgotten their recent experience with the tyranny of majorities in Parliament.

Burke's opposition to the Articles of Confederation marked the high tide of his states' rights philosophy. The pristine ideals of republicanism, as yet undisturbed by his service in a national body, provided a firm basis for judging the behavior of Congress. The states, especially North Carolina, seemed best to embody those ideals. Yet the dilemma of acting effectively as a delegate while opposing the power of Congress would not be easily resolved. During 1777 and 1778, Burke's commitment to Congress would remain tenuous and erratic. In time, new concerns would

66

alter his viewpoint and role as a delegate, at
first imperceptibly and then with obvious urgency.

PITFALLS OF PUBLIC SERVICE

If Congress had often proved ineffectual, it was in part the product of its onerous routine. Daily service in the meager confines of the Pennsylvania State House and evening duties on boards and committees encouraged fixations on small matters to the exclusion of larger concerns. Since there were few delegates in Congress and many varied items for their cognizance, the members were forced to familiarize themselves with a wide variety of topics. This was particularly true of committee assignments. On February 5, Burke had been added to the standing committee on Indian Affairs, and in March he was appointed to the Appeals Committee, where he served with John Adams.[1]

Adams had mixed feelings concerning his experience with the committee system. He later recalled that "the pleasantest part of my Labours for the four years I spent in Congress...was in the naval committee."[2] When the evening's business had been concluded, the elderly member from Rhode Island, Stephen Hopkins, mellow from drinking rum all evening, would entertain the group with "Wit, Humour, Anecdotes, Science, and Learning."[3] But Adams also recalled that he had been "incessantly employed" at other times, in regular sessions of Congress each afternoon and on committees during the evenings and even in the mornings. His memory of service on the Board of War was not as pleasant as that of the Naval Committee.

> The Duties of this Board kept me in Continual Employment not to say Drudgery from this 12th of June 1776 till the eleventh of November 1777 when I left Congress forever. Not only my Mornings and Evenings were filled with the Crowd of Business before that Board, but a great Part of my Time in Congress was engaged in making, explaining and justifying our reports and Proceedings.[4]

The delegates were forced to spend much of their time on details which otherwise might have been assigned to a department under a single, accountable head. Much of the critical financial and military business was first referred to special committees. This included letters sent to Congress by military commanders, state officials, and even private individuals. The diversity of these matters meant that an inordinate number of committees with terminal functions was created--William Livingston during his term in Congress had served on eleven such groups, and Thomas McKean had actually been assigned to thirty-three during a year, of which he was chairman of five. Thomas Burke also received a variety of terminal assignments ranging from propaganda to recruiting, to making up payrolls, and finally to the conduct of military officers. As a result of these assignments, he had the opportunity for close contact with men such as James Wilson, William Duer, and Richard Henry Lee. While some of the questions vitally concerned the conduct of the war, others might have been handled by a hired staff. In late May, for example, Burke was one of those appointed to form an estimate of the teams necessary to convey adequate provisions for General Washington's army. Some delegates agreed with Robert Morris that "so long as that respectable body [Congress] persist in the attempt to execute, as well as deliberate on their business, it will never be done as it ought."[5]

In June of 1775, Silas Deane, representing Connecticut, had observed that Congress "tho' not numerous, are yet a very unwieldy Body."[6] This was equally true in the spring of 1777. Although inundated by administrative detail, the Congress stubbornly preserved its ponderous, deliberative format. As a result, it was forced to deal in regular sessions with low priority items such as trivial expenditures and incoming correspondence. Varied details concerning imports, prisoners, manufactures, and military promotions, to name a few, all competed for their attention. In April of 1776, for example, Congress had spent valuable time devising a means for a Tory prisoner to get "the benefit of air in his room, and of walking

70

every morning in the yard."[7]   During the summer
of 1777, Congress was driven to take over much of
the responsibility for defending Philadelphia from
the ineffectual Pennsylvania government. On July
23, it empowered the Secret Committee to contact
bakers to make flour into brisket for the army,
and on July 25 they authorized the Board of War
to contract with the proper persons for supplying
the army with beer, cider, vegetables, soap, vine-
gar, and sauerkraut.[8]

As if this were not enough, the duties of
delegates in Congress included painstaking exertions on behalf of their individual states. When
John Penn left in May to join Burke in Congress,
Governor Caswell had instructed him to procure
250,000 dollars for North Carolina from her continental account. On June 10, the frantic Caswell,
not having received the money, appealed to Burke
"For God's sake let it [the money] be sent out
with the greatest dispatch."[9]   The money was to
be used for recruiting a new regiment, and lack
of funds had brought recruitment nearly to a standstill. On July 5, Burke reported that although
Penn had arrived and brought the necessary papers,
the Treasury was nearly exhausted. Nevertheless,
he and Penn had obtained an order from the Treasury
for the amount. The Continental printing press
was at Baltimore, and when the new currency was
printed and signed, the Board of War would have
it forwarded to North Carolina.

In addition, while Burke was in Baltimore,
his attention was drawn to the prisoners from
the Battle of Moore's Creek Bridge in North Carolina, who had been taken to Maryland for safekeep-
ing after their defeat in 1776. Upon their request, he gave them permission to have their parole in Frederick, Maryland. He also prevailed
on Congress at Caswell's request to take a new
battalion being raised in North Carolina and an
artillery company into continental pay. The Governor further called on him to obtain pay warrants
so that the North Carolina troops could be paid,
and he managed to secure this request as well.[10]

In addition, Burke received news and information from North Carolina. Letters from friends
at home periodically assured him that his wife
was in good health. There were also frequent accounts of what had taken place in sessions of the
General Assembly or of conditions in the state.
Yet the difficulties of communication and transportation created a gap in information. When Burke
informed Caswell that reports of infectious dis-
eases in North Carolina were circulating, the Governor replied that he had never heard anything
about them. On learning that North Carolina troops
undergoing innoculation at Alexandria were in need
of shoes, the North Carolina delegate had the
Clothier General forward the footwear to the troops
after their recuperation from the difficult innocu-
lations.[11]

Burke further transmitted a variety of impressions as well as demands. In March, he informed the Governor that their expenses in Philadelphia, where the Congress had recently moved,
were "incredible."[12] He also asked for a leave
of absence during the summer and suggested that
additional delegates be appointed to take his
place. Although the General Assembly ignored
his request, Caswell confided to Burke that it
would be proper for him to have a short leave of
absence. On July 5, intending to leave shortly
for home, he described to the Governor his reaction to two recent celebrations that marked the
first anniversary of the British defeat at Charleston and of the Declaration of Independence. At
both events, a Hessian band captured at Princeton
in December had performed "very delightfully,"
as the pleasure of the onlookers was enhanced "by
the reflection that they were hired by the British
Court for purposes very different from those to
which they were applied."[13] As for the North Carolina troops in continental service, Burke reported
that they were encamped a mile from the city under
the command of General Francis Nash, a neighbor
from Hillsborough, who was staying at his lodgings.
He also informed the Governor that his son, Captain William Caswell, was with the North Carolina
battalion and would be coming to dinner the following day.[14]

One task, the appointment of a major general, was not a subject for such casual reflections. Normally the General Assembly could be consulted on military appointments, but it was not in session. Burke had earlier sponsored a motion that officers of the army be obtained through promotion, the criteria being seniority, merit, and the state quota. Although the Commissions were to be signed by Congress, the promotions would be automatic. Burke was concerned by the power that Congress might exercise over the states if appointment of officers were left exclusively in its hands.[15]

Yet, he soon deviated from his own principles. With General Moore dead, a vacancy had to be filled. In early August, Burke took the unusual step of nominating an outsider, Dr. Edward Hand of Pennsylvania, as a General of the North Carolina battalion. His reasons for doing so are not clear, and he undoubtedly did not anticipate the storm of protest that would arise from the North Carolina officer corps. Opposition to state interests was hazardous, even for the champion of state sovereignty. It is very probable that Burke shared the oft-repeated impression of North Carolina officers as incompetent and felt compelled to depart from the normal practice. If, as he later stated, he was simply trying to obtain the most qualified candidate, he probably decided that the appointment of Hand was the only way of accomplishing this.[16]

On August 15, Burke was given a paper signed by North Carolina's senior officers protesting the appointment. The statement criticized his preference for a "country man" rather than an officer of the state that he represented. The officers insisted that their long and arduous service for the state should have merited better treatment by their delegate in Congress. They observed that Hand was "unknown to almost every person in North Carolina, except to Dr. Burke."[17] Since the appointment had not been publicly announced, they called on him to provide them with further information.[18]

Thomas Burke's response was as rapid as it was angry. It had been indicated that the statement had General Nash's approval, and as a result

Burke fired off a tirade to Nash. To Burke, the "scandalous charge of partiality, in the discharge of my duty," was a personal affront.[19] He bluntly informed Nash that he should have known "Partialities have never found place with me," and demanded to know whether Nash had endorsed the statement.[20]

Although no record exists of Nash's response, the incident appears to have hurt Burke's political standing. In the spring of 1777, his popularity in North Carolina had moved the General Assembly to name a county after him. By the following April, the Assembly in elections for Congress excluded him from the delegation. The incident was also unfortunate from a personal standpoint. Burke chose to regard the protest in a personal rather than a political sense. Always sensitive to insinuations concerning his character, he unnecessarily brought his friend, General Nash, into the squabble.[21]

Still, Burke's experience in Congress was somewhat more encouraging. Disillusioned at first by the attitudes he had encountered, he now became more hopeful. In addition to his states' rights amendment, the question of the recruiting service had again been raised, and this time his opinions had more effect. The North Carolina delegate had attributed the slowness of recruitment to the lack of state regulation, and the other delegates seemed to agree. They did not oppose the resolution which he now introduced. Indeed, despite rumors of an assault by the enemy on Philadelphia, Congress refused to leave, and the fainthearted among them were loudly ridiculed. Never one to flee from danger or controversy, Burke intended "to stay in the city, & give my best assistance for its defense."[22] In May, he found another encouraging sign that Congress had come to its senses. When a naval captain commanding a continental frigate wrote an insulting letter to the Governor of Maryland, Congress suspended him, a move that Burke strongly supported. Perhaps the delegates were finally "sensible that the honour and dignity of the Magistrates of the States ought to be preserved and inviolable."[23]

In early May, 1777, Burke followed up his amendment to the Articles with a more sweeping proposal, which almost amounted to a new plan of government. The essential feature of his scheme was a bicameral legislature, which Burke considered indispensable to sound government. A General Council of the states would be combined with an upper chamber known as the Council of State. The General Council would be composed of delegates from the states chosen in whatever manner they prescribed, while the Council of State would be composed of one delegate elected also from each state. Any legislation approved by both chambers would be binding on the states. Most decisions would be made by a simple majority except those involving a declaration of war. When there was neither an invasion nor a previous declaration of war by a hostile power, a majority of three-fourths would be necessary for such an action. Any state declining to participate would be required only to refuse assistance to the enemy, but would be exempted from the expenses involved as well as any benefits accruing from the war. Burke's proposal for the creation of a bicameral legislature with different types of representation foreshadowed the system adopted in 1787. His colleagues in Congress, however, were not ready for a radical change in the existing unicameral structure. Voted on as a question of whether the Congress should consist of two houses, Burke's proposal was rejected, and as a result the whole measure was dropped. The only reasons given were two vague notations suggesting that the extended legislative process would cause delays in executing business and that the plan was somehow reminiscent of the distinctions embodied in the British constitution.[24] Yet Burke had demonstrated, as he would in 1780 and 1781, that despite his opposition to unwarranted congressional powers, he was willing to accept a more elaborate structure at the national level. Indeed, Burke's system of bicameral legislature was more in keeping with republican canons of sound government than the makeshift arrangement of government which was being formalized in the Articles of Confederation.

On May 23, as the debate over the Articles
continued, Burke noted that Congress was experiencing difficulty in deciding "how to secure to
each State its separate independence, and give
each its proper weight in the public Councils."[25]
Burke despaired of the states, which were in so
many ways unequal, reconciling their inherent differences. He reckoned that it was not unlikely
that the agreement for Confederation would be
little more than a defensive alliance. This apparent divergence of interest had long troubled
the members of Congress, and Benjamin Franklin had
once remarked that a government with equal representation in Congress but without equal contributions "upon such iniquitous principles will never
last long."[26] It was later reported that John
Adams, when he saw the Confederation's imbalance,
had predicted that "before ten years, this confederation, like a rope of sand, will be found inadequate to the purpose, and its dissolution will
take place."[27] Adams had been upset over the
failure to obtain an increase in the interest rate
of the loan office certificates because of the
voting by states. He complained that "Nine gentlemen, representing about eight hundred thousand
people, against eight gentlemen, representing a
million and a half nearly determined the point."[28]
Although the large states fought to put through
a measure whereby each state could send one delegate for every 50,000 inhabitants, they were unsuccessful. The accommodation of large and small
states had to wait until 1787.[29]

Although Burke was lukewarm toward the Articles, Richard Henry Lee and his fellow nationalists
of 1777 were anxious to conclude the deliberations
and secure its approval. To them, the Confederation was a natural corollary of the Declaration of
Independence. Continental unity was the only means
by which the principles embodied in the Declaration could be assured. Toward those who delayed
its approval, they displayed thinly veiled disgust.
In lavishly praising the Articles, Lee suggested
that those who opposed it were disloyal and were
among those who had earlier fought independence.
The implication was that those who questioned the
Confederation secretly preferred to remain dependent upon Great Britain.

Lee's insinuations of disloyalty were indicative of the strife which had divided Congress almost from its inception. At the first Congress, the New England delegates had forged a political bond with Richard Henry Lee and part of his Virginia delegation. This tie was the most durable and dynamic in the early years of the Continental Congress. Initially, it led to commitments to support New England in case it was attacked by the British garrison at Boston. When an attack did occur at Lexington, the militants of New England and Virginia were able to bring about the establishment of a continental army and other measures for defense of the colonies. During 1776, the lines of opposition had been dictated by the campaign for independence; in June of that year, it was Richard Henry Lee who introduced the resolution calling for independence from Great Britain.

Not only did the activities of the Lee-Adams axis radicalize the Revolutionary movement, but it was also responsible for provoking enough resentment to bring about opposing groups. The crux of this opposition was the feeling that New England was attempting to dominate the other states and that Richard Henry Lee had betrayed southern interests. William Hooper, who as a native of Boston had been initially sympathetic to New England's pretensions, was soured by the high bounties and wages advocated for the army by the New Englanders, and Thomas Burke shared these feelings. Upon first arriving in Congress, he related that there were "some apprehensions of combination in the Eastern States to derive to themselves every possible advantage from the present war, at the expense of the rest."[30]

The willingness to accept independence had originally been an index of affiliation with the eastern axis. Since partisanship in the eighteenth century was regarded as selfish and unprincipled, it was customary to vindicate such activity with professions of noble objectives and to ascribe disloyal motives to opponents (as Lee did with those who opposed the Confederation). Although the experience of promoting independence was the source of pride and justification for alignment, the issue had changed in the spring of 1777 to military policy. Originally zealous advocates of military organization, the New England states were no longer immediately menaced by military invasion and could return to many of the anti-military attitudes which had characterized their controversy with Great Britain. In particular, they were critical of the military establishment which they had created and which had failed to live up to their expectations. Whereas General Charles Lee had once been their favorite, they were now touting General Horatio Gates. The commander of the continental troops in New York, General Phillip Schuyler, was considered by them the scourge of the American military effort.[31]

To offset the effect of the Lee-Adams interest, some of their opponents joined together periodically into makeshift opposition. The most enduring alliance was between New York and Maryland. This periodic combination occasionally included other states, such as North Carolina, Pennsylvania, New Jersey and Virginia. In 1777, the revitalized New York delegation, led by William Duer and James Duane, spearheaded the opposition. In June, Duane observed that many of their former allies were no longer in Congress--he mentioned William Hooper as one--and that he was attempting to cultivate the new delegates from the southern states. "The hospitable and cheerful manner we live in contributed," Duane reported, "for it was no time to consult parsimony."[32] Burke reported in the spring of 1778 that he had previously been on intimate terms with William Duer, so it may be assumed that he was feted by the New York delegates. Duane and Duer made it a rule of thumb not to overwhelm Congress with their demands. Rather than exhaust the reservoir of good will so carefully accumulated, they concentrated on single objectives which could be innocuously presented.[33]

The assault on General Schuyler by the New England delegates was of special concern, since Schuyler was a New Yorker and had only recently served a brief term in Congress. The resentment of New England against Schuyler had originally resulted from his treatment of the New England troops serving on the expedition to Canada in 1775. This offensive had failed, and the force had to retire, exposing the New England frontier to attack. Late in 1776, as criticism began to mount, Schuyler offered his resignation, which Congress refused. Instead a committee was dispatched to consult with Gates, who was second in command to Schuyler and in charge of defending Fort Ticonderoga. After Schuyler's dismissal in May, the revitalized New York delegation began a campaign to restore him to his command and to redress the injury to their state.[34]

Later in the month, William Duer elatedly reported that the New York delegation had obtained Schuyler's reinstatement. Despite the opposition of the eastern camp, his conduct was fully vindicated. In its campaign on the General's behalf, New York gained the support of the North Carolina delegates, and in the Virginia delegation, only Richard Henry Lee was opposed to Schuyler. Duer proudly confided about his lobbying activities that there had never been "a more difficult card to play."[35] Gates had been spreading ugly rumors concerning Schuyler, and only the delegates' realization of this had saved General Schuyler from oblivion.

In time, however, the campaign on behalf of Schuyler aroused the anger of General Gates, who had briefly taken command of the Northern Department when Schuyler was relieved. On June 18, Gates unexpectedly arrived in Philadelphia and went immediately to Congress, where he asked to be admitted. Once inside, he seated himself "in a very East Cavalier Posture on an Elbow Chair, and Began to Open his Budget."[36] After relating some unimportant news about the Indians, a pretext for his visit, Gates launched into the complaints of how he had been mistreated. Recalling his arduous exertions in the cause, he remarked that he had left an easy life for the rigors of a strenuous military career, and then, as if to prove his point, he began to make accusations against William Duane, who had so effectively opposed his command, and Duane in turn objected to references that Gates made to an earlier conversation between the two in New York.[37]

79

Fortunately for Duane, the New York delegates reaped the full harvest of their recently cemented alliances. First, it was a delegate from Maryland who became angered and moved that Gates be ordered to withdraw. After some of Gates' eastern friends tried to justify his conduct and prevent his expulsion, Burke along with other delegates jumped to his feet, and there was a resounding clamor for Gates to leave the room. Gates lamely attempted to interject some excuses, but was at length forced to get out, and Congress later decided that it would consider his grievances only if presented in writing.[38]

However, he did not have to wait long for redress. Within a month, Schuyler had been forced to evacuate Forts Ticonderoga and Crown Point in the face of General Burgoyne's advancing army. This led to a motion for Schuyler's recall, and Gates was given the chance to exploit Burgoyne's increasingly difficult position in upstate New York. Burke wrote Caswell that the loss of the forts was the fault of New England, which had failed to provide necessary troops for their defense. In his opinion, the easterners were anxious to make scapegoats of their commanding officers, and unwilling to acknowledge their role in the defeats.[39]

Burke was opposed to relieving either general of command, maintaining that the generals were not at fault and that Congress was in no position to establish their competence. As usual, he displayed a reluctance to interfere in the internal workings of the army, indicating that with the limited resources available, those in command could not be expected to win major victories. He was certain that the stationary defense of a position such as Ticonderoga could never hope to succeed, since even veteran troops would be unable to withstand an enemy assault from all sides. Still, Burke was not unoptimistic. If the finances were mended, particularly by means of taxation, the American capacity to make war would improve. As it was, the flood of money in circulation was causing rampant inflation, and the growing indebtedness gave the question of taxes a high level of priority. Although no financial remedies were in

sight and the armies were retreating, he anticipated that the British would be dealt a severe
setback and dared even to "look forward to an
end of the war, much sooner than has hitherto
appeared probable."[40]

Although Burke had hoped to leave in July,
he lingered into August. The British fleet had
recently set sail from Sandy Hook in New Jersey,
and many of Burke's colleagues feared that it was
destined for the Delaware River. Burke figured
with considerable logic that the British forces
in New Jersey planned to link up with the armies
that were invading from Canada and then divide
the country in two from New York City to the
Great Lakes. By the end of July, he reported that
there was growing certainty that Philadelphia was
the target of the recently launched British armada.
As the suspense increased, he continued to delay
his departure. For two weeks in August, the
British whereabouts was unknown until finally on
August 22, the frigates and troop carriers were
sighted in the Chesapeake Bay, obviously in a move
against the capital. Washington was quickly informed, while Congress immediately removed all
military supplies from the targeted area and
called upon the states of Delaware, Maryland, and
Virginia to send up the militia for reinforcements.
In addition, orders went out for the evacuation
of all boats, foodstuffs, wagons, horses, and
livestock from the enemy's probable line of
march.[41]

On Sunday, August 24, ten thousand troops
under the command of General Washington marched
through Philadelphia. Despite their impressive
numbers, many of the men were poorly clad and in-
sufficiently armed, wearing twigs of evergreen
in their hats to give them a uniform appearance.
Proceeding to the Common, they crossed the new
floating bridge over the Schuylkill and marched
down the road toward Chester and Wilmington. It
was hoped that their display would impress the
Tories and other disaffected who were thought to
threaten the security of the city. On the next
day, the North Carolina battalion under the command of General Nash, with whom Burke had fallen

out two weeks before, followed in Washington's line of march.[42]

General Howe landed in Maryland and moved slowly towards Wilmington, where the continental army was stationed. At first, it appeared that Howe and his 17,000 man force might succeed in pinning down the American army against the Delaware or driving them down the Delaware Peninsula. On September 3, he made an initial move towards the upper fords of the Delaware, but Washington was able to keep from being cut off. After several skirmishes, the armies maneuvered themselves into positions on opposite sides of Brandywine Creek near Chad's Ford. The object of the continental army was to prevent the British from crossing at one of the many fords, for if the enemy were able to do so, they would probably seize the main road into Philadelphia and march into the city. Washington had drawn himself into a secure position on the north bank and seemed anxious to entice the British into an engagement. Burke visiting the North Carolina regulars found them in excellent spirits and proclaimed that the continental army "is supposed superior, and the enemy is very shy."[43]

This, of course, was Burke's first contact with the army before battle, so that his optimism is understandable. During the summer, as he defended the military commanders and saw the British offensive unfolding from the perspective of congress, he had grown more hopeful about the prospects of victory. The high spirits of the troops at camp near Brandywine undoubtedly strengthened this belief, one that would soon be rudely shattered. Unfortunately for the Americans, neither Washington nor his senior commanders had a clear idea of the countryside surrounding the battle site, whereas Howe had the advantage of expert assistance from Loyalists in the vicinity.[44]

In the early morning of September 11, the engagement began. Burke had remained at the scene, reporting that the enemy appeared on the south side of Brandywine Creek and began to shell the American lines, which were located in a low

82

meadow and covered by artillery mounted on the
surrounding hills. Three hours later, at eleven
o'clock, the British guns had been silenced, and
their troops driven from the ground which they
had initially occupied. During the shelling,
the light troops made contact, and Burke felt
that the American side had gained the advantage.
A slight distance down the creek was the left
wing of Washington's army, and on the upstream
bank was the right wing commanded by General John
Sullivan. Washington intended to launch a full
frontal assault against the apparently retiring
enemy forces. Before ordering the attack, Washington received word that a party of the enemy
was marching upstream presumably to cross at
another ford. The commander erroneously thought
that the British would have to march twelve miles
in order to cross, and so he felt confident that
he could safely begin a frontal assault across
the creek.[45]

As the attack was being ordered, General Sullivan encountered a militia officer coming from
where the enemy was thought to be moving. When
the major reported no sign of the enemy, Sullivan
sent a dispatch to Washington with this information, and the commander withheld his orders for
the attack across Brandywine. Finally, at half
past two, after a major British flanking action
had been observed, Sullivan was ordered to join
with the units on the extreme right where the
British would first make contact. Instead of
marching directly, Sullivan took by mistake a more
circuitous route, going almost two miles out of
his way. Soon after arriving, he was confronted
with the British 7,000-man flanking party under
the command of Lord Cornwallis and accompanied
by Lord Howe. Before he could draw up his men
with the other divisions, the British attacked.
In response to the assault which threw the Americans right into confusion, Washington detached
the brigades of General Nathanael Greene and Frank
Nash from the center, and only fierce resistance
by these units along with Sullivan's kept the
British force from seizing the turnpike at Washington's rear and cutting off his only route of escape.[46]

Burke was on horseback during the battle
and apparently at some distance from the front
lines. Since the battle took place over an extensive front, an accurate impression of what was
occurring was hard to obtain, and only glimpses
emerge of Burke during the course of the battle.
After the disaster on the right wing, spying some
troops fleeing towards the rear, he attempted to
rally them, and in the frustration of the unexpected defeat, he heard officers, probably from
North Carolina and Maryland, criticizing General
Sullivan in the bitterest terms. Not familiar
with the orders and counter orders nor the uncertainty that was present in every quarter, Burke
was quick to blame the American debacle on those
commanding the right wing. He was told that
Sullivan had been given cavalry and light infantry
for reconnoitering the unfamiliar and rugged terrain and had been warned to expect a flanking movement. Perhaps unfairly, Burke held Sullivan responsible for being caught by surprise and also
for leading his troops on the circuitous march,
and for faltering under the British onslaught. He
believed that Sullivan was aware of the strong
possibility of a British flanking movement and
should not have accepted the report of the militia
officer. He concluded that while the enlisted men
and junior officers were competent, Washington's
major generals--and especially Sullivan--were not.
The disgruntled delegate was particularly upset
with Sullivan whom he characterized as "the Mar-
plot of our Army," and as a result, he now embarked
on a campaign in Congress to have him removed from
command.[47]

    His criticisms of Sullivan met with a sympa-
thetic ear in Congress. The General was already
under investigation for a costly raid he had led
on Staten Island, and his predicament at Brandywine
was reminiscent of what had happened in August of
1776 at the Battle of Long Island, where Sullivan
had been surprised and captured by a British flanking party. Besides this, the American defeat had
exposed Philadelphia to the British army, and the
Congress was again faced with the prospect of
exile. A scapegoat for such a disaster was perhaps inevitable, and Burke whose fond hopes of

victory had been shattered was in no mood to deal gently with the unfortunate General. Under the leadership of the North Carolina delegate and several colleagues, Congress voted to suspend Sullivan from his command. When Washington complained that he could not afford the loss of a senior commander, Congress relented, leaving the implementation of their will to the Commander's discretion.[48]

A Massachusetts delegate, James Lovell, was skeptical about the campaign against Sullivan, pointing out that neither Washington nor the others involved had attributed the debacle on the right wing to Sullivan. "But as he was under the Order of Congress for a Court of Enquiry as to Staten Island," Lovell concluded, "the Maryland Officers in his Division, the Delegates of that State, the great Burk, the Friend of St. Clair, and the connexion of Schuyler" had combined to secure his recall.[49] This partisan statement indicates that the factionalism in Congress was in part responsible for the campaign against Sullivan and connects Burke with the New York-Maryland group in Congress. After the New England onslaught against Schuyler, this faction had seized upon the defeat at Brandywine as a means of retaliation while getting rid of an incompetent general. Sullivan was from New Hampshire, and though not at all provincial in his political attachments, he did represent a measure of New England influence. For Burke, this attack on a continental officer meant a departure from his practice of refraining from attacks on commanding officers. No doubt the support of his friends in Congress as well as his intense disillusionment had influenced the change of heart.[50]

Yet Burke's controversy with the General was not terminated by the debates in Congress. On September 28, Sullivan sent a letter to Congress indignantly defending his military record and replying in kind to Burke's censures. He was disappointed with Congress for uncritically accepting the reports of disaffected officers and especially of Burke. "Nothing can be more mortifying," he complained, "Than to find the Representatives

85

Thereof...Loading him with Blame Infamy and Re-
proaches upon the false Representations of a Single Person who Don Quixot Like pranced at a Distance from the fight..."[51] He also questioned
whether "this warlike son of Achilles" could possibly have been aware of the difficulties in countering the unexpected assault of a superior force
along a broad line of advance.[52]

The thinly veiled insults drew an instant
reply from the volatile North Carolina delegate.
After demanding in Congress an explanation of
Sullivan's remarks, he addressed a letter to the
General which was savage in its blunt condemnation.
With cold precision, Burke reeled off the "miscar-
riages" for which the unlucky General was to blame.
He further reflected on Sullivan's military character, charging that he was "void of judgement and
foresight" and lacked the talent necessary for his
rank and assignment.[53] Moreover, if the pointed
insults in Sullivan's letters were meant for him,
the General was really quite mistaken, for he had
merely been doing his duty both at the battle and
in criticizing Sullivan. "My demeanour was," he
stated, "entirely devoid of parade and ostentation;"
the only time that he galloped his horse was in
an attempt to rally some of the General's "flying
troops."[54]

This letter provoked still another set of
studied insults from General Sullivan. He rejected Burke's demand to explain his comments about
the delegate from North Carolina and warned him
not to "meddle with my character." If Burke wished
redress against his insults, he would be more than
agreeable to a duel. In fact, Sullivan assured
him that "no man will be more rejoic'd to see you
than yr. Hum. Servt."[55]

The image of the two fiery Irishmen locked
in verbal combat and nearing a showdown must have
given observers some pause for reflection. Yet
when Sullivan's frustrating predicament is considered, the well chosen insults are not so incongruous. Chafing under what he regarded as
unjust criticism, Sullivan felt that nothing less
than his military career was at stake. Although

86

he had asked for a court of enquiry, the prolonged military crisis made this impractical. Exasperated by the delays, Sullivan submitted his resignation, on the grounds that a party had been formed against him in Congress. Unless he took action, the charges would be accepted as fact.[56] Finally, on October 12, a court of enquiry acquitted him of earlier charges and this was endorsed by Congress. Now, anxious to clear himself of the more recent charges from the Battle of Brandywine, he was trying to entice Burke into a duel.[57]

There is no question that Burke overstated the extent of Sullivan's responsibility for the defeat at Brandywine. As Sullivan himself observed, he had merely forwarded the fatal misinformation received from the militia officer without additional comment. The responsibility for what followed was in Washington's hands. If anything, Washington should have secured better intelligence in the days before the battle. Sullivan, who was at his post only during the day of the battle, had no opportunity to familiarize himself with the terrain. Yet Sullivan had displayed a lack of personal initiative. Burke was correct in criticizing the General for having transmitted the information of the militia major without a warning to Washington. If indeed he anticipated a flanking movement, he should have tried to obtain information about the surrounding countryside. Perhaps Sullivan, after being criticized for his actions in earlier battles, was reluctant to trust his own judgment.[58]

After the initial salvoes between Burke and Sullivan, their quarrel was gradually forced into the background. Sullivan wanted the duel to take place at the army camp, while his adversary anticipated that a more discreet location would be selected. Sullivan was still involved in military activities against the British, and Burke was anxious to start his long delayed trip to North Carolina. As a result, the meeting had to be postponed. When Burke returned to Congress the following March, the General had been transferred to Rhode Island. Although their correspondence did continue, the duel remained in limbo. The congressman's occasional letters to Sullivan gradually moderated, and at length their tone was almost cordial.[59]

Aside from the pettiness of the Burke-Sullivan controversy, there was a hint of Burke's earlier acrimony and impulsiveness. As in his recent conflict with the North Carolina officers, he had bared a streak of wrathfulness that flatly contradicted his eighteenth century norms. Such behavior instead evoked what was regarded as absurd, unnecessary, and even tragic in human nature--the inability of man to control his passions. In most respects, Thomas Burke was in harmony with his time. He had a logical and precise mind, nurtured on scientific principles and educated in the truths of the enlightenment. But, it seemed sometimes as if this intense rationalism necessitated a periodic release by the irrational side of his nature. The "candid" and "generous" qualities on which he prided himself could turn momentarily into resentment, pettiness, or in the case of General Sullivan to chilling insensibility. Human nature was like a prism which distorted the experience flowing into it, and what appeared to Burke as attempts to act rationally were often distorted by these ungovernable passions. The blind alleys into which these passions flowed indicated a darker side to human nature. Contradictory and unpredictable eruptions of the irrational, inner self placed in question the rationality on which his political principles were founded. Already the experience of the Revolutionary generation both individually and collectively was revealing its inherent limitations.

BURKE AND CONGRESS

After the defeat at Brandywine, a mood of fatalism characterized the proceedings of Congress. As the delegates nervously awaited the approach of the British, they hesitated to agree to persistent motions that Congress should adjourn to a safer location. On September 17, the question was informally resolved when a letter from Colonel Alexander Hamilton, an aide of Washington, suggested that the delegates would be safer elsewhere. According to Burke, the resulting exodus was "not by a vote, but by universal consent, for every member consulted his own particular safety."[1] Burke, who scoffed at the timidity of other members, was one of the last to leave. At two o'clock the next morning, he was awakened by a servant, and while acting deliberately, he did not withdraw precipitately. He crossed the Delaware at sunrise and at Burlington, New Jersey, stopped to await the news of further military actions. Perhaps reminded of the flight of Congress the previous December, he was convinced that the delegates had again acted in haste.[2]

The battle that Burke anticipated did not occur until October 4, and by then he was many miles away in Reading. This ensuing defeat at Germantown dealt his hopes of victory still another setback, and Burke was disillusioned. He believed that the debacle resulted once again from the incompetency of senior officers and a lack of discipline in the ranks. Even worse for North Carolina, their senior commander, General Francis Nash, had been fatally wounded behind the lines by a stray cannon shot. Despite his recent dispute with Nash, Burke described him as one of the most capable and respected officers in the American military and sincerely regretted his loss.[3]

While he lagged behind waiting for news of the fighting, Congress reconvened at Lancaster and then at York. Burke was impatient to leave for North Carolina, and so after finally reaching York, he only remained for a few days. This was.

long enough, however, to glean favorable reports
of victories from upper New York where American
troops resisted the British invaders under Burgoyne.
First, it was learned that the northern army under
Gates had defeated the British near Saratoga, and
then on October 20, the incredible news that Burgoyne had surrendered his entire army. With this
long-awaited reassurance, Burke was able to leave
for North Carolina after nearly a year away from
home.[4]

While at home, Burke served in the General
Assembly during December, where he presented his
objections to the Articles of Confederation.
After visiting home in Hillsborough, he returned
to Congress in February, arriving in York after
a hard journey of three weeks. He was again serving with Harnett, who had joined him the previous
summer. The sociable old politician had taken a
liking to Burke, and the two delegates had in
Burke's first term enjoyed the company of the
ladies in Philadelphia. While Burke was at home,
Harnett wrote that Elizabeth Trist was at Lancaster and " 'begs....to know what had become of our
friend Burke.' "[5] Mrs. Trist, later a confidante
of Thomas Jefferson and a visitor at Monticello,
had been living at her mother's boarding house in
Philadelphia, waiting to join her husband, who
was fighting for the British. Harnett reported
that they had planned a visit to York, and his
carriage had been sent to convey them, but "the
capricious vixens have put it off for another
day."[6]

Harnett's letters to Burke in North Carolina
were not always so frivolous. On December 16, he
urged his friend to push vigorous policies in
North Carolina: "For God's sake," he pleaded,
"fill up your Battalions, Lay Taxes, put a Stop
to the Sordid, & avaricious Spirit which has In-
fected all ranks & Conditions of Men--regulate
the Prices of all Commodities."[7] By the time
Burke returned, Harnett was suffering from gout
and fatigued from his duties. The location of
Congress at York was very uncongenial, and he
longed to sit "under my own vine and my own Fig
tree (for I have them both) at Poplar Grove where

none shall make me afraid except the boats of the
British cruisers."[8] York was a most "inhospitable
scandalous place," and he advised Thomas not to
bring Polly Burke, for they would be lucky to find
even a bed.[9]

The situation of the delegates at York, however, was far more bearable than the army's at
Valley Forge. Burke wrote Governor Caswell that
the worst shortages were that of meat, which he
deemed artificial. Even though supplies were
available in the vicinity, those who had them refused to sell except for windfall profits, and
without large expenditures, the countryside would
not yield up its bounty. Under these gloomy conditions, the weakened army would not be able to
undertake a spring offensive against the enemy,
and as a result the war would be prolonged. Burke
who believed strongly in taking the initiative
could see no alternative but remaining on the defensive.[10]

In North Carolina, Richard Caswell was doing
what he could to relieve the dire necessity of the
army at Valley Forge, responding to an appeal by
Washington with the promise of clothing, shoes,
leather, and blankets. Yet he complained bitterly
to Burke that he lacked the funds to pay the enlistment bounties necessary for recruiting troops
into the continental battalions. By the terms of
the state constitution, the Governor was denied
executive power, even to call a special session
of the Assembly. The touted republican philosophy of 1776 which Burke had endorsed, emphasizing
the legislature at the expense of the Governor
and circumscribing executive power, was proving
inadequate for the needs of war, as Thomas Burke
himself would discern when he became Governor in
1781.[11]

As the situation of both the army and state
government reached a low ebb, Washington too stood
in tenuous footing with regard to Congress. After
suffering major setbacks at Brandywine and Germantown, Washington's capacity as Commander was being
questioned, and the victory at Saratoga had established Horatio Gates in some minds as an alternative

to Washington. Congress, displaying a peevishness towards the Commander, ordered him in December to use his full powers to impress supplies from those friendly to the British and live off the countryside, implying also that Washington should initiate new military offensives against the British.

In November and December, the whispering campaign against Washington known as the "Conway Cabal" (after General Conway, the Inspector General) came to light. What impressed Washington's friends as an unseemly plot and later historians as exaggerated in importance was the cause of constant reverberations during the winter of 1778. Benjamin Harrison, the delegate from Virginia, writing to Burke in March, condemned the presumed conspiracy, which he laid at the door of the Lee-Adams connection in Congress. "Are the good and virtuous of you...taken in?" asked Harrison in wonderment.[12] As other key issues were debated in Congress, the controversy surrounding Washington was uneasily present and apt to intrude.

The prisoner question was before Congress from time to time, and the delegates still could not agree on the terms of exchange, even for General Charles Lee. On March 15, Thomas Burke on behalf of the North Carolina delegates wrote to Washington requesting his ideas on the subject as it concerned the southern theater. Burke made it clear that they considered it inadvisable to permit the exchange of non-military personnel, pointing out how easily the British could make prisoners of American civilians to exchange for loyalists. The man who himself would become a prisoner, classed with militia and noncombatants, ironically concluded that it was better to allow those falling into British hands to remain in captivity. Their confinement was scarcely as serious in Burke's thinking as giving the enemy incentive to capture more civilians, a situation which would be "attended with increase of ravages and Horror."[13]

The complex subject of prisoner exchange was coupled with the question of whether the continental officers should receive half-pay for life

when they retired. As the war dragged on, some
of the officers were forced to dip into their own
pocketbooks to support themselves and their families. After the unbelievable hardships at Valley
Forge, Washington strongly urged that the half-pay
provision was essential to the army's survival.
In response to some members of Congress, who insisted that patriotism by itself was adequate motivation, Washington argued that patriotism had to
be bulwarked by self-interest in order to work
over the long term. It was necessary to accept
human nature with its imperfections rather than
trying to reshape it. He dismissed the fears put
forward of standing armies, pointing out that the
interests of this non-professional army were iden-
tical to those of the larger society (unlike an
organization made up of mercenaries). Most important in Washington's view were the painful sacri-
fices which he himself had witnessed: "...Men
without Cloathes [*sic*] to cover their nakedness,
without Blankets to lay on, without Shoes, by
which their Marches might be traced by Blood from
their feet, and almost as often without Provisions
as with."[14]

Burke agreed with many of Washington's arguments. The threat of a standing army as a result
of half-pay was illusory, since so many civilians
were being drawn into military service who would
be anxious to return to peacetime pursuits. As
for the right of Congress to provide for officers
in peacetime, Burke pointed out that the temporary
wartime powers of the national government had not
stopped it from borrowing money, which would not
be repaid until long after the war had ended.
What bothered the apostle of states' rights, however, was the nagging fear that half-pay might
threaten the control of the states over their own
troops. In effect, Burke worried that the continental authorities would become the perpetual paymaster of the army, even in peacetime. Equally
important in his view was the potential burden
that this half-pay would place upon the states.
Only if the number of troops supported by the states
were reduced would he be in favor of the measure.[15]

During these discussions, a certain ambivalence distinguished the relationship of Burke and other delegates with Washington. There was a political need to display at least superficial loyalty to the selfless Commander. At the same time, the "Conway Cabal" and the sufferings at Valley Forge had created a feeling of tension with respect to this noble and commanding figure of Washington, leading in turn to an underlying need to demonstrate either inherent antagonism or support. Burke, while resisting some of Washington's proposals, strongly upheld the General's claim to respect from Congress. The delegate from North Carolina deeply admired him as "a good officer and most excellent Citizen, moved only the most amiable and disinterested Patriotism, [who] perseveres in encountering extreme difficulties, dangers and fatigues under which he seems sensible of no uneasiness but from the Misfortunes of his Country and of no pleasure but from her success."[16] He added that the only defects observable in Washington's character were excesses of his positive attributes. Since his youth, Burke had reacted intensely to strong personalities, starting with his uncle in Ireland, sometimes accepting and often rejecting. Curiously, his involvement with the General would result in the defense of his own rights against the collective tyranny of Congress, a temporary merging of Thomas Burke's tenuous and independent stance in Congress with the powerful figure of George Washington.

What brought matters to a boil were the conditions placed by Congress on the exchange of prisoners and the anguished outcry of the commander. Besides the restrictions on exchange of loyalists and stipulations regarding General Lee, Congress had added further qualifications. All accounts for supplies given the British soldiers had to be liquidated before the exchange of prisoners and in gold and silver equal to the value of the inflated continental currency. Congress repeated its dictum that the loyalist prisoners be returned to the states to stand trial as traitors.[17]

Convinced that this would be unacceptable to the British, Washington complained bitterly to Congress that their unrealistic conditions were making the "cartel" inoperable, adding that the legal obstacles to negotiations should be "suffered to sleep."[18] Burke found Washington's position unacceptable and anticipated that the majority in Congress would oppose it.

Washington's letter was referred to a special three-man committee which was to draft a reply. On April 10, the members--Francis Dana, Samuel Chase, and William Duer--laid their response before Congress. It began on a conciliatory note, reassuring Washington that Congress intended no personal affront or indignity. After this gesture to Washington's pride and official position, the language of the letter grew arrogant and prolix, and the General was at points reprimanded for violating the will of Congress. The committee also criticized Washington for agreeing to permit British prisoners to go on parole before Americans, implying that Washington was naive and careless in trusting the enemy. Finally, they condemned the plan to exchange Colonel Ethan Allen for a designated British officer before the more prestigious Charles Lee was released.[19]

It is well to remember that the report was written by William Duer of New York, who had reason to dislike Ethan Allen. The state of New York was trying to prevent Allen from converting territory that it claimed into the independent state of Vermont. Yet the letter was more notorious for its tone rather than its content. Despite his objections to Washington's policies, Burke deemed it a further insult to the gallant commander, finding particularly objectionable the implied censure of Washington. The North Carolina delegate was joined by two allies, Joseph Reed of Pennsylvania and William Drayton of South Carolina, in his attack on the objectionable parts. The ensuing debate was slow and tedious, one paragraph of the letter consuming the entire afternoon, and in the evening the committee members wasted more time on "extraneous matters" until finally Burke and his supporters were able to amend the paragraph so that it was given a different context.[20]

It was after ten o'clock in the evening, but
still the committee members insisted on completing
the letter before adjournment. Burke was suffering with a cold and fever, and during the endless
debates he had developed a headache as well. Cornelius Harnett, still afflicted with gout, was
not present, leaving Burke as the only representative of North Carolina, and his presence was necessary for a quorum, since only the minimum nine
states were present.[21]

After a motion for adjournment, a roll call
was finally begun, but Burke soon saw that it would
be defeated. As it came his turn to vote, he decided to withdraw from the chamber "if no other
way was left, to prevent our proceeding so impro-
perly on business of such Importance."[22] Burke,
followed by Edward Langworthy of Georgia, walked
out of the chamber, returning to their lodgings
at Mrs. Moore's boarding house where they prepared
for bed. Congress, unwilling to halt the proceedings over the objections of only two delegates,
sent a messenger to recall the errant members.
When he reached the rooming house, he found Burke
and Langworthy together, and the dialogue was
brief and to the point.

> 'Gentlemen, your attendance is desired
> in Congress.' Mr. Burke replied, 'Devil
> a foot will I go to night.'
> He [the messenger] then addressed Mr.
> Langworthy in particular.
> Mr. Langworthy said, 'I do not know
> whether I will go. Who sent you' To
> which the messenger replied 'The Secre-
> tary.'
> Mr. Burke then said, 'It is too late
> and too unreasonable.'[23]

After returning to Congress, the messenger
was sent back with a message from the Secretary
to Edward Langworthy and a verbal postscript from
William Duer to the Georgia delegate. The messenger later testified that the messages had been
received as if from Congress; yet Burke apparently
thought the first message had also been from William Duer with whom he had been on close terms.

As a result, he had been careless in his language: when the messenger first arrived, Burke reportedly mumbled that the "Devil take him if he would come, it was too late and too unreasonable," and this was later changed in the testimony to "Devil a foot will I go to night."[24]

Whatever the exact words, they did not sit well with Congress. When he appeared in Congress the next day, Burke found that he had stumbled into a den of howling jackals. The chairman of the special committee, Francis Dana, warned of dangers and inconveniences if such conduct were allowed. The North Carolina delegate quickly responded, pointing to his sickness and fatigue from the all-day marathon in Congress. He had felt unable to perform his duty adequately--and he had seen other delegates who were also tired. It was unreasonable to keep a delegate at such late hours--"in my opinion Tyrannical," Burke added.[25] What he failed to realize was that Congress had received his angry response from the messenger and by defending himself he was adding injury to insult.

Burke's sin in the eyes of Congress was now compounded, since he had failed to follow etiquette and appear contrite. Duer, Chase, and Dana led the attack on the wayward delegate, provoking him at one point to charge that his attackers were in a "Combination" against him.[26] Some delegates went so far as to suggest expelling Burke or throwing him into jail. Burke angrily replied that he would not "submit to a tyranny of a majority of this Congress, which would keep him here at unreasonable hours."[27] As the dispute continued, Burke challenged the right of Congress to coerce its members. Unless Congress wished to use force against him, he would attend only at times which he deemed reasonable. As for the charge that he insulted Congress, it was untenable; if for no other reason than the fact that Congress, lacking a quorum after he left, was no longer in session. If he had given affront, he had done so to private individuals, and this required no public apology. He absolutely refused on April 11 to make any kind of apology, loftily

maintaining that any improper behavior on his
part was the business only of his state.[28]

Although Congress was a voluntary assemblage,
it was implicitly accepted that the delegates
would obey the traditional rules of parliamentary
order. The proceedings of Congress were like a
game in which each participant is expected to abide
by the ground rules. While eccentricity might be
tolerated, complete individualism could not be.
Burke had violated the delicate balance maintained
between the states in Congress, and his actions
if carried further might threaten the existence
of Congress. He had unintentionally stripped from
Congress its pretense of durability and exposed its
fragile and tenuous qualities.[29]

As a result, his rebellion caused great con-
sternation. James Lovell reported that "The Sickness or *Will* of one man out of those now here
destroys its existence."[30] On the Sunday after
the episode with Burke, the delegates informally
drew up an engagement for orderly and punctual
meetings at hours designated by Congress, and it
was agreed that no one would speak for more than
ten minutes at one time nor more than twice on
any subject, and that all would "unite in supporting order and preserving decency and politeness
in debate."[31] Thomas Burke's signature was notably absent.

Having reinforced their delicate framework,
the delegates turned again to their colleague.
His violation of the implicit taboos could not
be tolerated; his act of exposing Congress in its
weakness had to be punished. For the next two
weeks, Congress periodically devoted itself to
what Burke described as making "a Mountain of
this Mole-hill."[32] After the charges and counter-
charges on the morning of April 11, his critics
compiled an account of the incident and entered
it in the Journals of Congress with the remarks
that they had made. At length, it was decided
to allow the miscreant to present his side of
the story in writing, and he was given the week-
end in which to prepare a statement.[33]

98

Meanwhile, Congress examined witnesses in connection with the incident and entered the answers in the Journals. The rules of judicial procedure were followed, and Burke was allowed to question the witnesses. Edward Langworthy of Georgia, who had withdrawn with him, testified that he had been suffering from a cold and was not hearing acutely. Perhaps misled by Burke's departure, he thought that Congress was adjourning and left the chamber. It appeared that he too had assumed that the messenger came from William Duer--as well as from the Secretary of Congress. Thinking Congress adjourned, he concluded that Duer was sending him a piece of news or private message. When the messenger came a second time, Langworthy recalled that Burke was still in the room but could not say whether the North Carolina delegate had heard the message. At this point, Langworthy had returned to Congress.[34]

After Langworthy's testimony, Duer and the Secretary of Congress, Charles Thomson, were called to the stand, and their testimony supported some of Burke's contentions:

> Mr. Duer sworn. Questions. Did you on the evening of the 10, send a message to Mr. Burke and Mr. Langworthy or either of them? A. I sent a private message to Mr. Langworthy after the messenger returned...and desired him particularly to come. I also think I mentioned some thing to the secretary the first time. I do not particularly recollect it....

The secretary, sworn says:

> When the order passed I went out to send the messenger for the members. Mr. Duer followed me and at the door desired me to send a message in his name to Mr. Langworthy and desire him to come. I delivered the order of the house to the messenger.

> As he was going down the steps, I
> told him he might tell Mr. Langworthy
> that Mr. Duer desired him to come. I
> did not know that the messenger was
> sent a second time.[35]

Following the testimony, it was decided to
bring the entire question to a vote. Burke immediately protested submitting to any jurisdiction
besides North Carolina's. When a motion was
made that his words be taken down, he again rose
to repeat his objection with only the qualification, "except so far as the power of Congress
compell [*sic*] my attendance at reasonable hours."[36]
It was then decided to appoint a committee to report on the incident, and here the malice or im-
patience of Congress knew no bounds. Burke's
inquisitors--Duer, Chase, and Dana--were appointed
to sit in judgment of him.[37]

The committee took until April 25 to conclude its report, and the result was not unexpected:

> Resolve, That the manner in which
> Mr. Burke withdrew, on the evening of
> the said tenth instant, was disorderly
> and contemptuous; and that the answer
> then returned by him was indecent.
> That the principle upon which he had
> attempted to justify his withdrawing
> ...is dangerous, because it strikes at
> the very existence of the house, and,
> as in the present case actually happened,
> would enable a single member to put an
> instant stop to the most important pro-
> ceedings of Congress.[38]

On April 28, the wayward delegate swallowed
his pride and addressed a conciliatory letter to
the President of Congress, Henry Laurens. Osten-
sibly he wrote to protest the clause in the resolution condemning his attempt to justify his abrupt
departure; he pointed out that he was merely trying to indicate the special circumstances surrounding his withdrawal and that other members
had been allowed that same privilege on occasion.

He reemphasized that he had not meant to speak
rudely to the Congress, since he thought he
was responding only to the delegate from New
York, and in making his official reply, this
had not seemed worth mentioning. Laurens was
to understand that Burke regretted the incident and hoped to keep the gentlemen for whom
he had "esteem and respect" from having the
wrong impression of him. If his language or
manner were disrespectful to Congress, he
hoped that it would be attributed to inatten-
tion rather than design.[39]

There are several reasons why Burke might
have abandoned his uncompromising position in
the letter to Laurens. It had been a fortnight
since the incident, and his temper had probably
cooled. Because he believed in the sincerity
of his motives, he hated to be misunderstood,
and Congress had evidently misconstrued his behavior. Somewhat naively perhaps, he seems to
have thought that if his motives were understood,
then his actions would be forgiven.

Having reached the end of his annual term
in Congress, Burke was anxious to leave for North
Carolina. With vindictive formality, he insisted
first on consulting the Congress in order that
"his departure would not be considered a breach
of order." But what would have been a mere formality in the case of any other delegate became
a matter of intense deliberation in Congress.
While painfully aware of his recent impertinence,
Congress was doubtless worried that North Carolina
would not be represented, since Harnett had left
a short time before. It was moved that Burke be
directed to attend to his duties in Congress, and
when the motion failed, it was proposed that he
be considered a delegate until his state legislature directed otherwise. This also failed, as
did a motion to declare that Burke was no longer
a member of the house.[40]

Although Congress refused to give an inch,
Burke's position was later endorsed by the General
Assembly of North Carolina. A special committee
chaired by William Hooper was supplied with the

101

documents relating to Burke's withdrawal and letters from both Burke and the President of Congress,
and their report was critical of Congress for exaggerating the importance of what had happened
and for disregarding Burke's rights. The conservative Hooper, author of the report, criticized
the delegates for attempting to sit in judgment
of Burke and for ignoring his right of free speech.
The arguments were taken, however, from the statements which Burke had drawn up to justify his behavior. The report even endorsed Burke's viewpoint on the threat to basic freedoms implicit in
the actions of majorities in Congress, but having
served in Congress William Hooper was perhaps
aware of the indignities to which a recalcitrant
might be subjected. The General Assembly approved
the report and then proceeded to make amends for
not re-electing Burke in April. No doubt in response to his heroic defense, the General Assembly
elected him to still another term, thrusting their
enfant terrible back into the lap of Congress.[41]

Although he had made a *de facto* apology to
the President of Congress, Burke was scarcely
contrite, still regarding his position as the defense of a just principle. In his mind, this experience was a practical example of the tyranny
of majorities in Congress. The delegates had
been guilty of violating the "grand Principle of
Whiggism,"--the right of a free man "to judge of
the reasonableness or unreasonableness of any
act of power, and even to resist it if unreasonable."[42] He was suddenly the living embodiment
of the states' rights principle. Just as his
rights as an individual might be placed in jeop-
ardy, so also the right of his state might be ignored. The actions of Congress towards Burke were
a frightening example of the dangers that he had
been warning against.

Even more, the encounter revealed a lack of
clarity surrounding the principles of republicanism. John Locke had thought almost exclusively
in terms of conflicts involving legislatures and
overbearing executives. His laws of politics
were on the side of majorities, since only a majority could justifiably and effectively oppose

an unlawful monarch. From that vantage, individuals such as Burke in Congress or minorities were
not particularly relevant. For political thinkers
such as Locke, the use of "consent" was merely a
convenient device. The people or at least a majority, not the individual, had sanctioned the government initially, and the emphasis by the revolutionary generation on the rights of American society
at large towards the British ministry or the King
also reduced the individual to a cipher within
the body politic. Within the new republican ideology, it had not yet been determined whether individuals like Burke might be coerced by the majority.[43]

Yet the Whig concepts coupled with the traditional English protection of basic rights could
relate to the individual. If the character of the
political body applied to one of its members, then
he too should be able to defy the tyrannies of
unjust authority. Personal rights could no more
be violated by a majority than whole societies
could be unjustly governed by a corrupt monarch.

In this instance, Congress rather than the
British had worn the clothes of the despot, and
Thomas Burke could legitimately claim the role
of being the wronged member of society. It was
his right, he implied, to judge what injustice
had been done to him and to defend himself. Whatever obligations he had to Congress, in Burke's
view, were superceded by his obligation to resist.[44]

Burke was further alarmed by the disregard
of his right of free speech, and in preparing his
case for the General Assembly, he dwelled at length
on this point. It was apparent, at the very least,
that Congress was seizing on certain expressions
he had made out of context, and they had criticized the manner of his expression rather than its
content. He scornfully observed that the "language
Such as I usually Speak which tho' perhaps not re-
fined enough for the Courts of Princes, might escape Censure in a Republican Assembly."[45]

Typically, he also saw the violation of his
free speech as related to the disregard of states'

sovereignty. In the Articles of Confederation, freedom of speech in Congress was not to be impugned outside of that body.[46] Burke interpreted this ambiguous clause to imply that the states could not criticize proceedings in Congress nor discipline their delegates for statements therein; if this were true, the members of Congress would become the sole judges. In his opinion, the states had no reason to limit a freedom that would be used in their own interest, whereas Congress might find it advantageous to restrain the free speech of its members. If Congress were the sole arbiter of its own proceedings--and Burke was perhaps stretching the language of the clause--it would have the power of being judge, jury, and executioner. Political power had to be available, as he readily acknowledged, but its use should ultimately be judged by an independent agency. It was Burke's continuing belief that this agency should be a lawful assembly acting under the tangible restraints of a written constitution.[47]

In the case of Congress, Burke saw that its philosophy was still being controlled by the dead hand of British parliamentary tradition. Most of the members had been conditioned by their legislative service in the miniature parliaments of the thirteen colonies and were unconsciously trying to adapt the British practices to Congress. In contrast, the former Irishman sensed that institutions are shaped and given meaning by the objects with which they are in tension or conflict. He was able to discern, therefore, that parliamentary practice had grown out of the struggle to restrain and control the British monarch where Parliament had a need for extraordinary powers in order "to protect itself from fraud or Violence of a Hereditary, Controling [sic] Magistrate."[48] Congress was, Burke implied, the sole organ of national authority. Untrammeled by executive encroachments, the Congress did not require these powers, and the delegates were making claims on himself and his state out of habit rather than necessity. Their blindness, of which Burke was so uncomfortably aware, was perhaps symbolic of the difficulty of transposing British revolutionary ideology, including the ideas of philosophers like

John Locke, to the new and expanding American republican experience.

Burke was better equipped than most to grasp these incongruities. At a turning point in American thought and constitutional practice, he had the correct mixture of theory and experience to perceive what was taking place. Still a relatively young man, his viewpoint had not been calcified by service under the old colonial system, and he had stepped only recently into the politics of the American Revolution. Up to this point, the interests of his state had been the controlling factor in his responses, and he had seen no particular reason to acquiesce in strengthening the central government. This factor, however, was soon to change.

Thomas Burke's act of rebellion and his confrontation with Congress marked a turning point in his political career. The pathological response of the delegates and his own isolation had perhaps demonstrated the futility of acting as the conscience of Congress. Henceforth, he was to shed the role of detached critic and begin to identify himself with the goals and interests of Congress.

THE TURNING POINT

Burke was re-elected to Congress in August, but did not immediately leave for Philadelphia. Prompted by complaints of the delegates, the General Assembly had enlarged the North Carolina legislative quota from three to five, and since only three representatives had to be in Congress at a single time, the burden on individual delegates diminished. As a result, Burke devoted the autumn of 1778 to his own neglected livelihood.[1]

In October, Burke went to Williamsburg to help Judge Richard Henderson secure title to vast claims of land in Kentucky which Henderson and his associates had purchased from the Cherokee Indians. In 1774, the Judge and his Hillsborough associates had formed the Louisa Company for large-scale speculation in western lands. Louisa partners had included the Orange County establishment, the lawyers and entrepreneurs who controlled local politics from the courthouse in Hillsborough. Some of the group were earlier targets of the Regulators in 1768; and Henderson's brother-in-law, John Williams, and Thomas Hart, later friends of Burke, had been beaten by the rioters.[2]

Henderson's claim was based on the Treaty of Sycamore Shoals of 1774, by which twenty million acres of land had been obtained in exchange for ten wagon loads of spirits, firearms, and trinkets. In 1775, Henderson hired Daniel Boone and a band of frontiersmen to clear a path, and then himself led a party of settlers to Fort Boone or Boonesborough, as it was later called. It was soon learned that other groups from Pennsylvania had already established settlements that conflicted with his claims. Unperturbed, Henderson and Williams went as delegates from "Transylvania," the name given their holdings, to the Second Continental Congress in Philadelphia, seeking recognition for their claims. In the meantime, the Virginia provincial convention, responding to the requests of disgruntled settlers, took over jurisdiction of the lands. "Henderson and Company" was left without a colony or compensation.[3]

For the next two years, the North Carolina
speculators tried to persuade the Virginia Assembly to recognize their claims. For land speculators it was helpful to have political connections
among the state legislators who normally disposed
of unoccupied lands. Unfortunately for the Louisa group, its influence was limited to North Carolina, and the Virginia Assembly stubbornly refused to consider its claims. Unable to make any
headway, it was only logical to hire Thomas Burke,
who had resided and practised law in Virginia, to
represent their interests before the Virginia Assembly. After numerous setbacks, Henderson was now
requesting only a partial compensation for his
once grandiose claims. Although certain that
Burke would do them justice before the Assembly,
he was still pessimistic about the outcome; "so
prevalent is Interest, in what ever mankind under-
takes," he reflected, "that the Eloquence of ten
Thousand Cicero's and Demosthenes, could not have
prevailed."[4]

Soon afterwards, Henderson was elated to
learn that the Assembly had agreed to hear their
claim, and for his concession, he gave credit to
their new lobbyist. "It is universally given up
on all hands," he proclaimed, "that Mr. Burke did
Justice to the Cause, and for my own part think
we could not have been better served on or off
the Continent."[5]

Burke returned to Orange County, but was back
in Williamsburg on November 19 speaking before the
Virginia House of Delegates on behalf of the Transylvania proprietors. Although the Assembly had
voided the claims, there was still the chance that
some compensation could be obtained from the state
of Virginia. In his speech, Burke acknowledged
the right of Virginia over the lands in question
but carefully distinguished between jurisdiction
of the state government and private ownership of
real estate. The state had inherited its right
of jurisdiction from royal treaties with the Cherokees, whereas the claim of the Henderson company
had evolved from a private contract at Sycamore
Shoals. The right to administer rather than to
sell belonged to the government; the right to the

108

soil had been retained by the Indians and as a
result was properly conveyed to the Henderson
Associates. In other words, the Indians had been
permitted to keep ownership of their lands so that
they could turn around and cede them to Richard
Henderson.[6]

The rest of Burke's speech pertained to objections that had been raised to the Transylvania
claims. He denied, for example, that the claims
had been invalidated by the Crown Proclamation of
1763, which had prohibited settlement beyond the
Appalachian Mountains. The rights of citizenship
should have application wherever the subject went
(in this case the North American wilderness), so
that the British proclamation had violated a basic
principle of imperial practice. Deeming the proclamation unlawful, the Henderson Associates had
refused to be bound by it, and they had acted on
the assumption that it was invalid. As a result,
Burke argued, they should not be penalized for
the honest beliefs on which their purchases and
investments were based.[7]

The lobbyist further answered objections to
the vast extent of land that Henderson had engrossed,
pointing out that there was no law against purchasing
land in large quantities. He gently reminded the
legislators that Henderson and Company had generously offered to relinquish all the land, content-
ing themselves to receive a portion as a gift from
the state. Nevertheless, the company had invested
effort and expense in promoting exploration and
settlement, and some recompense was due. In response to Burke's pleas, the Assembly decided the
Associates should be reimbursed, though the details
were left for future settlement.[8]

Burke was generously rewarded by a draft
of £1000 on which he would draw for the support
of himself and his wife during 1778 and 1779.[9]
Unlike his earlier trips to Philadelphia, he was
accompanied when he set out for the north in late
November by his wife Polly and a party that included
Whitmill Hill, a new delegate, the daughter of a
friend in Hillsborough, a servant, and a phaeton
to transport them.

On December 14, the North Carolina delegates
took their seats in Congress, and Burke was to
spend most of this term in the capital engaged in
public business. In doing so, he was to become
more at ease in Congress and more willing to oper-
ate within its framework. Even his criticisms
were directed at individuals and states rather
than at Congress as a body. Cornelius Harnett
once remarked that it required "a *young man* of
Genius, ability, and *application*, three months
at least to make himself well acquainted with the
business of Congress."[10] He might have added
that even more time was necessary in order for him
to contribute to Congress rather than merely to
protect the interests of his state.

For Burke, this term in Congress meant a
longer period of residence in the city of Philadelphia. Since he later talked of returning to
the city permanently, it appears that he came to
feel at home there. From December of 1778 until
he left Congress in April, 1781, Burke's friends
ranged from men of national prominence like Robert
Morris and General Anthony Wayne to the lesser
known merchants and professional people of Philadelphia. One of the most unusual of his acquain-
tances, whom he had met during his first term,
was a poetic Quaker girl named Anne Emlen.[11]

Nancy, as she was called, was a striking
blend of refinement and religion. Tall though not
beautiful, she was charming to Quaker and non-
Quaker alike, which was remarkable, since her most
apparent trait was an almost obsessive sense of
pietistic morality. The Quaker diarist, Anne Warder, described her mind as "a perfect symmetry
of heavenly love."[12] A French traveller who met
her commented on her mildness, modesty and yet
capacity for entertaining conversation.[13]

During the summer of 1777, Thomas Burke and
Nancy Emlen exchanged a series of poems under
the pseudonyms Collin and Chloe.[14] Before Burke
withdrew from Philadelphia in Setpember, as the
British approached, he received a letter from
Nancy in which she lectured him on Christian and
civic virtue. Observing the degeneracy of mankind,

she held up the precepts of Christianity as a
cure for the moral dilemmas of the world.[15] In
response to Burke's poetic criticisms of the British, she expressed hope that the violence which
he pictured in the British would never be justly
ascribed to the Americans. Through the humilia-
tion of temporary conquest, God would make the
faithful suffer in order to attain a level of
virtue that would then merit divine protection.
Mixing her pious injunctions with an aristocratic
tone of haughtiness and condescension, she called
forth from Burke virtue of heroic proportions.[16]

> remember Collin [Burke] those who are
> placed in conspicuous stations, owe
> the duty of a right Example to that
> of a Multitude, which is ever looking
> up, for imitation, to the manner of
> its Superiors.[17]

It is doubtful that Burke was inspired to
that "pitch of virtue" which his Quaker friend's
ideals required. He was not particularly religious
and by this time possibly deistic in his beliefs.
A friend writing to him in April of 1779 made the
following observation: "But you are a Philosopher,
and therefore more *merciful* than Religious."[18]
In addition, he was a slaveholder at a time when
Quakers were in the vanguard of emancipation.
During 1779 and 1780, bills for gradual emancipation were being considered by the Pennsylvania
legislature, and even Nancy Emlen was in time to
marry the Quaker abolitionist, Warner Mifflin.[19]
At a time when slavery was being questioned in
Pennsylvania, the North Carolina Assembly was chas-
tising certain Quakers for having freed their
slaves. While Burke may have had earlier doubts
concerning slavery, there is no indication that
he now differed from the prevailing sentiment within his state nor that he in any way sympathized
with emancipation.[20]

In February of 1779, Nancy's moral perfection-
ism caused a rupture in their friendship. She had
detected in Burke's conversation what she considered unacceptable frivolity, primarily in reference to his use of the word "luxury," which she

apparently regarded as sensual and excessive.
Burke, who had withstood the collective will of
Congress, contritely apologized for his indis-
cretion. [21]

> I was betray'd into this Indecorum
> by not sufficiently attending the dif-
> ference of those lights by which you
> and I Survey moral objects. You have
> the advantage of pure Inspiration, and
> I am by divine Providence left entirely
> to more human reason under all the
> prejudices of habit and Education. [22]

The gulf between earth and heaven was too
great for Burke, and when Nancy Emlen asked never
to see him again, he reluctantly consented. Professing himself too deeply affected for any live-
lier thoughts, he still could acknowledge to her
his "most affectionate esteem" and pointed out that
he could only act from reason and experience until
God at his discretion endowed him with a greater
awareness. [23] Any further contacts between them
are not recorded.

If Burke failed to appreciate moral nuances,
he was far more acute in his political transactions.
He was careful, for example, to avoid controversy
with the North Carolina military establishment.
In early January, the question of appointing briga-
dier generals again arose. The General Assembly
had instructed the delegates to nominate Colonels
Clark and Sumner. Both Burke and Whitmill Hill
felt that the promotions should be made according
to seniority of rank rather than by the arbitrary
choice of the state legislature. As a result,
they informed Congress of the rank of the North
Carolina officers in the Continental line. The
implication of their action was that the delegates
should disregard the instructions from North Carolina and select the two brigadiers according to
seniority. Not surprisingly, Congress complied
and nominated Colonel Hogan as an additional candidate. [24]

Having conciliated the military by deferring
to seniority, Burke then voted for Clark as in-

structed. In this manner, he obeyed his instructions, while at the same time acceding to the
wishes of the officers. Since Hogan and Sumner
were elected, the military lobby was satisfied,
and Burke avoided the criticism levelled at him
in August of 1777. In April, he was informed that
he was more popular with the North Carolina military men than he had ever been unpopular.[25]

In debates involving finance, Burke zealously
defended North Carolina interests. When he and
Hill arrived, Congress was trying to reorganize
its shaky financial structure. Both the state
and the continental currency had become increasingly unstable, and counterfeiting of paper currency
and monopolizing on scarce goods were causing
prices to rise at an alarming rate. Judge Samuel
Ashe of North Carolina observed that he would pre-
fer to receive eight pounds of goods at their
former prices than a hundred dollars of his sal-
ary in depreciated currency.[26] The reaction of
the delegates in Congress was as much moral as
analytical. There was a constant murmuring
against the shadowy specter of war profiteering,
criticisms which were to rise in 1779 to a frenzied
pitch. Most of the delegates, too, were upset by
the burden placed upon their own standard of living. Frelinghuysen of New Jersey vowed not to
complain until his last farthing had been spent in
the service of his country. Then at least he would
have the consolation of knowing that his poverty
was the "characteristic of a *honest* man."[27]

Since November, Congress had been considering
in committee on the whole the recommendations of
a special committee on finance. Burke objected
to the proposal that forty-six million dollars of
currency, the product of earlier emissions, be
retired by Congress. Characteristically, he viewed
this measure as an encroachment on state authority.
To declare bills of credit void "implies a power
to destroy at pleasure the security which the
people have in all the property vested in paper
money."[28] The states should be permitted to enact
their own laws of tender and to schedule times for
their operation. Burke pointed out that the relatively brief period for withdrawing the former

issues was unsuited to North Carolina, where the population was scattered. In a letter to Governor Caswell, he recalled that he had long opposed allowing Congress the power to emit currency or borrow money. "I am persuaded [it] will always be used," he stated, "for purposes partial, and unjust, and either to serve particular States, or Individuals to the prejudice of the whole community."[29]

In support of these views, Burke fought a fierce rear guard action against the will of the majority. He frequently used his privilege of demanding a roll call, hoping perhaps to discourage members who were uncertain. On January 1, after the questions had been earlier resolved, the issue of retiring bills of credit was revived. After debate and a preliminary roll call, he invoked the state privilege of postponing business for a day. On January 2, however, the vote was taken, and despite a roll call demanded by Burke, the motion for further consideration was defeated. The vote was decidedly sectional; every southern state, including Maryland, voted for reconsideration.[30]

He and his colleagues from North Carolina were consistently opposed to the proposed changes. It was not that Burke wished to abolish the financial authority of Congress, nor was there a strictly constitutional objection on his part. He strongly suspected that the measures would favor the interests of the "monied [sic] states."[31] Under the new regulations, the old currency could be exchanged for loan office certificates as well as for new bills of credit. The interest and principal of the certificates, in his opinion, would eventually be paid off in money that was not depreciated. This would enable the states which now were furnishing supplies at extravagant prices to receive a further premium. Representing a state with little capital and resources that were strained to their capacity, he was reluctant to see any increment paid to the money producing states of the north. The South already showed signs of having a debtor economy which could be placed in bondage to the more commercial interests of the North.[32]

Although he also criticized the taxation
clause of the new financial program, it was because he felt the sum was too great for the collective resources of the states. By summer, as
the financial conditions further deteriorated,
Burke became an ardent advocate of taxation.[33]
As it was, the effect of the proposals to retire
forty-six million was neutralized by the continuing scarcity of public funds. Congress had only
intended to issue fifty million in place of the
money it was withdrawing, but it was soon forced
to resort to further expedients. On February 2,
a proposal was voted on to issue twenty million
dollars in loan office certificates. Burke again
demanded a roll call and then voted against it.
So pressing was the need for money, however, that
only Burke, John Penn, and two of the Virginia
delegates opposed the measure. Learning soon afterwards that the Treasury was almost bankrupt,
Congress fell upon the palliative of still another
currency emission.[34]

As policy in the war of finance was hammered
out, the military situation was undergoing an
ominous change. In September, as a British expedition was about to embark from New York, Congress called upon North Carolina to send troops
to South Carolina. As added incentive, Governor
Caswell was designated as commander with the rank
of General.[35] Burke, Harnett, and Allen Jones
saw this request as unnecessary, since no one knew
for certain where the British were destined. "We
have always been haughtily treated by South Carolina," Allen Jones complained, "till they wanted
our assistance, and then we are sisters, but as
soon as their turn is served, all relationship
ceases."[36] Despite Caswell's efforts to comply,
many of the troops requested by Congress could not
be adequately outfitted, and some of the officers
even refused to march their poorly armed troops
to South Carolina. By the first of the year, it
was evident that the initial phase of the southern
campaign would take place in Georgia, and on January 20, a letter from General Benjamin Lincoln
informed Congress of the fall of Savannah.[37]

A few months earlier, events had taken place
that would involve Burke in questions of national
authority, but with different results than before.
In September, a British sloop, the *Active* had been
brought into port by the Pennsylvania brig *Convention*.[38] Earlier in the month, a Connecticut fisher-
man named Gideon Olmstead and three others had
been captured by the British and taken to Jamaica.
Placed on board the *Active*, they were forced to
help navigate a cargo of arms and supplies to New
York, which was occupied by the enemy. Once at
sea, Olmstead and his friends surprised the captain and crew of the sloop and took over the ship.
Although outnumbered more than three to one, the
fishermen were able to confine the British to the
cabin and head the vessel for Little Egg Harbor
in New Jersey.[39]

But the prisoners proved equally ingenious.
Melting pewter spoons into bullets, they forced
open the hatches and raked the decks with fire.
Although wounded, Olmstead saved the day by turning
a swivel gun down a companionway and countering
their fire. The British then made a hole in the
stern and jammed the rudder, so that Olmstead could
not steer. At length, weakened by their hunger,
the enemy prisoners were forced to give up the
struggle.

As the unlucky Olmstead was in sight of land,
however, he was overtaken by the *Convention* and
against his will forced into the port of Philadelphia. The captains of the *Convention* and the
Gerard, a privateer which had assisted, both claimed
the *Active* as their prize. It was alleged that the
Connecticut fishermen did not have the ship in complete control when they were encountered by the *Convention*. The question of dividing the prize was
referred to the admiralty jurisdiction of the state
of Pennsylvania, and the case was tried by a jury
presided over by Judge George Ross, soon to be a
friend of Thomas Burke.

The decision greatly favored the Pennsylvania
claimants. The jury, which had only recently been
required in admiralty cases, found that Olmstead
and his friends were entitled to only one quarter

of the proceeds from the prize, the remainder to
be split between the state of Pennsylvania and
those connected with the *Convention* and the *Gerard*.
Although sympathetic with Olmstead and his fellow
claimants, Judge Ross upheld the finding of the
jury.

Under the procedures established by Congress,
the case was then referred to "The Courts of Commissioners of Appeals for the United States of
America," otherwise known as the standing Committee of Appeals. After reviewing the case, the
Appeals Committee reversed the findings of the
Pennsylvania court. The marshal of the state court
was ordered to sell the prize and pay the proceeds
to the Connecticut fishermen. The large number of
claimants now included the military commander of
Philadelphia, General Benedict Arnold, who had purchased a share in Olmstead's claim. Arnold's participation increased the political nature of the
controversy.[40]

The state refused to comply with the order
of the Appeals Committee of Congress and remit
the money to the Olmstead group. Instead, the
proceeds were paid, in anticipation of sale, to
Judge Ross by the marshal of the court. The Appeals Committee countered by issuing an order
enjoining the marshal to keep possession of all
monies from the sale of the *Active* and its cargo.
The marshal submitted in reply a copy of the re-
ceipt given him by Judge Ross and otherwise disregarded the order. The Commissioners of Appeal
then refused to pursue the matter any further,
admitting in effect their helplessness. It was
now a question of whether the Congress had any
authority to reverse the decision of a state
court. Looming in the background was the larger
question regarding the right of Congress to over-
ride the will of a state if the state refused to
comply.[41]

Congress referred these delicate issues arising from the case of the *Active* to a special committee made up of Burke, Paca, Duer, and Smith.
Burke was apparently the chairman, for the correspondence regarding the question was directed to

him. He received, for example, a note from Judge Ross stating his views concerning the reversal by the Committee of Appeals. The Judge distinguished between trial by jury and trial by "*Witnesses*," which had been the practice before the Revolution under the English civil law. Congress had directed that in admiralty courts the facts should be established by juries. If the jury's finding was set aside, their express intention would be violated. Ross pointed out that if facts were determined on appeal (rather than determination of questions of law), then a civil law procedure would be in effect, as the facts in legal cases would be established by the judges from the depositions of witness rather than by a jury. Ross felt that limits should be placed on the right to appeal such decisions. Under his approach, the jury would be sovereign in the smallest as well as the largest details in admiralty litigation.[42]

The institution of juries in admiralty cases was a matter of gnawing concern. One of the minor, but persistent, grievances against the British had been their use of civil law admiralty courts to enforce unpopular customs regulations. An axiom of contemporary thought was the right of an individual to be secure in his property. Only the traditional right of trial by jury was a sufficient guarantee of due process. Although the *Active* did not fall precisely within these limits, it raised the question of how far the rights for which the war was being fought actually extended. Was trial by jury an absolute and unimpeachable right?[43]

During the committee's deliberations, Burke was careful to minimize the sources of conflict. In reply to a letter from Joseph Reed, the president of Pennsylvania, he agreed that the judicial power of Congress was not at issue, expressing confidence that the state legislature had fully investigated all relevant principles of law. "None of us conceive their affair," wrote Burke, "to have proceeded from any thing but those imperfections of human language and human understanding from which no rank or condition of men is exempt."[44]

Nevertheless, the committee upheld the authority of Congress. Its report, which was presented on February 2, was in Burke's handwriting and contained several characteristic Burkean references to the "Law of Nations." The "Supreme Court by Appeal" over admiralty jurisdiction was justified on the basis of collective necessity. In order to have a "just and uniform" foreign policy, it was essential that Congress control the decisions of juries as well as judges.[45] In absence of this control, juries would be in a position of exercising "the Law of Nations," and who then would be able to restrain arbitrary acts on their part?[46] The committee foresaw that Congressional authority in foreign affairs might be rendered impotent and absurd. What if juries could involve the United States in controversies with foreign nations or prevent relations between them? What would happen if juries, in effect, exercised the same rights as Congress? The potential for mischief was endless, even to the point of involving the United States in unsolicited wars.

The committee thereby made an important distinction between the authority of a state in domestic as opposed to matters involving foreign nations. Although the former was understood, Congress could not "divest" itself of the latter.[47] Juries as well as other institutions of government had to comply with this principle. In effect, the members of the committee perceived the opportunities for chaos if the doctrines of local and state sovereignty were carried to extremes.

On March 6, Congress approved the report, affirming its right to determine questions of fact as well as law. Nevertheless, the resolution of Congress did not dissolve the obstinacy of the Pennsylvania state government. Burke on behalf of Congress corresponded and conferred with President Reed and the Supreme Executive Council of Pennsylvania, but all to no avail. Congress even sent copies of its resolution to all the states, requesting them to enact the necessary legislation for complying.[48]

As a matter of fact, the controversy outlived Burke by twenty-five years, and it was not until 1808 that the case was finally resolved. However, it required a federal writ from John Marshall, which the state of Pennsylvania then attempted to block by force. A near confrontation between a federal marshal and the state militia finally convinced Pennsylvania to back down. The Chief Justice of the State Supreme Court reluctantly conceded that the federal courts were successors to the Continental admiralty jurisdiction. The authority of the national government was at last vindicated.[49]

The year 1779 was not 1808, and the Continental Congress was well advised at that time not to force the issue. Trial by jury in admiralty cases was soon abandoned, even by its most zealous advocates. In 1780, the year after the controversy with Congress, the state of Pennsylvania returned to civil law procedure. Moreover, the framers of the Constitution of 1787 carefully reserved to the judicial authority of the United States all cases arising under admiralty and maritime jurisdiction. Yet, it had been Thomas Burke, the champion of states' rights, who had written the committee report of February, 1779, supporting the Continental Congress over the state of Pennsylvania.[50]

For Burke, this position represented a shift away from support of state sovereignty. In his "Notes on the Confederation," Burke avoided criticizing the admiralty jurisdiction of Congress under the Articles. He looked with disapproval, however, upon the proposed role of Congress as a court of mediation between the states.[51] Burke did not, strictly speaking, alter his principles in regard to admiralty jurisdiction. Yet, he did, for the first time, favor the authority of the national government when the right of a state was in question. If only as a reflection of shifting priorities, this was an important step.

The year 1779 was a harbinger of change. The Congress, faced with problems of unprecedented magnitude, saw its authority and prestige considerably diminished by its failure to find effective solutions. The case of the *Active* was an indication of both its decline and of underlying weaknesses. The year 1779 was also the beginning of the southern campaign. The security of North Carolina and the salvation of its beleaguered neighbors to the south depended on their ability to act in unison as well as the effectiveness of Congress in rendering them support. This meant a shift in priorities, both political and material. Although Burke's attitudes were already in flux, the renewed fighting in the South was a catalyst to further change.

BURKE AND THE SOUTHERN CHAMPION

From the start of his congressional service, Burke had made his presence felt. At first, he demonstrated a tendency to criticize and even to disrupt, which in April of 1778 had produced a rare congressional consensus for censuring his actions. Yet his relationship with institutions as with men was apt to be highly personal, and in these relationships there were also opportunities for constructive group behavior. Burke was innately social in outlook, reserving an independent course for situations where personal or political tensions existed. In 1779, the *enfant terrible* of 1778 no longer looked at Congress as a stranger in residence, and his insatiable need for opposition was channeled into accepted parliamentary practice. As a result, the North Carolina delegate was cast in a more statesmanlike role.

During the winter and spring of 1779, Burke was exposed to the national emergency from numerous vantages. Almost all of the issues which engaged the energies of Congress in 1779 came before Burke. Besides considering the case of the *Active*, he sat on committees to draft peace proposals and to examine problems resulting from the conflict between Arthur Lee and Silas Deane. In addition, he drafted a report in May recommending domestic loans. On a smaller scale, he was one of those assigned to consider the grievances growing out of the controversy between the state of Pennsylvania and the military commander of Philadelphia, Benedict Arnold. His most consistent assignments, however, were on committees to examine and make recommendations concerning the military situation in the South.[1]

In December, Burke met with Washington when the General was in Philadelphia to confer with Congress, and during March, on behalf of two committees, Burke corresponded with the Commander. Though still bothered by the dangers of exchanging loyalist prisoners, he now had other concerns. One of his letters discussed the wisdom of giving higher bounties for enlistment of state and continental troops. Washington advised against it, counseling that the system of giving bounties for short enlistments was both expensive and demoralizing. In August, when the question of half-pay for officers was revived, Burke was one of those who proposed that it be extended to the lifetime of the officers. This represented a distinct change on his part. While he had sympathized with the proposal in 1778, he had then found in it elements which seemed detrimental to his state.[2]

Serving on committees to consider the military situation in the South, Burke was invariably thrown with the influential delegate from South Carolina, Henry Laurens. After the appearance of the British in Georgia, the vulnerable and exposed condition of Laurens' state was often brought home to the members of Congress. In compliance with the alarmed pleas of that state, Congress had dutifully voted to call upon North Carolina and Virginia to raise additional troops for defense of South Carolina and Georgia. Although some objections had been heard from North Carolina regarding demands on its resources, the state officials approached these requests with an attitude of readiness and good will best summarized by Cornelius Harnett. "I am one of those old Politicians," reflected Harnett, "who had much rather see my neighbor's house on fire than my own, but at the same time would lend every assistance in my power to quench the flame."[3]

Between Burke and Laurens, however, this spirit of charity was strained to the limit. The episode of Burke's withdrawal, during which Laurens was President of Congress, probably left a residue of antipathy. More important was the fact that Laurens frequently voted with the Adams-Lee axis in Congress, turning his back on the southern group with which North Carolina was allied. For this apostasy, Laurens was known disparagingly as "the Southern Champion."[4] A serious and often emotional man, Laurens was dedicated so completely to the American cause that he occasionally lost his perspective. Like Burke, he had a sensitive streak and a need for public esteem that made him

particularly vulnerable to criticism. He had resigned in December as President of Congress so
that he could engage himself in the debate over
the activities of Silas Deane.

The controversy in Congress over terms of
peace brought the relations between Laurens and
the North Carolina delegates to the verge of
open conflict. During February and March, this
question emerged as a matter of deepest concern
for Burke as well as many other members of Congress. On February 14, Count Gerard, the French
minister, had informed Congress that Spain might
be willing to ally with the United States. Spain
had offered to mediate the dispute between America
and Great Britain providing that England acknowledged American independence. Failing in this,
the Spanish would go to war with Great Britain.
In the meantime, the United States should lose no
time in formulating terms of peace, for, Gerard
hinted, an alliance with the Spanish might bring
a subsidy to replenish the empty continental treasury. It was necessary, however, that the United
States offer concessions to Spain, in particular
the right to receive East and West Florida from
the British who currently possessed them. The
Spanish would also feel more secure, he advised,
if the right of navigating the Mississippi River
were closed to the Americans. Gerard's information was referred to a committee on which Burke
was included.[5]

The committee in its report rejected Gerard's
proposal that American independence should be the
primary term of negotiations. While insisting on
an acknowledgement by Britain of independence before beginning peace talks, the committee urged
that other demands should also be non-negotiable.
These included boundaries, British evacuation of
occupied territory, fishing rights, navigation of
the Mississippi River, and the right to use the
ports below the American southern boundary. Almost
as an afterthought, the committee included less
crucial issues that were to be considered negotia-
ble, ones which the United States had little reason to hope for, such as the possession of Nova
Scotia and Bermuda.[6]

The Congress reached agreement on boundaries in relatively short order, but the other issues affecting state and regional interests were more difficult to resolve. When the right to navigate the Mississippi came before the Congress, the southern delegates had particular reason to make this a requirement for peace. On this issue, Burke never lost sight of peace as the ultimate goal. Supported by Drayton of South Carolina, he proposed that the allies of America should first declare themselves able to provide help for pursuing this objective. Nevertheless, Burke's article was defeated.[7]

The possession of fishing rights proved even more treacherous. Regarded as essential by New England, it was debated from March until April, with Burke fighting the eastern attempts to have it included as an ultimatum in the peace terms. For example, he attempted to reduce drastically the area in which American fishing rights could be exercised. Instead of the right to fish in and around Newfoundland, the Gulf of St. Lawrence, the coast of Labrador, and the straits of Belleville, the limits would include only the fishing banks east of Cape Breton Island and Nova Scotia, which had been ceded to Great Britain in the earlier treaties of Utrecht and Paris. Burke felt that the United States had no right under the "Law of Nations" to claim such an extensive area. Besides, Great Britain would never yield what was so indispensable to her interests, since the fisheries were regarded as an economic advantage and also an effective means for training seamen. He also sensed that the United States was not yet strong enough to demand fringe benefits such as this in peace negotiations. With the South in danger, the North Carolina delegate considered peace too desirable to be postponed for minor objectives.[8]

Despite his opposition, Burke could appreciate the peculiar interests of New England which compelled it to hold out for fishing rights. However, he was sharply critical of Pennsylvania and Delaware who had no interest in the fisheries for supporting the New England position. The case of Henry Laurens of South Carolina, who had also

voted for fishing rights, raised even more contempt. Congress was again planning to send further levies of troops to South Carolina for its
defense. Since he knew that both North Carolina
and Congress were straining to support Laurens'
state, Burke could not understand why the former
president of Congress would vote to prolong the
war.[9]

Early in April, Burke and his colleagues,
John Penn and Whitmill Hill, decided to take
action. The North Carolina delegates wrote a
letter to their South Carolina counterparts, ob-
jecting to their position on the fisheries. Their
target was Laurens, since Drayton had taken little
part in the fisheries debate. South Carolina,
they observed, was "deemed so feeble" that the
neighboring states had to assist in defending her,
and that an inordinate share in this defense fell
to North Carolina from "her circumstances and con-
tiguos [sic] situation."[10] Continuation of the
present hostilities could only expose South Carolina to the horrors of a brutal enemy, slave re-
bellions, and Indian raids.

The delegates also wrote a letter to Governor
Caswell, a copy of which was sent to Henry Laurens.
The letter was particularly critical of the incon-
sistencies in Laurens' manner of voting. Even if
France were unwilling to continue its assistance
or if independence could be obtained, Laurens
would postpone peace in his quest for fishing
rights. No rational individual would expose his
state to additional ravages and bloodshed. The
implication was, therefore, that Laurens either
lacked judgment or was misrepresenting the condition of his state.

We therefore conclude that his Country
[South Carolina] is strong and powerful
in resources, which are unknown to us,
and that confident of this, he defies
all these difficulties which arise from
our decayed and almost annihilated Finances, our ruined Commerce, our want of
manufactures, our obstructed agriculture,
our wasted forces, and our slaughtered

127

fellow citizens, from our want of resources of Men, Arms, ammunition provisions or equipments, difficulties
which appear to us almost ready to
overwhelm our exhausted country.[11]

It was possible, as Laurens himself charged,
that the attack had been engineered by William
Henry Drayton, his colleague from South Carolina.
The two delegates were at odds both in their political and personal relations. While Laurens often
sided with the New England bloc, Drayton usually
voted with their opponents. The growing peril to
the South had contributed a new consciousness of
southern interests and a rationale for acting in
concert. The tendency of the New Englanders and
their allies to combine in their own narrow interest had stiffened the backbones of their opponents.
As a result, the war experience was creating a
new loyalty with respect to geographical sections
as well as new attitudes on issues like state sovereignty and national union. Drayton was on friendly terms with the North Carolinians and had more in
common with Penn, Hill, and Burke than he did with
Henry Laurens. With this heightened awareness of
their common interests, it is possible that Drayton
and the North Carolina delegates may have conspired
together to embarrass the apostate from the southern
cause.

If Drayton did encourage the North Carolina
gambit, he could only have been pleased with the
result. Laurens reacted with alacrity, first
writing a letter to his colleague in which he
requested an "explicit and candid opinion" of the
actions of the North Carolina delegates.[12] This
attempt at unity failed miserably and to Laurens'
chagrin, Drayton refused to comply, pointing out
that he had already petitioned the North Carolina
delegation not to send their letter. Since the
subject of the fisheries had been thoroughly discussed in Congress, Drayton saw no point in re-
viving an issue over which he was in disagreement
with Laurens. He doubted that he could influence
Laurens and was willing to let the matter drop.
Suddenly Laurens found himself estranged, not only
from Burke, Penn, and Hill, but from Drayton as

well. His reply to Drayton bristled with indigna-
tion. In it, he implied that the state of South
Carolina had been insulted and subjected to in-
timidation, and he displayed bitter frustration
at Drayton's refusal to meet with him to discuss
the issue. No love or even understanding was lost
between the two South Carolina delegates. Asked
why he always voted contrary to Laurens, Drayton
wryly responded: "We vote systematically"--meaning
presumably that each delegate had his own system.[13]

Having failed in his first attempt, Laurens
prepared a counter statement for Governor Caswell
to vindicate his conduct. The strained relations
between Burke and Laurens were abundantly evident.
Laurens urged that whether or not he was in error,
the North Carolina delegates had exaggerated the
importance of his voting. Referring perhaps to
Burke's mercurial temperament, Laurens charged
that these gentlemen were "under the government
of Passion, I will not say any thing worse," and
suggested that he was being pressured by "sophistry, misrepresentation, and menaces."[14]

> Could I have expected such attempts from
> Gentlemen whose daily and laudable boasts
> are,
>   'I am accountable to my own State and
> will be goverened by my own Judgement'
>   'fiat Justitia ruat coleum.'
>   'I have my own feeling and I am not
> answerable to any Man or set of Men but
> to my self and my Constituents, etc. etc.
> etc. etc. etc.'[15]

Laurens accused the North Carolina delegation
of committing "heinos [sic] Crimes," and in particular of menacing a free citizen in order to bias
his vote.[16] They had advocated that South Carolina be abandoned to the enemy and even violated
the congressional rule of secrecy by publicizing
details of the debate over the peace terms, thereby endangering national security. Finally, Laurens
hinted darkly at what he saw as "a settled Plan
and has been for some time past 'to hunt me down!'"
The letter concluded with a lofty quote from Francis Bacon celebrating with "Vantage ground of
truth."[17]

The inexhaustible Laurens wrote still another
letter to the North Carolina delegates, acknowledging their most recent communications and lamenting
the unwillingness of Drayton to stand behind him.
He did not have to wait long for a reply from
Burke and his colleagues, who had by this time
also read his letter to Governor Caswell. Through
the veneer of precise formality, a condescending
and yet conciliatory tone suggested that Penn,
Hill, and Burke were not unduly upset by Laurens'
wild response. Each point of his letter was carefully rebutted. They regretted his differences
with Drayton, which had occasioned separate re-
plies expressing contrary sentiments; Laurens
was to be assured that Drayton had played no part
in their letter to him. On an issue as crucial
as the fisheries, they had wished, not to intimidate Laurens, but to remove any misapprehensions
which might have influenced his vote. It was
silly to imagine, in view of the resources that
South Carolina must surely possess, that she was
being abandoned. The obligation of public secrecy,
in its turn, did not supercede what was more impor-
tant--"a Tie to our Country [state] Superior to
any which Congress can lay us under."[18]

As for the "Plan to hunt you down," Laurens
was patently in error.[19] There were no delegates
in Congress either important or dangerous enough
for such villainy. On the contrary, the North
Carolina delegates felt no sense of resentment
against him and were not subject to the passions
which Laurens ascribed to them. It was suggested,
however, that the North Carolina delegates had some
doubts about Laurens. "The Paragraph in your letter, beginning with the quotation from Lord Bacon,"
they observed, "is too figurative and misterious
[sic] for our Comprehension."[20]

The care of the delegates not to deepen the
rift nor slip into public vilifications restored a
facade of harmony between themselves and Laurens.
In turn, Laurens' response was still more temperate
as he regretted the differences with Drayton and
made a conventional reference to his intermittent
bouts with the gout.[21] Laurens was pleased to
note that his conciliatory approach had produced

"many assurances of good will and esteem" from
Burke, Penn, and Hill, interpreting these signs
of friendliness as a personal triumph.[22] In a
letter to his son, John Laurens, he discarded the
cloak of humility which he had adopted. Coupling
his insults with a derogatory reference to North
Carolina, he boasted that he had both "humbled"
and "hobbled" the "Censors from the Land of Tur-
pentine."[23]

> they felt the pressure of the Cord in
> which they had entangled themselves; at
> first they kicked violently... I had
> every advantage over them that could
> have been wished for by a vindictive
> mind, and have disdain'd to insult Men
> who have surrendered.[24]

Nor were the North Carolina delegates wholly
reconciled to Laurens. Whitmill Hill thought him
lacking a sense of shame and undone by his colos-
sal vanity. Unlike Laurens, Samuel Adams and
Richard Henry Lee had great ambitions which dominated their actions, but "our Southern Champion is
duped by their flattery, an artillery which he
cannot oppose."[25]

The fisheries dispute, which had generated
the quarrel between the North Carolina delegation
and Laurens, refused to die. In May, the question
was again brought to the floor. On the 27th, the
southern bloc was able to reduce the fisheries
ultimatum to a bare acknowledgement of the neces-
ity of not relinquishing them in a peace treaty.[26]
On June 3, Elbridge Gerry, a member of the anti-
Gallican party, as the French ambassador, Gerard,
called the New England bloc, retaliated, intro-
ducing a set of resolutions designed to restore
the force of the ultimatum. For the next two
months, whenever time permitted, the question
was bitterly contested.[27]

Burke, voting with a faction that included
Gouverneur Morris, Smith, and Drayton, fought a
determined parliamentary campaign against the
Gerry motions. Every tactic was utilized, among
them roll calls, motions for the previous ques-

tion, and time consuming substitutes for amendments already on the floor. Even single words and short phrases were the targets of their persistent motions for amending. On various occasions, Burke tried unsuccessfully to have words like "explanatory," "continue to," and "acknowledge," struck out or altered.[28] Occasionally, he succeeded in making an alteration, and the parliamentary struggle delayed consideration of the other Gerry proposals. Some of Burke's larger motions, all of which were defeated, would have entirely changed the meaning of the original motion. On July 1, he proposed that the war should under no condition be continued on behalf of fishing rights. If his amendment had carried, the right of independence would have been the sole objective for which the war was being fought.

Burke persisted even after debate had concluded and a draft was unveiled of the instructions to the peace commissioners. It was provided in the draft that preliminary to negotiations Great Britain would have to acknowledge American independence. He tried to change the thrust of this clause by stipulating that the invitation to negotiate would be rejected only if the King openly repudiated independence.[29] Congress, as usual, defeated his proposal, preferring to allow the troublesome issues to remain at rest.

While the debates dragged on, Congress was arguing also over the credentials of its infant diplomatic corps, and not surprisingly, the smoldering feud between Burke and Laurens was rekindled. The latest controversy had begun as a dispute between Silas Deane and Arthur Lee, or what Burke had prematurely described as "this little fracas."[30] Silas Deane had published a public address shortly before in which he had made in Burke's opinion "some very home accusations."[31] Until recalled by Congress in late 1777, Deane was purchasing agent and later a commissioner for the United States in Europe. After his return, Deane had become the center of factional struggles which had arisen over charges that he had misused public funds and misrepresented contacts with the French. The charges flowed from the pen

of Arthur Lee, who was also one of the commissioners and a brother of Richard Henry Lee. As a result, the conflict gravitated into existing factional channels. Richard Henry Lee, Henry Laurens,
and the New England delegates supported Arthur
Lee, while their opponents including Burke defended Deane.[32]

At length, a committee of one member from
each state, including Burke, was appointed to
investigate the difficulties involving Deane,
Lee, and the other diplomats. In March, the committee presented its long awaited report, cata-
loguing the labyrinth of accusations and recommending that all diplomatic appointments be va-
cated. In late April, Congress began to consider
which of the envoys ought to be retained and
finally decided that Benjamin Franklin should
remain as commissioner in France. Although Burke
and John Penn held Franklin in high esteem, they
voted for his recall, arguing that it was necessary to summon everyone connected with the dispute in order to have an effective investigation.[33]

In the case of Arthur Lee, there was a further question of his abilities as a diplomat.
On April 21, Burke and Thomas Nelson of Virginia
visited the French minister, Gerard, and Burke
carefully recorded what he said. The Frenchman
reported that Arthur Lee no longer had the confidence of the court. Lee was both hostile to
France and diplomatically indiscreet. He kept
in touch with important British politicians,
and his only close associate in France was a
nobleman who hated the French government and to
whom Lee had leaked classified information. "I
must confess," Gerard observed, "that Mr. Arthur
Lee was suspected by People of all ranks...of
being unfriendly both to France and America, and
the Ministry were solicited to exclude him from
all Negotiations."[34]

The French government's distrust of Lee flowed
from many of the same cross currents which had produced the Lee-Deane controversy. From the start,
Lee had been suspicious of the mercantile activities of Deane and his associates. He had discovered

the record of a premium payment on an insurance speculation, on which Deane was wagering on the likelihood of war between Britain, France, and Spain. He had reason to believe that Deane and those around him were using confidential information and public funds in still other speculations. Besides, Lee claimed to have initiated the commercial contract with France in 1776, for which Deane now took credit. Deane's colleagues had systematically excluded Lee from their diplomacy and even attempted to discredit him, the latter not being difficult since he lacked the qualities of either a diplomat or a politician.

From April 26 until May 8, Congress struggled to decide whether Arthur Lee should be recalled. The southern-middle state coalition, led by Deane, Paca, Drayton, and Burke, fought to obtain his recall. In fact, their joint policy was to recall all of the American diplomats in Europe, which led opponents such as Richard Henry Lee to insinuate that the pro-Deane group was merely trying to open up diplomatic positions for its members. Vitriol dripped from the pages of the Philadelphia newspapers and into the private conversations of delegates. Even Burke was drawn into this vortex by his recent adversary in the fishing rights controversy, Henry Laurens of South Carolina, who insinuated that Burke had a financial connection with Deane.[35]

> In a letter from a Mr. Brakenridge to
> Mr. Drayton [Burke wrote Laurens], I
> find my name mentioned as one reported
> to have some interest in a Commercial
> Concern with Mr. Deane the design and
> tendency whereof is supposed to be
> injurious to the political interests
> of America and that the report origin-
> ated from you.[36]

Burke indignantly denied the accusation. He had not injured the political interests of the United States. As for being involved with Deane, he studiously ignored Laurens' insinuation. He made it clear that his private dealings, if not harmful to the public, were his own business and

134

could only matter to his friends, who already knew
his reputation. Burke's friends did include such
men as Benjamin Harrison, who like Deane were
associated with Robert Morris. There is no evidence, however, that Burke was their business
partner.

This was undoubtedly another tactic in the
campaign to discredit the pro-Deane faction.
Charles Carroll, writing from Maryland in May,
reported a concerted effort to smear the Deane
supporters. "The faction of the Lees is indus-
triously propagating that their opponents, or
most of them," he wrote, "are engaged in mercantile activities with Dean [*sic*] and others."[37]

Meanwhile, Laurens designed another ploy.
He offered to vote for Lee's recall if Silas Deane
were detained in America to support his charges
against Lee. Since Deane had strongly indicated
a desire to return to Europe and put his accounts
in order, the pro-Deane faction seemed reluctant
to force him to stay. But how then, asked Laurens,
would the conflict be resolved if Deane was in
Europe while Lee was pressing his charges in
America? "Mr. Lee and Mr. Deane," Laurens asserted,
"will be reduced to the state of two Buckets alter-
nately going up and down a Well meeting only mid-
way."[38]

Burke decided to take Laurens at his word.
The next morning, before debate opened, he showed
Laurens a written motion which he planned to present to Congress. The motion stipulated that "Mr.
Deane be ordered not to depart from America until
the Hon'ble Arthur Lee shall arrive' etc."[39] Accepting this as a tactical challenge, Laurens qualified his offer. Deane would have to furnish security for staying in America until Lee returned.

According to Laurens, Burke then presented
this motion. Laurens rose to demand that Deane
give security, and while he was speaking, Burke
withdrew his motion. From Laurens' viewpoint,
another challenge by the pro-Deane faction had
been frustrated. Later in the day, the final vote
was held on whether to recall Lee. Although twenty-

two of the thirty-six delegates voted for his recall, the vote was by states: four states favored the motion, four opposed it, and two delegations were split. As a result of the tie, the motion lost.[40]

Burke's disagreement with Laurens over Silas Deane was paralleled by a similar question involving Benedict Arnold. As commander of the forces in Philadelphia, Arnold was accused of eight categories of misconduct, the most serious being the misappropriation of public goods. He was also condemned for purchasing a half share in the *Active* dispute at a notoriously low price and for trading on his own account, all of which he hotly denied. Burke supported Arnold as resolutely as he had Deane. This led to more quarrels, this time with Joseph Reed, the President of Pennsylvania, whom Burke disliked, and Elbridge Gerry, the delegate from Massachusetts, whom he had opposed on the issue of fishing rights. On April 3, during a heated debate, Burke charged that the Supreme Executive Council of Pennsylvania had acted toward Arnold in a "waspish, peevish and childish manner."[41] Elbridge Gerry then moved that Burke be called to order, but was overruled by John Jay, President of Congress, who declared that Burke was not out of order, and the motion was then dropped.[42]

From the vantage point of history, Henry Laurens and Burke's other adversaries had the best of the argument. Unknown to Thomas Burke and his friends, the armor of their two champions, Silas Deane and Benedict Arnold, was more tarnished than ever they could have imagined. Deane had already delivered state secrets to his secretary, a British agent, and in 1781, he would suddenly appear in England working as a propagandist for the British government. Arnold had been doing business in goods purchased for public use and was about to embark on the course that led to his betrayal of the American cause. Of course, Thomas Burke had no way of knowing this. The merits of the two cases, as they stood in 1779, merely placed the word of each group with its champion against that of the other. As Burke himself remarked about the Lee-Deane controversy, the accusations against Arthur Lee "were no better supported [than those against Deane], and he himself was not present to answer."[43]

Burke had again showed that his penchant for personal antagonism was alive and well in the session of 1779. Yet the controversies with Laurens and over Arnold did not degenerate into the shouting matches that had typified earlier disputes. Instead, Burke had opposed from within the factional system and with less concern for his personal image. If the arguments at times became petty or trivial, the issues that spawned them seemed particularly vital. The military threat to the South had given the North Carolina criticism of Laurens an arch priority, even if it overflowed into other issues like the Lee-Deane affair. As in the case of states' rights, the feuds that had preoccupied Burke earlier were luxuries that neither he nor Congress could afford in the critical days of 1779 and 1780. Like Burke, Congress was gravitating toward a new set of priorities.

THE AGONY OF CONGRESS

The role of Congress, charted in 1775, was
to create and maintain a national military effort.
By 1780, the burden on Congress was too great and
could not be indefinitely tolerated. Government
as practiced in 1779 had failed to meet the needs
of the national constituency. The financial breakdown and the deterioration of the means to supply
the army forced Congress to seek new alternatives.
Now, either the states would have to relinquish
more authority to Congress or take more responsibility upon themselves. As it turned out, the
overload on the continental authorities was shoved
back upon the states and the military.

Burke now had compelling reasons to support
effective government at the national level. As
the British subdued South Carolina in 1780, the
ability of the Congress and its continental army
were their only beacon of hope. With the Articles
of Confederation still not ratified and no machinery to force compliance, Congress was totally dependent on the cooperation of the states. Yet the
prestige of Congress rested on its capacity to
fund the operations of the military. When Congress was no longer able to make good its economic
commitments, its stock dropped accordingly. James
Madison, with his keen eye for constitutional relationships, saw this change soon after he arrived
in Congress. He carefully described it to Thomas
Jefferson in May of 1780.

It is to be observed that the situation
of Congress has undergone a total change
from what it originally was. Whilst they
exercised the indefinite power of emitting
money on the credit of their constituents
they had the whole wealth and resources of
the continent within their command, and
could go on with their affairs independently
and as they pleased. Since the resolution
passed for shutting the [printing] press,
this power has been entirely given up and
they are now as dependent on the States as
the King of England is on the parliament.[1]

When Burke and Allen Jones arrived in December, the financial situation was in visible disarray. Jones found "our money depreciated beyond bounds and Congress taken up in finding out Ways and means to remedy the Evil."[2] He added that every solution attempted previously had made matters worse. The year of 1780 would be no exception.

Earlier in 1779, before his return to North Carolina, Burke had found himself in the unfamiliar position of advocating stronger financial measures by Congress. His position had changed drastically from only a few months before when he had opposed new issues of loan certificates. In June of 1779, for example, a report which he had drawn up advocated that additional funds be raised by borrowing rather than the use of currency. New incentives were proposed for the same class of borrower which he had once dismissed as the monied interests. In the roll calls that followed, Burke had displayed a further willingness to reward the money lenders for providing funds. On one vote, he diverged from his fellow delegate, John Penn, on the question of raising interest rates proportionally to the depreciation of the currency. He also favored heavier taxation. During May, Congress had resolved to call upon the states to contribute quotas totalling forty-five million dollars, and Burke voted to require an even higher sum of sixty million dollars, again differing from the other North Carolina delegates.[3]

However, by early 1780, Congress was on the brink of abandoning its reliance on currency altogether. On February 20, the North Carolina delegates wrote to Governor Caswell enthusiastically endorsing Congress' new plans. The letter, in Burke's handwriting, pointed out that the money standard of measuring taxes had not worked effectively. The merchants and brokers from whom goods were purchased only served to force up the prices, and remoter areas could not find enough cash to make up their quotas. In place of these inequities, the letter proposed, the state should contribute in actual goods rather than currency.[4]

A system of specific contributions by the
states, they thought, would be a self-adjusting
mechanism that would be free of the inequities
and in turn related to the output of each state
and its inhabitants. Indeed, it would eliminate
the abuses of a numerous bureaucracy, of high
prices caused by temporary local necessity, and
precarious supplies of food for the army. Even
the value of money would be stabilized. Stimulated by his notions of Newtonian economics,
Burke foresaw that in time prices could find their
natural level and that the value of paper money
would be tied to economic productivity.[5]

Once Congress had given up responsibility
to the states, however, it was difficult to dic-
tate the value of the goods that each was to
contribute. Burke contended that Congress had
allowed generous prices to be assigned for each
article of specific goods to be contributed,
taking as the base year, 1774, before the war
had driven prices upward and calculating the
values in specie rather than in currency. As
it turned out, however, the clocklike mechanism
that he envisioned simply palled before the
patchwork of local interests in the United States.
A New Hampshire delegate felt, for example, that
his state was bearing too much of the burden, insisting that excessive prices were being paid in
the southern states for certain commodities and
that these prices were established by political
maneuvering in Congress rather than by intrinsic
worth. In his moralistic view, the root of the
problem was lack of "virtue" at the national level.
The public had been groaning under the burden of
"Supporting Legions of Continental Sinecures who
appear in Swarms like Locusts upon the Land of
Egypt."[6] Not only were they draining public resources, but were "rioting upon the blood and
Treasures of the virtuous Citizens (if any Such
there be) in these United States."[7]

Despite the scarcities, competition for the
dollars and credits of Congress was still fierce
and unrelenting. For a state like North Carolina,
poor in resources and menaced by the enemy, it
was essential to obtain as much public assistance

141

as possible. Burke tried to persuade Congress to assume all reasonable expenses for raising militia as well as continental troops. He proposed a plan by which the total expense of raising, equipping, and maintaining the militia would be divided among the states. The motion, however, was defeated.[8]

The reform of the currency system, as James Madison pointed out, further confused the role of Congress in relation to the states. On March 18, a new plan was unveiled for revaluing the debilitated bills of credit, marking the end of attempts to finance the war by printing money. Congress now resolved that the states retire the bills that were in circulation. A new issue of currency was to be printed, and each time that a state brought in forty of the old bills, two new ones would be emitted. Four-tenths of this amount would be given to Congress and the remainder to the states. The Congress optimistically pegged the value of the new issue at forty to one, higher than the rate at which the currency was circulating. To the empty promises of Congress were now added the empty purses of the states. Congress merely gave up what remained of its tenuous claim to respect as the paymaster of the Continental Army.[9]

The most farsighted idea to emerge from the debates on finance was presented by Burke and Allen Jones. On March 18, the same day the new financial program was adopted, Burke proposed a national impost. Under his plan, Congress would request the states to pass laws authorizing a duty of one percent on imports and exports. The revenue which it produced would be used to retire the old currency and to pay for essential supplies. It would continue in effect until all the previous issues of currency were retired.[10]

Burke's motion provoked very little interest, and it was quickly put aside. Yet within a year, Congress would yield to the inescapable logic of his proposal and look to the necessity of strengthening the central government. It is ironic that the one-time advocate of state sovereignty was indirectly an architect of American nationalism—though later proposals went farther than Burke's

142

motion. His gradual progress away from states'
rights indicates how service in the Revolutionary cause was potentially a nationalizing experience and how the course of the war, now centered
in the South, was a determinant of basic political positions. The paradox of the war situation
in 1780, however, was that the continuing crisis
was establishing a need for national powers while
engendering the practice of independent statehood. Since Burke had been animated at various
times by both of these tendencies, it would appear
that each represented an opposite strain of the
same experience.

Burke recognized that one problem before
Congress threatened the individual interests of
the states and indirectly the war effort. That
was the question of the New Hampshire Grants or
what was later called Vermont. The inhabitants
of the Grants were still attempting to obtain
statehood and refused even to permit Congress to
arbitrate their dispute. James Lovell reported
that both New York and New Hampshire were finally
willing to proceed with arbitration, yet there
were other difficulties. One involved "Ellery
and Burke who *will not* believe that they have
any right whatever to discuss the Independ'ce of
Vermont."[11] Other delegates wanted to postpone
the discussion indefinitely.

On May 23, Scott of New York introduced a
lengthy set of resolutions reviewing the controversy and urging the disinterested states in Congress to mediate. A motion was passed, however,
postponing consideration. Then Burke, seconded
by Allen Jones, offered a motion guaranteeing
ownership of lands within the United States to
the individual states. This principle was designed
to protect states with indefinite western claims
which included North Carolina, from being forced
to surrender their charter rights. Maryland had
persistently refused to ratify the Articles of
Confederation until the landed states gave up their
western territories. Besides, it would disqualify
the claims of separatists like the inhabitants of
the New Hampshire Grants. It would place a lid on
the refractory forces in the unpredictable American environment.[12]

But Burke went even further. His motion also stipulated that Congress was "bound to employ the common forces and common powers in support of the jurisdiction of any of the said states, whenever the same shall be invaded or infringed."[13] Burke was again emphasizing the idea of national authority. With no references to despotism or tyranny, he now wanted to use the continental army to protect the states from opposition to their jurisdiction. This was a significant extension of the policing power from the states to Congress. He had travelled far from his erstwhile conception of the national government as a diplomatic alliance. Ironically though, he only accepted the need for stronger central government as that authority was slipping away to the states.[14]

Burke saw the constitutional impasse of 1780 as a specialist on state matters. Much of his committee service involved questions related directly to the states. He was the author, for example, of a report setting tentative state contributions or quotas for the year. Letters from the Governors of Massachusetts, South Carolina, New Jersey and Maryland were referred as background material to the committees on which he served, and in April, he was one of those appointed to reconsider an address by Congress to the states. The new version of the address, composed by Burke, was also rejected, with a notation on the draft indicating that certain statements were considered unrestrained.[15]

In December, he had written in an official capacity to President Joseph Reed of Pennsylvania appealing for help in supplying the needs of the army. The delegate from North Carolina was particularly concerned about the lack of food supplies and forage. Though desperately hoping for greater efforts by the governors of the other states, Burke was full of praise for "General Reed," in contrast to his earlier criticisms of the Pennsylvania executive.[16] Later, in May of 1780, another acute crisis developed around the need for meat and flour to supply the Continental army and the French fleet. Washington and Congress appealed to Pennsylvania, and on June 1, it was reported

144

that the state had offered all the assistance in its power. Burke then proposed a motion that the thanks of Congress be extended to the President and Supreme Executive Council of Pennsylvania. Petty disputes of the previous year were all but forgotten in this hour of need.[17]

With this new sense of urgency, Burke sometimes came dangerously close to affirming those acts which he had once condemned as tyrannical. On April 3, Elbridge Gerry of Massachusetts tried to place a letter before Congress on behalf of his favorite project, a committee from Congress to go to army headquarters. When Gerry asked for a roll call on a question of order, the delegates declared him out of order. Not long before the assembly had passed a resolution guaranteeing members with grievances the right to be heard at least once, and Gerry was upset that they had disregarded their own guideline. He was particularly critical of Burke. When the North Carolina delegate had become embroiled with Congress in 1778, Gerry had been one of the few who had risen to defend him:

> an Instance of this happened at York
> Town, and may occur to the Memory of a
> Gentleman now in Congress, who will do
> me the Justice to acknowledge, that
> with him I then opposed such ungenerous
> proceedings.[18]

Burke had seen a shadow of his own image and had unmistakably rejected it. The business of Congress was now as important to him as it had been to his colleagues in April of 1778. His concern was how to expedite the defense of the South. The idea of a committee of Congress at headquarters, as Gerry was urging, did not sit well with Burke. To increase the authority of Congress during a crisis was one thing, but to decentralize that same authority seems to have been quite another.

Still, the changing relationship between Congress and the states had an immediate relevance to the continental army. Although now to be directly supplied by the states, the army was still attached to the apron strings of Congress. Yet congressional delay and impotence were acutely felt at headquarters. The slowness of Congress and its remoteness from the army made it necessary to consider decentralization of the military as well. On April 3, Washington wrote to Congress warning of dire consequences from the lack of administrative uniformity. He noted that invidious differences existed in enlistment bounties, terms of service, and provisioning by the states, and in addition, the depreciation of the pay scales had become a source of discontent. Washington reported that the officers were angry with their states and Congress, and many were resigning. For the enlisted personnel, who shared their grievances, there was not the safety valve of resignation. The General ominously mentioned the potential for these men "to enter into seditious combinations."[19]

At the same time, General Nathanael Greene, the Quartermaster General, was in Philadelphia trying to persuade the Congress to decentralize the operations of his department. Greene asked that the lengthy procedure for settling accounts be changed. Instead of submitting each account to the Board of Treasury, the Quartermaster should have authority to pay vouchers and accounts that were presented to him. Greene also advised Congress to send a committee to headquarters. This committee should be permitted to make necessary revisions in the operating procedures of the army.[20]

Congress had employed the committee at headquarters (or committee at camp) as far back as 1775. It was originally designed to bridge the gap in communications between the Congress and the army. In January, a new plan had been broached for using a camp committee to undertake reforms in military administration. Congress was reluctant to delegate authority over the child of its creation, even to its own committee, and the plan was rejected. The letter from Washington and the visit of Greene to Philadelphia, however, again revived the proposal.[21]

Burke was far from enthusiastic. To start with, he and some of his colleagues were opposed to Greene's recommendations and perhaps annoyed also that the General should take up their valuable time. The Board of Treasury on which he now served frowned on Greene's request for an independent settlement of accounts. They felt that it was not only "inexpedient," but also "dangerous" to relinquish so much power.[22] Burke confided to Cornelius Harnett that in Greene's "personal qualities and Individual Utility and importance Congress have found much business and much altercation and embarassment [sic]."[23] Curiously, Thomas Burke would find two years later that the awkwardness of his own situation would cause Greene much difficulty and bring the two men into an unsolicited friendship.

Not only political controversies but the viability of independence now more than ever seemed to hinge on the effectiveness of American arms. Spain had now begun its long awaited attempts at mediation, and the prospects were not encouraging. It was learned in January that a compulsory settlement might be arbitrated on the principle of *uti possedis* or the territory occupied at the time of arbitration. The future of the American union as well as the South's independence might rest upon the outcome of the current campaign.[24]

Burke and Jones made every effort to obtain military support for the defense of the South. In March, Burke presented a resolution calling for troops to be detached from Washington's army and sent to the southern department. The Board of War, to which the measure was submitted, deemed it unwise, but agreed to submit his idea to the discretion of the Commander. In May, responding to periodic attempts to economize by limiting the military complex, Burke moved that it was not advisable to reduce even partially the size of the continental army.[25]

In his abortive letter to the states, he had asked for contributions to assure that the upcoming campaigns against the British would result in an honorable peace settlement.[26] If the states failed in this obligation, he observed, they would be faced with the gloomy prospect of a "victorious, Insulting and remorseless Enemy ravaging our Country, sacking our Towns, and slaughtering our fellow Citizens."[27] On June 1, news arrived that brought the latter prospect alarmingly near. The city of Charleston with its almost 5500 troops had surrendered to the British on the 12th of May. The fire in their neighbor's house, in Harnett's homespun metaphor, was spreading perilously close to North Carolina. At the request of Burke and Jones, Congress agreed to send 3000 arms and twice that number of military stores to North Carolina.[28]

On June 13, Thomas Burke again moved that Major General Horatio Gates take command of the southern department. The hero of Saratoga was given 30,000 dollars to defray his personal expenses and 100,000 more for his military chest. In addition, he was authorized to call upon the four southern states for whatever militia and supplies he needed. Despite the reputation that preceded him, Gates would prove a sad disappointment, and Burke, in particular, would have personal reasons to regret his nomination.[29]

Yet the connection between politics and the army was particularly intimate, since Congress elected the officers of the Continental line. While promotions were not often contested, the opposition of a delegate or faction in Congress could interfere with the officer's career. The antagonism of New England to Schuyler in 1777 or Burke's attack on Sullivan demonstrated the dangers of offending members of Congress. As a result, the senior officers tried to have at least one friend in Congress to promote their interest. Even Washington had a friend and confidant in Joseph Jones of Virginia, through whom he lobbied and expressed opinions. Burke attended to the interests of his friend, General Wayne. With dreams of glory himself, Burke admired the General's spectacular military accomplishments. On July 19, 1779, Burke congratulated Wayne on "the Signal and brilliant Success of your enterprise against Stony Point."[30] Even his battle report to Washington was "a Just model of martial eloquence equal'd by none but Caesar's *veni vidi vici.*"[31]

148

Yet the symbiotic tie between Congress and the military was a potential source of tension. On June 5, Burke was sitting with Wayne at the dinner table of Dr. Hugh Shiel, relaxing from a busy session in Congress. He was approached by Major Henry Lee, the daring cavalry commander from Virginia. The intense young officer began to press him on a matter related to public business. Burke hinted that Lee should defer his concern until a more convenient time. At length, the delegate let it be known that the matter was being dragged out "beyond the line of good breeding."[32] When Lee persisted, Burke dismissed him with the curt reply, "allow me to trifle when it is my hour for trifling."[33]

Lee was highly insulted by this remark. Angrily interpreting it as a breach of honor, he demanded an immediate explanation. Burke intimated that he did not intend to comply until he could "cooly, consider what had passed and distinguish between captious petulance, and the feelings of a man of honor."[34] He had no sense of having offended Lee and had only meant to suggest that serious conversation was not agreeable at mealtime.[35]

With Lee's honor at stake and Thomas Burke as a protagonist, a duel clearly loomed in the foreground. Fortunately, Anthony Wayne was agreed to as an arbitrator. For his part, Burke left it to the General to determine whether his words or manner had implied any offense to the youthful officer. After hearing Burke's side, Wayne made it clear to Lee that he was acting out of "esteem & friendship for both you & Doctor Burke."[36] With these assurances, the matter was laid to rest.

Burke was relieved to settle this unsolicited quarrel. He emphasized that they were fortunate to have Anthony Wayne as arbitrator. Otherwise, the result might have proved "unhappy" (and incalculable for posterity since Henry Lee was to be the father of Robert E. Lee). Burke made it plain that his esteem for Lee was as great as before the incident. As for Wayne, he deserved whatever fortune he had available, including "the fondness of an *enamoured mistress*."[37]

The "enamoured mistress" was not merely a figure of speech. She was also a protege of Burke, and her name was Mary Vining. Attractive and engaging, she was fully worthy of Wayne's "merits" and "ambitions." Burke had known her since the previous year when they lodged at the same house while she visited Philadelphia with her aunt. All the North Carolina delegates--Burke, Whitmill Hill, and even old Cornelius Harnett--were charmed by the Vinings. Burke had even written a poem "To Mrs. Vining on his departure from Philadelphia, August, 1779."

No more, returning from the Statesman's Toils
At thy kind Accents and benignant Smiles
The jarring Tumults of my Breast shall cease
and to mild gen'rous Sympathies give Place.[38]

If the statesman revered the aunt, the soldier worshipped the niece. The middle aged Wayne, who was comfortably married, was smitten like an adolescent. He confessed to his friend, in replying to his lavish congratulations in 1779, that the shafts of love were far more dangerous than any weapons devised by the British. Mary Vining was to haunt him the remainder of his life. In 1796, after his wife died, he became engaged to her and died at Presque Isle on Lake Erie just before they were to be married.[39]

Burke seems to have thrived in this social atmosphere. He confessed to Harnett that "another year's close application in Congress would make [me] a perpetual citizen in Philadelphia, and give me a right to the soil from whence nothing short of the Final Judgement of the World could eject me."[40] Only the living accommodations had not measured up to the quality of the company.

Gen. Allen Jones and myself continued at our old quarters until about ten days ago, and had the pleasure of our old agreeable friends, Mrs. and Miss Vining. But even their Society could not render our situation any longer tolerable, and we changed our quarters to the house

150

formerly occupied by our friend, George
Ross, which we have taken ready furnished. We live there as comfortably
as we wish.[41]

Yet another season in Philadelphia was drawing to a conclusion. On June 21, Burke once more
took leave of Congress and started his trip back
to North Carolina.[42] His "hour for trifling" was
soon to end; he was ready to make the first steps
toward the final tragic *cul-de-sac* of his political career.

BURKE ASCENDANT

> I now write you, supposing you to be
> devoted to Mars, and at the head of
> some victorious Party warm in pursuit
> of their fugitive enemies.[1]

So, Whitmill Hill in Philadelphia grasped at
the rumor of American victories in South Carolina. Ironically, as he penned these optimistic
lines to Burke at Hillsborough, the condition of
the American army was at its lowest ebb.

Not long before, on July 25, 1780, Horatio
Gates had taken command of the Southern Department, and as Burke soon discovered, the army was
in confusion. Reinforcements of militia from
Virginia and North Carolina arrived, but no provision was made for supplying them. As a result,
the army commissaries had resorted to impressment
of crops and livestock, and this practice had
caused widespread unrest. In some instances, they
were guilty of extreme negligence, such as wreck-
ing fields of grain by turning horses into them,
and Burke hinted to Gates that the conduct of the
procurers had been so rude and insulting that it
threatened the loyalty of otherwise good patriots.[2]
He singled out one officer operating in the vicinity of Hillsborough who, claiming to be authorized
by Gates himself, was sending out "some very worth-
less persons" who were not even giving out the
usual certificates guaranteeing future payment.[3]
Burke warned the General that these practices
would drive otherwise patriotic citizens into the
protective arms of the British.

The hero of Saratoga was more concerned, however, with forcing a military showdown. From upper
North Carolina, Gates' army proceeded directly
towards Lord Rawdon's at Camden. When they finally came within range, the troops were suffering
from dysentery and general malnourishment. On the
night of August 15, the American commander ordered
his army to set out for Camden. Before dawn, they
made contact with the British under Cornwallis who

153

were also marching by night. At daybreak, the
armies engaged, and the result was disastrous for
Gates' army. The undisciplined militia fled in
disorder, and Gates and Richard Caswell, the ex-
Governor of North Carolina, briskly followed pace.
Baron De Kalb, who tenaciously held the line with
his Maryland and Delaware veterans, received a
fatal wound on the field of battle, while Banastre
Tarleton, the coldly efficient cavalry commander,
pursued the retreating American army for twenty
miles.[4]

On August 25, 700 ragged continentals, all
that remained of Gates' legion, reassembled at
Hillsborough. Although the American commander
had taken two weeks to march to Camden, he had
returned roughly the same distance in three days.
Again, the scarcity of provisions was a problem.
In July, Burke had written to Congress describing
the misconduct of the commissaries and lack of
supplies.[5] Now, he wrote another letter, this
one highly critical of Gates. Whitmill Hill replied in October that he had observed "with pain"
Burke's strictures on Gates' actions, but had since
"prevailed on Congress to direct Genl. Washington
to order a Court of Enquiry into his Conduct and
to send a proper Officer to succeed him."[6]

His days of command numbered, Gates wrote to
Burke humbly requesting advice. Did he credit the
report that Cornwallis intended to withdraw most
of the garrison at Camden and embark for the Cape
Fear River? Burke replied that he did not think
so. After carefully describing the geography of
North Carolina, he predicted that the British would
invade western North Carolina, for they had no need
to occupy the Cape Fear River or the areas around
the Chesapeake Bay since their fleet was always
available. They would attempt instead to destroy
communications between the east and the west, and
Burke advised Gates to post his forces in the interior of the state. If the British attempted to
seal off the western part of the state and employ
large numbers of Tories in pacification, Gates
could perhaps attack them from the rear.[7]

154

Meanwhile, impressment of supplies had been
resumed, and Burke bitterly denounced Gates for
allowing what he called "rapine without remedy."[8]
As Burke described it, wagons were sent out under
the supervision of junior officers or non-commissioned officers. No notice was given to the landowner, and as much was taken as the army personnel
chose to expropriate. Even if the owner was present, he was rarely consulted regarding price or
quantity. Though a certificate might be given to
the proprietor, Burke regarded it more as an insult.[9]

Ironically, the misfortune that he had so
precisely described was soon visited upon Burke
himself. A brigade order had been issued for ob-
taining straw and cornstalks to cover the huts
at camp, and the procurement detail then stopped
at Tyaquin. Permission to enter was refused by
Burke's overseer, but the officer in command simply
rebuked the overseer and went ahead with the detail.
Incensed when he learned of it, Burke sent a stern
protest which was forwarded to the officer of the
detail by Colonel Otho Williams. In reply, the
officer weakly protested that he was "very Conscious of the Supremacy of the Civil Power" and
merely trying to put that power on "a permanent
foundation."[10]

Unwilling to let the matter rest, Burke wrote
a still more outraged protest to Gates, threatening
to place the matter before Congress. He re-emphasized that the state's inhabitants were burdened
by a heavy specific tax and could not stand such
exactions. Was it or was it not in Gates' power
to curtail the abuses of impressment? If it was,
he assumed that Gates would correct the abuses.
But if not, Burke would request Congress to delegate the powers necessary to govern his army.[11]

His disgust went beyond concern over his own
personal interests. In July, when he first had
encountered the abuses of impressment, he had risked
his own credit to support financially those who
furnished the much needed supplies, and in his subsequent letter to Congress, Burke had asked that
the government honor his engagements. Congress

gave lukewarm approval to his actions and agreed
that all those citizens of the state who made contributions would be reimbursed by the government.
It is not known whether this statement of good
intentions relieved Burke from making payments out
of his own pocket.[12]

Overshadowing the abuse of military power was
the fact that Gates' defeat at Camden had opened
North Carolina to the British, and in September,
their armies invaded the western part of the state.
As Cornwallis prepared to seek out the remnant of
Gates' army at Hillsborough, however, the Tory
detachments in his west were annihilated by back-
woods militia at King's Mountain. With his flank
unprotected, Cornwallis had to retire from Charlotte to South Carolina. Yet the day of reckoning
had only been postponed.[13]

As Burke returned to Philadelphia in late 1780,
the conditions in North Carolina were particularly
alarming. Not only had the military situation
deteriorated, but the scarcities of manpower, agri-
cultural production, and trade were a source of
constant concern. Despite the numerous problems,
Burke still managed to keep a facade of optimism.
Writing to John Adams in Europe, he extolled the
indomitable North Carolinians who continued to
resist despite defeats and privations. After Camden, the inhabitants "flew to arms," determined
that North Carolina would not become an easy prey.[14]
"The war may impoverish and distress us, we may be
at many times unsuccessful, our Armies may be dis-
persed, our finance deranged," he maintained, "but
a people pervaded by such a spirit as animates all
America can never be conquered."[15]

Even if Burke were correct, the end of 1780
presented a bleak prospect for American arms. In
October, Benedict Arnold had deserted to the British in what Whitmill Hill described to Burke as
"yr. Friend Arnold's Treason."[16] The demoralized
American army in the South was beginning the new
year with little prospect of defeating the superior forces of Lord Cornwallis. In addition, Washington's army in the North was experiencing their
most severe winter since Valley Forge. On New

156

Year's Day, 1781, the troops of Pennsylvania line stationed at Morristown, New Jersey, mutinied, shot one of their officers, and marched off toward Princeton. Besides being meagerly clad and poorly fed, they had not been paid for a year. When the Pennsylvania mutineers were coming to terms in late January, the New Jersey line rebelled. The mutiny was brutally suppressed as twelve conspirators were forced to execute two of their own leaders.[17] What Whitmill Hill had written to Burke in October, 1780, seemed even more true in January and February of the following year.

> ...for a moment view this Continent contending with the most powerful people on Earth, without one Shilling of Money in the Treasury, no public Magazines of Provisions, Forage, etc., laid up for the Army, which during this campaign have been ten times without Bread, and as often without mouthful of Meat....Are you not alarmed at our Situation?[18]

As Burke confronted these problems in 1781, his last session in Congress, his role and influence were expanded from previous terms. He was chairman of a committee to prepare diplomatic instructions for Benjamin Franklin to guide him in any future peace negotiations. During 1780, he had played a crucial role in finance, and after serving on several related committees, he was appointed in March to the influential Board of Treasury. A month later, his candidate for secretary to the Board won over the New Hampshire nominee.[19]

In January of 1781, Burke was approached by William Bingham, the powerful merchant and protege of Robert Morris, who asked if the North Carolina delegate considered him qualified for the newly created position of secretary for foreign affairs. Burke replied that Bingham was eminently qualified and that he would make inquiries regarding Bingham's candidacy. After sampling opinion, he reported that James Madison would probably be elected; "he is a young Gentleman of Industry and Abilities," the North Carolinian reflected, "but

I fear a little deficient in the Experience Necessary for rendering immediate Service in that department."[20] However, Madison's Virginia background
made him more acceptable to the South.[21] The
southern delegate had no objection to Bingham but
merely to choosing so many officers from the state
of Pennsylvania. Burke himself reflected that it
was difficult in a young republic such as the United
States to avoid such jealousies.[22] As it turned
out, the contest was between Arthur Lee and Robert
Livingston, and after three ballots, Livingston
was elected to the post. James Madison had to
wait for twenty years until 1801 when he became
Secretary of State in the Jefferson Administration.[23]

By 1781, the membership of Congress had altered dramatically, and this undoubtedly contributed
to Thomas Burke's growing importance. Arthur Lee,
for example, complained that many of his old supporters were no longer in Congress. "Toryism,"
he complained, "is triumphant here," and he included Burke among those who had replaced the good
Whigs of previous sessions.[24] In truth, many of
both his former friends and enemies were no longer
in attendance. Drayton had died, Duer was in New
York, and Paca had been elected to the Court of
Appeals. Henry Laurens, the "Southern Champion,"
had fallen into the hands of the British on his
way to Holland and languished in the Tower of London. Arthur Lee's brother, Richard Henry Lee, had
temporarily retired in Virginia, and even the previously solid bloc of New England delegates was
rent by the emergence of new delegates who were
less partisan and more conservative. The image
of the obstreperous Thomas Burke of 1777 and 1778
was now dim. Few remained who had greater longev-
ity or more legislative experience than the North
Carolina delegate.[25]

One of the delegates who had arrived in Burke's
absence did recall vividly his encounter in 1777
with the North Carolinian. That was General John
Sullivan of New Hampshire, one of the few, independent spirits from New England. Suddenly, the possibility emerged of holding their long-delayed duel.
Taking the initiative, Burke asked for a resolution

of their quarrel, but left open the possibility of
a peaceful solution. Although the feud had cooled
from the white heat of 1777, there was still a
residue of ill will from repeated innuendoes made
during their separation.[26]

In reply to Burke's demand for a showdown,
Sullivan proposed that their seconds decide what
should be done, and Burke reluctantly agreed.
His second held a conference with Sullivan, the
result of which was less satisfactory than he
had anticipated. "I expected that the discussion
would be liberal, candid and ingenuous," he complained, "and apprehended nothing like the refine-
ments and Subtleties which you tell me are Insisted on."[27] Nonetheless, an elaborate fiction
was resorted to for settling the dispute, in which
Burke stated that he had not intended to insult
Sullivan personally and conceded that he had grown
to appreciate Sullivan's talents after seeing him
at work in Congress. The New Hampshire delegate
through his second let it be known that he had
not been referring to Burke as the "warlike son
of Achilles" who at Brandywine "Don Quixot Like
pranced at a Distance from the fight."[28] Thus
Burke and Sullivan were enabled to coexist peace-
fully in the close confines of Congress.

Inside Congress, Burke's colleagues now accorded him the respect that had eluded him in 1777
and 1778. Thomas Rodney of Delaware, a relative
newcomer, left an appraisal of the delegates' abilities. Rodney cautioned that their deliberations
"are not Conducted by the ablest talants [*sic*] and
men of first abilities."[29] The delegates also
lacked "the most true, disinterested and amiable
spirit of Patriotism."[30] Yet, the present Congress
approached its duties with good intentions, and
Thomas Burke was the most capable member in attendance.

Doct'r Burk [*sic*] of N. Carolina, tho not
equal to many who have been in Congress,
may justly be stiled [*sic*] the ablest and
most useful member there at present. He
had been in Congress five Years, is very
attentive and well acquainted with business,

is nervous tho not Eloquent in his
language. He is Correct and pointed
in his debates, possesses the Honest
Integrity of a republican and is for
preserving inviolable the rights of
the people without being lured away
by power. Yet he is some times not
fully guarded from Dictatorial language and does not attend sufficiently
to system, order and management, in a
general view but confines himself too
much to particular Objects.[31]

Yet Burke still found himself periodically
at odds with the majority in Congress. In January of 1781, the delegates were considering modi-
fication of the instructions given to the envoy
in Spain, John Jay, which meant giving up the
right of navigation on the lower Mississippi. If
Congress complied, then Spain might pledge itself
not to make peace without American consent and
would offer the generous stipend which it had so
long dangled before their hungry eyes. The pledge
not to make peace would prevent the Spanish from
negotiating peace on the basis of *uti possidetis*.
Burke refused to submit to Spanish coercion, even
though North Carolina might soon fall into British
hands and funds were needed for the ailing American economy. In this unsuccessful effort, he
was supported by James Lovell of Massachusetts,
a sign that the old factional lines had relaxed.[32]

On the question of voting procedure, Burke was
more successful. Ratification of the Articles of
Confederation was finally completed as Maryland
at last agreed under pressure by the French minister to consent to the Articles. On March 2, the
Articles having officially taken effect, New Hampshire and Rhode Island lost their vote because they
only had one delegate in Congress, and the Articles required at least two. John Sullivan then
proposed that Congress appoint a committee of the
states, as authorized in the Articles, and adjourn
until the two states could send another delegate
to represent them. If this was not agreeable,
Congress should allow the delegates of Rhode Island and New Hampshire to vote until their dele-

gations were complete. Thomas Rodney recorded that
"all their Arguments were abley confuted by Mr.
Burke of N.C. and others, and the absurdity of the
motion fully pointed out, so that the question
passed off without a Division."[33]   It was agreed
that the disqualified delegates could still sit
in Congress, even if they no longer could vote.

The Confederation further stipulated that the
votes of nine states were necessary in favor of
important measures such as declaring war or making
financial regulations, with other measures to be
decided by a majority vote of the thirteen states.[34]
A number of delegates with varying political views
and from different sections of the country--Duane,
Madison, Lovell, and Witherspoon--interpreted this
to mean that a quorum of ordinary questions should
consist of nine states with a majority requiring
the votes of only five states. Under this interpretation of the Articles, doing business in Congress would be far less vulnerable to insufficient
members in attendance. The proponents of this
broad construction cited examples from British
parliamentary practice and other sources. Thomas
Rodney cynically observed that the broad construc-
tionists spared "no Species of artful reasoning
within reach of a Law[y]er."[35] The delegate from
Delaware had the uneasy feeling that he was witnes-
sing an attempt to increase the power of Congress
beyond what the states had contemplated in the
Confederation.

The controversy was reminiscent of early 1777,
and Burke was again on the side of strictly interpreting the rules. Rodney reported that "all their
Arguments were so fully answered by Mr. Burke of
N. Carolina that Mr. [Wolcott] of Connecticut came
over to the same opinion."[36] The delegate from
North Carolina recalled the arguments in Congress
when the Confederation was being debated. Congress
then considered seven as a majority. They deliberately omitted reference to a specific number because Canada was expected to join the Confederation, and seven would no longer be a majority.
Burke observed that the clause was so clear and
unequivocal that he failed to see how it could be
otherwise interpreted. To allow any other inter-

pretation would only invite a minority of five states to thwart the will of the others if several were unrepresented. As it turned out, this construction of the rules would have fateful results. Absenteeism and lack of quorums in Congress would contribute to the demise of the Articles and the Confederation. Thus, in an unintended way, Burke was leaving an imprint on Congress and the Confederation to be felt long after his departure.[37]

Even with his uncharacteristic emphasis on majorities, Burke's arguments demonstrated that he had not abandoned his civil sensibilities. Despite new priorities, he still could rally to the support of open and constitutional proceedings. In March of 1781, for example, while pushing for a more nationalized economy, he voted for printing the Journal of Congress and insisted also that the roll calls be included. Immediately after being appointed to the Board of Treasury, Burke moved that a majority of seven states be required for any such appointment. If Burke took this type of stand less often, it was because he sensed new dangers appearing from other directions. He could help his state more by promoting the effectiveness of continental government. Tyranny from within was now less serious than the threat of external conquest or disintegration of the national union.[38]

Burke and many of his colleagues had come to realize that the way to a viable national government lay in the creation of a sound economy; yet the financial policies gyrated uncertainly. The formula of all financial power to the states had proved less successful than the system of limited continental authority that had preceded it. The scheme of March 18, 1781, for retiring the old currency, had abjectly failed. Few states proved capable of generating the revenue to redeem the old bills, and only a token amount had been called in.[39]

One reason was that Congress had bound the state economies and their resources to its system of debt. The states were saturated with unredeemed promises of payment, which none could afford to overlook. Quartermaster and commissary certificates, for example, had been given up by the army in return for voluntary contributions and seizures of supplies. As Burke's experience with Gates illustrated, the army virtually lived off the land. The result was a glut of certificates in the hands of the general public. Congress had allowed the states to accept the certificates in payment of taxes levied for retiring the old money. The taxes were unproductive, and with few resources themselves, the states were unable to pay off the debts.[40]

On March 7, the New York delegates requested that Congress make the new issue of money available for retiring its certificates. New York was asking Congress to ignore its depreciated bills and to return, in effect, to financing by means of the printing press. Burke warned that this expedient would subvert the intention of the March 18 resolution, because the old money must first be retired. William Duane pleaded that it was beyond the capacity of New York to call in the old money. He estimated that there were two million dollars worth of certificates outstanding in New York and that the state was pledged to redeem them. In opposition to his erstwhile ally, Burke insisted that Congress keep the public faith as stated in the resolution of March 18. His position was perhaps influenced by the fact that North Carolina had never subscribed to this resolution and was under no obligation to comply with its terms. Nevertheless, in the vote that followed, his position was upheld.[41]

Wherever Congress looked, its options were circumscribed. The credit of the United States was no exception. On the same day as the certificates controversy, General Sullivan proposed that munitions be paid for by borrowing. Burke and Thomas McKean of Delaware replied that this would be ruinous, for the United States would be paying in specie bills of exchange for products whose prices were quoted in depreciated currency. Later in March, when Congress tried to draw bills of exchange on its commissioners in Paris, the French

163

minister, Luzerne, objected. The credit of France
was limited, and its use should be confined to
the expense of equipping the French army and fleet
in America. Congress should not draw any more
bills of exchange without the approval of France.[42]

    At length, a weary Congress decided to aban-
don the scheme of March 18, 1780. By setting their
own rates of exchange between the old and new currency, the states were contributing to depreciation, and speculation in differential money values
was only accelerating the spiral of inflation. On
March 16, the delegates nearly unanimously called
for repeal of the state legal tender laws. As a
result, the old currency began a dizzying depreciation until by April and May it was valued at as
much as two hundred to one, and Congress could
only try to cushion the effect. A committee report in Burke's handwriting sought to ensure that
the staff officers of the army would be compen-
sated for their personal losses from depreciation.
This would be done, but only as soon as circumstances permitted. Looking at their predicament,
Burke's present colleague in the North Carolina
delegation, Samuel Johnston, observed: "Never
was a poor fly more completely entangled in a cob-
web than Congress in their paper currency."[43]

    Still the Congress was struggling towards a
new philosophy. With the failure of the state
strategy, many crossed over to Burke's position
on the import duty or actually went beyond his
plan of the previous year. In August, November,
and again in December, this expedient had been
suggested and then spurned. On the last occasion,
Burke's old foe, John Sullivan, had been chairman
of a committee which had revived the proposal.[44]

    On January 31, the Committee of the Whole
Congress recommended a five percent duty on all
imports and prize captures. Three days later,
John Witherspoon, seconded by Burke, placed a
lengthy motion before Congress granting the United
States additional powers over commerce of the states
as well as calling for an "impost." Unlike Burke's
earlier motion, which had called for state import

duties, the later proposal involved granting new powers to the national government. It was stipulated that the impost would apply uniformly to all the states and would also be self-liquidating, lasting only so long as it was needed. Despite the apparent need for a desperate remedy, Burke and Witherspoon could only carry two states besides their own.[45]

As with state sovereignty, once Burke fixed upon an idea or ideal, he pursued it relentlessly to a logical or sometimes illogical conclusion. Whether Burke anticipated a permanently strong central government is beside the point. He and many of his colleagues, out of their Revolutionary experience, had committed themselves to the conception of a stronger national government. In 1781, this idea was still amorphous and lacking in wide support. It represented only one of several stages and numerous variations resulting from the experience of the American Revolution. Had Burke remained at the national level, it is likely that he would have followed the inexorable logic of nationalism, as it was conceived in the 1780's, towards the Philadelphia Convention of 1787. As it was, he was diverted into an undefined and less sanguine course. Thomas Burke stood on the threshold of an individual odyssey that would lead him away from both states' rights and the road to federalism.

Meanwhile, a less elaborate motion than that sponsored by Witherspoon and Burke was passed on February 2. Without reference to authority over commerce, the act requested the states to vest Congress with the power to levy a duty of five percent on all imports. The duty was to be *ad valorem* and used only for the purpose of discharging the public debt.[46] On February 10, Burke attempted to make the duty payable in specie rather than currency and loan certificates. However, the Committee of the Whole put the motion aside, and it was never brought to a vote.[47]

While opting for an impost, Congress was also preparing to divide the legislative and administrative functions. The proponents of scientific

165

management, usually businessmen like Robert Morris, had long urged Congress to place administration in separate hands. Burke, too, had moved toward acceptance of discrete administrative powers. The change on his part was a microcosm of what had occurred among those who were in national service. It also reflected the close association of the southern delegates and especially Thomas Burke with the mercantile lobby both inside Congress and without.[48]

With the exception of Henry Laurens and Richard Henry Lee, the southern delegates were always friendly towards Robert Morris and his commercial clique, and in 1781, this was more true than ever. Samuel Johnston wrote Burke in June from Congress mentioning "your friend, R. Morris," and Morris referred to their friendship when making requests of Burke as Governor of North Carolina.[49] In addition, Burke was well acquainted with George Clymer, Samuel Inglis, and Benjamin Harrison, who were business associates of Morris.[50]

It comes as no surprise, therefore, that Burke supported attempts to make Robert Morris the first Superintendent of Finance. During January and early February, Congress had been reorganizing its administration along the lines that Morris had urged. The decision was finally made to create independent departments of war, marine, finance, and foreign affairs under separate heads who would be accountable only to Congress, and on February 20, Morris was designated as Superintendent of Finance.[51]

But the delegates were forced to consider a larger grant of executive autonomy than they had imagined. Morris now stipulated conditions to which Congress must agree before he would accept. These included permission to keep his business connections as well as authority to appoint and dismiss officers for his department. On Tuesday, March 13, Congress took up the subject of Morris' demands. Burke moved to exempt Morris from the requirement that he dissolve his commercial connections. A roll call was demanded by Samuel Adams, and the motion failed to receive a clear majority. All was not lost, for a similar motion won approval later in the day, after Maryland agreed to switch her vote.[52]

On Wednesday, the remainder of Morris' request came before Congress. Matthews of South Carolina, seconded by Burke, moved that Morris be given full discretion over appointments and dismissals. The only qualification was that Congress authorize any new posts and set the salaries for them. The motion passed despite the solid opposition of Samuel Adams and his colleagues from New England who earlier displayed that same hostility towards the mercantile tendencies of Silas Deane. This seems to have represented not only sectional loyalties, but also hostility to the idea of the large merchant. To the Revolutionary puritan, such as Adams, the mercantile style of life appeared to be incompatible with his image of the saintly revolutionist.[53]

While Congress assessed the future of national union, the battle for the South was taking place in North Carolina. In December, Nathanael Greene had taken command from Gates. Eschewing the costly strategy of confrontation, so disastrous at Camden, the new commander resorted to guerilla-like tactics. On January 17, Daniel Morgan and his detachment from Greene's army outwitted and severely defeated the British under Tarleton at Cowpens. For the next two months, a cat and mouse game between the impatient Cornwallis and his nimble American counterpart led the British commander on a frustrating pursuit away from his base of supply. On February 9, Whitmill Hill wrote to Burke that Cornwallis had burned his baggage, indicating that he had given up any idea of retreating. Hill reported that the militia was assembling and predicted a decisive battle within a few days. Not until March 15, however, did Greene allow the encounter to take place and then on a choice site at Guilford Court House. The result was a pyrrhic victory for Cornwallis who after a fierce struggle forced Greene to execute a well ordered retreat. The British lost so heavily that their plan of crushing Greene and subjugating North Carolina had to be abandoned.[54]

In February, the British army had briefly occupied Hillsborough, and the loss to Burke and his neighbors was considerable.[55] Andrew Armstrong, a loyal friend who looked after Burke's interests in Hillsborough, was charged with evacuating Polly Burke, her sister, and as many of Burke's possessions as possible. He reported that Polly Burke showed great concern for the safety of his valuable papers and books. As for Armstrong, the ladies treated him with far less regard.[56] On the evening that he learned the British were at Salisbury, he rushed to tell Polly and her sister to begin packing immediately. The sister, Frances McCarrel, laughed at his nervousness and reminded him of "the Strength of Genl. Greene's Army," and again the next day she complained of the expense of moving when there was no real necessity.[57]

After "many foolish altercations," Armstrong persuaded them to accompany him. Hiring wagons, he collected Burke's slaves and horses, and then travelled to the relative safety of Taylor's Ferry.[58] Here, the wagoneers wished to turn back, but Mrs. Burke insisted on going farther, and despite Armstrong's protests and counter-proposals, she obtained a military order threatening the wagoneers with impressment if they did not accompany her. Seeing no alternative, Armstrong proceeded for two days and twenty miles until a place was found that suited her. He then gave the women a small supply of cash, sugar, and coffee, and hurried back to reach Hillsborough before the enemy arrived. The needless procrastination of Polly and her sister had unfortunately cost him that chance, for the enemy were too close now. Understandably depressed, he bitterly poured out to Burke his misgivings about the Revolution and his view of the Revolutionary underside of chaos and distress.

> I cannot help thinking that those at home who give the provocation to begin this war and those who was too easily provoked deserves a damned threshing either in this World or the Next. Its impossible to give you any Idea of the distress that appears at this place. Numbers leaving there [sic] property behind them and as Surely causing a famine where they go.[59]

The North Carolina delegate would soon have first-hand experience with these problems. His third consecutive term in Congress was expiring, and under the newly ratified Confederation he was ineligible to serve any longer. His friend Armstrong advised that his presence would be more useful in North Carolina, where troops were being raised to oppose the enemy: "I think you would be of more service to be there Now," he reflected, "than you possibly can be in Congress."[60]

Burke had indeed witnessed the beginnings of much that he had sponsored or promoted while in Congress. Even the Confederation may not have been so unwelcome as it once had been. On March 5, Philadelphia had celebrated the long awaited ratification. Cannons were exploded on land and from ships on the Delaware, and the bells of the city rang out the good news. The President of Congress invited the delegates, as well as state officials and legislators of Pennsylvania, to his house where "they partook of a Cold collation." Later that day, Captain John Paul Jones fired "a *Fue de joy*" from his ship, the *Ariel*.[61] In the evening, the festivities were climaxed by a fireworks display. To a Congress and a nation, starved for hope, the Confederation offered a reason to rejoice.

On April 13, Burke left for North Carolina. After five years of intermittent service in Congress, he was anxious to be relieved of his public burdens. Unable to practice law and already in debt, he undoubtedly suffered from the depreciation in continental money. In October of 1780, he had executed a mortgage on his land and even considered selling Tyaquin. Now he looked forward to recouping his eroded fortunes.[62]

Apparently Burke did not intend to remain permanently in North Carolina. In August of 1781, he wrote to friends in Philadelphia reporting that his plans to return there had been delayed; he also spoke of residing again in Norfolk. With his close contacts among the Morris group, he probably intended to embark on mercantile ventures or utilize his friendships to re-establish a practice in commercial law. He had no intention of making himself available for further public service.[63]

On June 25, less than two months after his
return, he received the startling news that he had
been elected to succeed Abner Nash as Governor of
North Carolina. Suddenly the accumulated burdens
of six years of war, the exhaustion of the state,
and the weakness of the Continent were shoved unsolicited into his hands. If this meant that he
was the first citizen of North Carolina, it was
somehow devoid of honor and fraught with many unhappy possibilities. Burke's career was taking
a sad and tragic turn.[64]

BURKE'S ORDEAL

On receiving notification of his election, Burke wrote to the Assembly accepting its offer, took the oath, and was invested with the symbols of office in the presence of the Assembly. Burke's term as governor would serve as the ultimate test of his political principles. The champion of republican institutions was now the chief officer of the republic that he had helped to found. With a touch of irony, the conservative Samuel Strudwick made reference to this in writing to congratulate him. "If it is true that 'salus populi suprema dea est,'" Strudwick politely observed, "then we are happy in having at our head, the Man who best understands, and will most promote this desirable End."[1]

Yet Burke stood at the head of a shattered edifice. Nearly a year of fighting within and around the borders of North Carolina had left the state physically weak and politically unhinged. The state government, lacking resources and unified leadership, had partially abdicated to the militia and the local civil authorities. Guerilla bands of Loyalists roaming the back areas attacked isolated communities, robbing, destroying, and occasionally murdering, while the state forces replied fully in kind. Those who abstained from violence were more often indifferent or intimidated rather than obedient to central authority. The marches and countermarches, raids and ransacking, impressments and involuntary militia duty made nonparticipants political casualties, fearful of coercion by either side.

On June 29, Burke was ready to present his ideas to the General Assembly. He recognized that the prospects for his administration were anything but encouraging. Given the civil strife and physical derangement, a systematic and categoric mind like Burke's could see little possibility of military resistance without a drastic change in the system.

171

I perceive the Country [North Caro-
lina], everywhere unprepared for defense, without arms, without discipline,
without arrangements, even the habits
of civil order, and obedience to Laws,
changed into a licentious contempt of
authority, and a disorderly indulgence
of Violent propensities.[2]

In order to restore orderly and rational
administration, the Governor had to revitalize
the military effort. This, in turn, required a
more efficient use of the militia and a better
system of support. In place of the short terms
of enlistment, he proposed the creation of a
skeleton force composed mainly of officers and
non-commissioned officers, an experienced legion
which could expand or contract as circumstances
and the supply of manpower dictated. In addition,
Burke urged that a corps of artificers be organized
from the militia to avoid the scarcity of supply.
As for arms, ammunition, and more specialized items,
Burke acknowledged that these could only be obtained
from abroad. He advised that the best method would
be by contract with private merchants, and he suggested John Holker, the French consul in America
and also an associate of Robert Morris. Holker
was already serving as agent for the state of
Maryland and had earlier assured Burke that he
would act in the same capacity for North Carolina.[3]

Burke was particularly concerned with the
problem of state finance and taxation. He urged
the adoption of a more rigorous and meticulous
approach towards the collection of taxes and payment of private contracts. The new Governor complained that "the numberless hands at present employed in the collecting of public revenues exhaust
much of the product."[4] The General Assembly should
take the initiative by calling to account all the
public collectors and accountants as well as by
providing taxes for the performance of public contracts. After his experience with impressment,
Burke insisted upon the strict adherence to all
contracts made with private parties. Since the
people of the state had no redress in case of public seizures, they would only cooperate if they

172

trusted the assurances of the government. Above all, he emphasized, force should not be used to obtain what should be in the interests of private individuals to supply. [5]

The Governor further addressed himself to the absence of commerce within the state. Merchants were estranged by the impressment of tobacco, which had damaged the mechanism of commerce. Since the state no longer protected their property nor provided a profitable source of trade, the merchants had ceased to cooperate. As in other states, the regulations against speculation had only served to dislocate the economy. With his belief in self-regulating economies, he proposed that it be "put on a footing that might secure it from violence, and leave it in everything else to the energy of private enterprise and natural operations of its own principles." [6] On the following day, Burke informed the Assembly that large quantities of lead and other materials were now available at the coast, and he felt sure that if the government could offer a market price and pay in marketable commodities such as tobacco, these imported goods would be brought forward by the merchants who controlled them. [7]

In his inaugural address, he also referred to the breakdown of order and state authority. He called for a revision of the militia laws henceforth be designed to place the militia under more stringent discipline. This was to prevent the trend towards revenge and blood lust. Burke called for an end to the excesses and a policy of conciliation towards the disaffected.

> I find myself obliged to trespass a little further on the patience of the Assembly, to request their attention to the peculiar distress arising from that internal war which is raging with intemperate fury, in some parts of the State, between the well affected and the ill-affected citizens, and which has produced enormities dangerous in their example to all good Government and cruelly fatal to individuals. Perhaps the

173

most humane as well as the most pru-
dent counsel would be to reclaim all
that are reclaimable of our ill advised and deluded citizens, and expel
the incorrigable [*sic*] by force of
arms.[8]

No matter how systematic, his program still
had to contend with centrifugal forces beyond the
control of a single individual. Governor Nelson
of Virginia, a former colleague in Congress, commented that it would require a "Magnus Apollo" to
create order from the confusion in North Carolina,
and Burke writing to Nelson spoke of the "habit
of neglect and disobedience so prevalent among
our People."[9] Appeals to the General Assembly by
his predecessor, Abner Nash, had produced a negli-
gible effect. During the emergencies of 1780 and
1781, the Assembly even presided over dismantling
the executive authority. Governor Nash became a
supernumerary, his military powers assigned to an
independent Board of War. Even after the Board's
dissolution, the Assembly faced with graver crises
was unwilling to entrust the governor with powers
equal to the emergency. Nash wryly observed that
the executive authority had been "so divided and
subdivided that like the rays of the sun it lost
its force and men not knowing who to obey obeyed
nobody."[10] Burke, however, was determined to avoid
all such limitations. Confronted with a legislative check on his power to send troops out of the
state, his response was firm and pointed. He would
accept no restraints on his power to call out or
dispose of troops--"as I should be very unwilling
to be a distrusted or mutilated Magistrate."[11]

Yet, he also felt obligated to protect the
state constitution from encroachment or subversion.
He was disturbed, for example, by a statute setting
up courts of *oyer* and *terminer*, the chief object of
this act being speedy trial of those who had taken
up arms against the state. Burke saw this act as a
threat to the principle of separation of powers
required by the constitution. The Assembly had
authorized the Governor to appoint judges, as Burke
pointed out, for cases involving capital punishment.
The Governor called attention to those sections of

the constitution providing for election of judges
by the Assembly to hold office "during good behavior." The Assembly had made their appointments
temporary and therefore subject to revocation.
Burke warned of the tyranny that might result if
the legislative branch should ever become "so corrupt and wicked" as to refuse to honor the independence of the judiciary.[12]

With his constitutional scruples, Burke refused to take part in carrying out the act. As
Governor he could not execute a statute which
opened the door to executive tyranny by which the
underpinnings of liberty might be destroyed.[13] He
could only suppose that the urgency of public affairs had blinded the Assembly to a situation that
he characterized as "dangerous to the principles
of a free Republic."[14] In a highly revealing
aside, Burke declared how "sensible" he was "of the
Imperfections of human nature."[15] Presumably he
would have approved of legislation that included a
clause for tenure "during good behavior" rather
than making the officials subject to recall.

Once back in state government, even as chief
executive officer, Burke demonstrated that he retained his sense of constitutional propriety and
a nagging fear of tyranny. Yet the problem of
political evil now appeared greater at the state
than at the national level. The lack of confor-
mity to rules of all kinds was to establish itself
as the major threat to Burke's republican principles. At length, it would jeopardize his commitment to the ideals of the American Revolution.[16]

From the start, North Carolina's perilous
position absorbed much of Burke's energy. The withdrawal of Cornwallis with his army into Virginia
afforded the state little relief. Besides the Tory
partisans, the government had to concern itself with
the presence of British forces which had held Wilmington since the previous January. Serving as a
base and source of supplies for Loyalists, the British garrison at Wilmington was a dagger aimed at
the mid-section of the state. The British commander, Major James Craig, was attempting to exploit
the loyal population against the feeble state govern-

ment. Guerilla bands and raiding parties struck
boldly into Cumberland, Duplin, Bladen, and Anson
Counties.

Heretofore, the Tory strategy of the British
had consistently run into difficulties. But the
British had exploited the loyal population only
in the conventional, military manner, sacrificing
the initiative to the better organized and more
numerous rebels. With a garrison of only four
hundred, Craig could scarcely fall prey to Cornwallis' grand illusions of a massive Tory uprising
occurring in the wake of his army. However, with
irregulars like the feared Loyalist David Fanning,
he could prepare the way for the ultimate defeat
of the rebels at a later point when more troops
were available.

On July 5, Craig acknowledged the new strategy
by making Fanning a colonel in the loyal militia.
Fanning's previous war experience uniquely qualified him for desperate and unconventional expedients. Once after accompanying an abortive expedition to East Florida, Fanning subsisted for six
weeks off the uncertain bounty of the Georgia wilderness. More recently he had conducted raids
against the enemy in Duplin County. Like the
guerillas of the twentieth century, he sensed the
requirements of irregular warfare--particularly
the necessity of quickness, mobility, deception
and improvisation.[17]

One of his first raids as a loyalist officer
was directed against the county court at Pittsboro,
where several Loyalists were to be tried. Catching
their adversaries totally unprepared, the Tory
guerillas took fifty-three prisoners, including a
Continental major, colonel, and captain, nearly
all the county militia officers, and three delegates to the General Assembly. As was customary
in eighteenth century warfare, most of the prisoners were paroled. Only fourteen most loathsome
to the Tories for their past deeds were delivered
to Major Craig at Wilmington. Such captives, far
from being a nuisance, were useful as pawns for
securing the exchange of British officers.[18]

Tory successes had a psychological effect on both sides. Fanning found no difficulty in recruiting partisans, more in fact than were feasible for his mobile band of guerillas. Like his twentieth century counterparts, he struck at the local governments by threatening their chief political and military officials. In his brilliantly executed descent on Pittsboro, Fanning had captured Colonel Philip Alston, a notorious persecutor of Tories. Where the civil and military authorities were subject to surprise attacks, there was a marked reluctance to press countermeasures against the Tories. Fanning's tactics, moreover, defied suppression. His clandestine movements, executed usually by night over remote and difficult terrain, were exceptionally hard to contain. After a surprise raid or ambush, Colonel Fanning could move his small column quickly off toward Wilmington where the British offered sanctuary and a source of supply.[19]

Burke readily perceived the multi-faceted threat posed by the enemy. District and county commanders relayed alarming messages reporting robberies and murders in the Tory infested regions. In some counties, the enemy seemed to parody the Whigs, holding their own troop musters and conducting a thriving trade with the British at Wilmington. One officer wrote from Bladen County warning of "a large party of Tories and robbers that is daily plundering and destroying our stock of cattle, and robbing our houses of everything they can get."[20] There were even reports of Tories plundering five or six miles from Burke's town of Hillsborough. Farther south in Cumberland County, the civil process was in disarray. Colonel Robert Rowan described an impending breakdown in government.

> There is now in the county of Cumberland a set of fellows that bids defiance to the Civil law. Several horrid murders & robberies having been committed there lately with impunity. It is dangerous for a Justice of the Peace to issue a warrant against one of these villains and no man will be so hardy as to attempt the execution of it.[21]

If their woes had stemmed solely from such "villains," the burden on the executive would have been challenging enough. Burke encountered, however, a more sinister undercurrent in the state's distress. Almost as often as he received reports of enemy activity, Burke was confronted with senseless atrocities committed by his own side. A letter from some of the prisoners taken at Pittsboro, very probably cued by Fanning, catalogued a number of known brutalities committed against the Loyalists. From informants in Halifax, the Governor learned that an unarmed Tory prisoner was shot to death by the man assigned to guard him. In addition, General William Caswell, in routine operations near Cross Creek, allowed his men to butcher Tories.[22] Horrified by these incidents, the patriot General Stephen Drayton, wrote indignantly to Burke.

> Civil Wars are always attended with something horrid. The bare Idea of Friend against a Friend & nearest Relatives in armed opposition shocks human nature! But good God! Sir, let us not countenance barbarities that would disgrace the Savage! If we cannot totally stop, yet we may check the wanton exercise of cruelty.[23]

Burke carefully instructed his military officers to avoid unnecessary violence. Perhaps more than Fanning, he consciously understood the role of a stable, reliable government as a vital component of counterinsurgency. Besieged with requests for fifty or a hundred reinforcements, the Governor began to realize the ultimate futility of dispatching small forces to provide temporary relief for the civil authority.[24] He was observing an underground enemy of the countryside, who, in the words of General Nathanael Greene, "act in small Parties, and appear in so many shapes, and have so many hiding places and secret springs of intelligence that you may wear out an army and still be unable to subdue them."[25] Yet Burke in his systematic way was grasping towards a fundamental remedy.

No plan could afford to overlook the lack of materials and personnel available, and Burke had already encountered the obstacles which disillusioned Governor Nash and doomed his administration to failure. The Council of State, necessary for executive action, was dilatory in assembling, and Burke complained that the councillors seemed "utterly regardless of their Country."[26] The specific tax, paid in lieu of cash, had already been exhausted in the western regions of the state. Voluntary contributions, seen by the Governor as an alternative to impressments, were not forthcoming.[27] The state militia and its commanders, incapable of facing any competent adversary, showed indifference to central authority. One district commander, without official consent, had decided to conclude a truce with the enemy.[28] Another officer completely lost control of his troops who refused to comply with orders to join General Greene's army, and then unceremoniously left camp for home.[29] It is no wonder that contemporaries voiced concern over North Carolina's chronic failure to perform. Captain Josiah Parker, writing from Virginia, feared that "a lethargic languor has seized so many of her virtuous sons which I hope is now expelled and their efforts will be exerted with a gigantick [sic] force."[30]

General Allen Jones was soon able to reassure Parker that Burke would restore effective government. The "gigantick force" of Captain Parker was an apt description of what the Governor now contemplated. To reduce the enemy's support, he planned to pardon those who would submit to legitimate authority, and a proclamation would be issued offering protection from violence to the disaffected who would swear allegiance. To prod the recalcitrant, Burke would raise a substantial force of militia for a period of six months. The militia terms of duty would be staggered to avoid the discontinuum caused by short enlistments, and supply magazines would be placed at intervals across the countryside. As a guarantee of success, he also hoped to employ the powerful presence of General Anthony Wayne and his Pennsylvania continentals, who were soon to march across the state to join General Greene. Burke's planning, in this respect, was premature, for it was by no means certain that Wayne or his superiors would have allowed the badly

needed regulars to be diverted from the South Carolina theater of war to chase the wily guerillas or
their patrons in Wilmington.[31]

This tenuous strategy, however, ultimately
hinged on the actions of the regular British forces.
Lord Cornwallis' methodic retreat toward the Chesapeake threatened that the British armies would use
North Carolina for returning troops to Charleston.
In mid-July, the Marquis de Lafayette cautioned
General Jethro Sumner to prepare for the movement
of Tarleton's cavalry across the state.[32] Although this threat did not immediately materialize,
the British conducted two substantial raids into
the northern and northwestern parts of the state.
To Burke, these were further indications of an impending descent by the cavalry toward South Carolina
and rumors were rife that the rest of the army was
soon to embark for New York to reinforce Sir Henry
Clinton against Washington and Rochambeau.[33]

The British forces at Wilmington were also
in motion, for at the start of August, Major Craig's
own pacification program went into effect. His
version of the Governor's expeditionary force set
out on a scorched earth campaign across the inner
coastal zone toward New Bern. Fearing annihilation
of the undisciplined militia, Burke ordered Generals Caswell and Lillington and the district commanders to avoid major engagements and to fight a
defensive campaign until his plans matured.[34]

All his energies were now consumed by his preparations. To compensate for the state's inertia,
he determined to manage the arrangements for the
military expedition and then personally take command. In anticipation, the Governor sent out urgent requests for inventories of troop strengths
and pleas for arms and ammunition.[35] He also resolved upon direct supervision of planning. By
shifting the executive branch wherever he was
needed, he could oversee the recruiting of troops
and the collection of supplies. Before his personal
dynamics could dissolve the corrosive apathy, however, the unexpected began to bedevil him. On
August 13, while setting out for Halifax, Burke's
horses ran out of control, breaking his carriage

and throwing him to the ground. The Chief of
State suffered bruises on his body, and his face
was cut. His departure had to be delayed.[36]

Reports from the southern regions were scarcely any solace for his political and physical afflic-
tions. On the 14th of August, Fanning, Ray, and
McNeil fell upon Campbleton and captured the local
leaders. Soon afterwards the British under Major
Craig occupied New Bern, while Hector McNeil with
a sizeable guerilla force was descending on Cross
Creek. So desperate was the need for ammunition
that the lead was removed from the Governor'a palace before the evacuation of New Bern. According
to General Caswell, the inhabitants below the British line of march were intemperately flocking to
the British standards, while those behind his lines,
seeing no relief in sight, had abandoned their
homes. There was even a rumor, inconspicuously
couched in a letter to the Governor, that the enemy
were conspiring to capture Burke himself. There is
no evidence, however, that he paid any attention
to the warning. His expeditionary force claimed
first priority.[37]

Anticipating General Wayne's arrival, Burke
had ordered out the militia from the Hillsborough
and Granville districts. As he was preparing for
the first troop musters, news arrived that deflect-
ed his efforts. The Marquis de Lafayette wrote
late in August that Cornwallis, hemmed in by the
Americans in the James River basin, was likely to
wheel and retreat through North Carolina.[38] All
boats, horses, carriages, and livestock had to be
collected and rushed to points of relative safety.
The men and supplies, heretofore marked for his
own project, had to be ordered to fords on the
Roanoke, the Dan, the Tar, and the Neuse Rivers.[39]
Burke's time was taken up by this new contingency.
When the Commander of Chatham requested his approval
for acting without formal confirmation by the Assembly, the Governor abstractedly replied: "Go on
and prosper in God's name do all the good you can
under any form or title you please."[40]

Events were outstripping Burke's capacity to
command initiatives; he was being manipulated by

181

The South, 1781

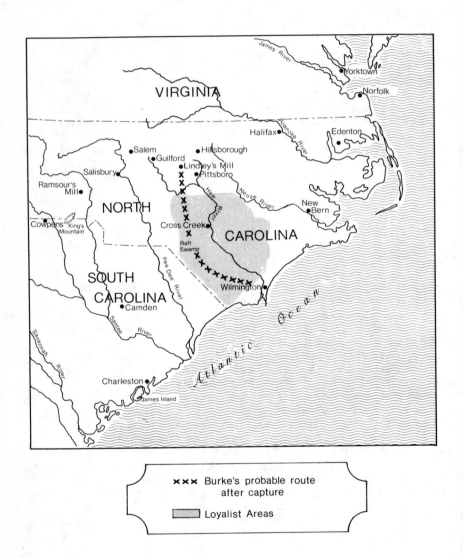

××× Burke's probable route
after capture

▓ Loyalist Areas

182

the actions of others who were often beyond his sources of information and far beyond his control. On the night of September 2, he was informed that a French fleet of twenty-seven vessels had arrived at Hampton Roads. Now that Cornwallis was blocked from retreat or supply by sea, it was even more likely that he would retreat through the state. Burke arranged for beacons along the rivers to be lit when the British made their crossing and stationed watchers in trees to look out for the fiery signals. Although Cornwallis' retreat was sealed off by September 3, the laggard communications system did not relay the news to Burke until late on September 5 or early the next morning. On the 3rd, as Burke rode from Halifax west toward Granville County, he could hear the cannonading on the James River, and his nervous mind imagined an attempt by Cornwallis to cross over the James and flee toward North Carolina.[41]

Even the great events to the north could not take his mind off the more local irritants. Again he was finding to his disgust that the nerves of government would not respond to his relentless impulses. A system of express riders that had been ordered days before in Halifax had not gone into effect. A scheduled meeting of General Allen Jones' subordinates was attended by only one officer, and "like an ass he is, dismissed his men because he did not find orders ready for him."[42] Burke confessed to Jones his fear that "systematic misbehavior" in every sector of government might drive him to arbitrary actions, which would taint his administration with "an air of Tyranny--though no man living is more averse to it."[43] Despotism, in his eighteenth century political terms, would fill the vacuum formed by civic irresponsibility. Burke in his correspondence appears to have been fatigued and harried, his patience and vitality sapped by a succession of crises. Increasingly, the Governor acted as if he and he alone was the sole vessel of the public will. Swimming against the tide of confusion and governmental infirmity, he sometimes seemed on the brink of being engulfed by it.

In Granville County on September 5, he learned not only of Cornwallis' predicament, but also that his old friend, Anthony Wayne, would be detained in Virginia. Wayne's attention was absorbed by the plight of "poor Cornwallis," and though recently shot in the thigh by an American militia sentry, he still counted on sharing "the glory of *Burgoyning* Lord Cornwallis."[44] For Burke the American success was proving costly. The encirclement of Cornwallis, the capital feat of the Revolution, was ironically contributing to his own demise.

Still he pressed forward. The orders to the district and county commanders were countermanded, but the militia were to be kept in the field for the upcoming expedition. On September 7, the Governor set out for Hillsborough, where he had rented a house in town and arranged to be joined by Polly who had been with him in Granville. James Iredell, temporarily laid up with an ailment, was unable to accompany Burke as planned. To his wife, Iredell related the Governor's kindness to him in attending to his illness.[45] Of his own welfare, Burke continued to be indifferent. With respect to a military escort, a precaution suggested by friends, he adopted a casual attitude, concluding that "if nobody has any greater apprehensions than I have myself it will hardly be worthwhile giving him [the militia officer] the trouble."[46]

Burke had already been marked for capture by David Fanning and Major James Craig--at least that was what Fanning later claimed.[47] From the moment they occupied Wilmington, the British had pursued an aggressive policy of trapping the Whig elite. The program had already produced an impressive list of captives, some of whom like his old friend Cornelius Harnett had died from mistreatment. The Loyalists were, however, numerous enough in Orange and surrounding counties to supply food and intelligence of the Governor's whereabouts.[48] On September 10, Burke wrote General John Butler, the district military head, that Tories had been collecting horses and assembling near town. With elliptical accuracy, he predicted that the Tories were planning "some stroke."

Typically careless of his own welfare, he supposed they would strike at Butler rather than
attack Hillsborough. "They will make a rapid
movement on horseback and if possible surprise
you," he ironically presaged.[49]

At 7:00 a.m. on the morning of September 13,
the guerillas appeared on the outskirts of Hillsborough. A dark night and an early morning fog
had permitted the columns to elude the patrols and
encircle the town. Exploiting fully his capacity
for mobility and deception, Fanning bypassed General Butler's militia and moved against the unde-
fended state government. In this respect, Burke
resembled the spider caught in his own web. The
"wretched Tories," thought to be on the verge of
defeat, had turned the tables on their potential
captor.[50]

Burke and his party of state officials fought
back, exchanging fire with the Tories. But the
battle was uneven. With few arms and the handful
of townsmen scattered in their homes, there was
little resistance. The Governor's house quickly
became the Tories' main object. Escape and even
resistance appeared futile, yet what they gleaned
of their assailants, "the savage manners and appearance," made them reluctant to capitulate. At length,
his aide-de-camp, John Read, left the house and
brought back "a gentleman in the uniform of a British Officer."[51] Assured of fair treatment, Burke
surrendered his sword. Once in the company of the
guerillas, however, the gentleman in question was
hard put to protect his prisoner. Fortunately,
Burke was rescued by some Scotch highlanders, formerly made prisoner by the Governor, who recalled
being treated with "humanity."[52]

All morning the guerillas of Fanning and
his confederate, Hector McNeil, remained in
Hillsborough, first emptying the jail of Tory
prisoners and then looting houses, or in a
few cases getting drunk. In the early afternoon, the Tories left town with their prisoners.
By noon the next day they had travelled twenty-six
miles to Lindley's Mill on Cane Creek. Contrary
to the modern canons of guerilla warfare, Colonel

McNeil's men, in front of the oversized column, had neglected to post an advance guard. McNeil paid dearly for this omission. Fanning later asserted that he was at the point of questioning McNeil about it when suddenly they were ambushed by General Butler. Before McNeil could respond, he was dead.[53]

The encounter lasted for several hours, and the result was a standoff. Following the ambush, Fanning had secured the prisoners, retreated, and chosen a battle site. After reorganizing his troops, he personally led an encircling movement around the Whig flank, and during the ensuing battle, he was severely wounded in the arm. Meanwhile, the prisoners, who were confined inside a nearby house, were subjected to periodic threats. One guerilla swore, according to Eli Carruthers' later accounts, that if the Tories were outmaneuvered by Butler, he would put all the captives to death.[54] Perhaps fortunately, the Whig attempts to outflank the guerillas were unsuccessful, and after four hours of fighting, both sides disengaged. Of the approximately nine hundred Tories, twenty-seven were killed and sixty seriously wounded. Fanning's broken arm resulted in so much loss of blood that he had to be left behind hidden in the woods.[55]

The prisoners were entrusted by Fanning to other hands, and the party moved toward far-off Wilmington. Their route led through the most desolate and remote areas of the state--marshes like the Raft Swamp which Burke later described as "vast pathless tracts of intermingled Sand and Swamp very thinly inhabited and which ought not to be inhabited at all."[56] Their possessions stolen, their clothes torn and soiled, they arrived at Wilmington, 160 miles from their starting point, after ten days of march. Somewhere along the way, perhaps just before the battle at Cane Creek or after resuming their march, the prisoners were offered paroles. Burke, confident of rescue and still unsure of his violent captors, refused the parole. His companions, Continental officers captured at Hillsborough, loyally followed suit, a gesture which moved Burke deeply.[57]

186

At Wilmington, Burke was turned over to Major Craig. While the latter was courteous, he was also determined to keep a jealous eye on his prize catch --so determined in fact that he isolated the Governor in a house within the lines and denied him access to anyone except a sergeant assigned to watch over him and a guard to prevent his escape. Burke humorously noted the defects in his lodgings.

> This room is always dry in fair weather,
> and warm when the sun shines, and the
> wind is southerly, it has all the advan-
> tage of the North East winds which may
> enter freely and must go out the same
> way; in short it seems calculated to
> answer the end of a grotto in winter
> and a hothouse in summer.[58]

Held incommunicado in this bare, comfortless dwelling, Burke searched for some model to give meaning to this illogical encounter with fate. With true eighteenth century stoicism, he turned his mind to antiquity in quest of "lacedemonian virtue" forcing his mind back "through the history of that patient austere people in search of some person whom I might propose for my model."[59] At length, Major Craig allowed Captain Read, Burke's aide-de-camp, to stay with the prisoner. Unfortunately, the officer, whose scrupulous code of honor exceeded his common sense, refused to divulge the vital news of the day for fear that he might violate the terms of his own parole. Burke could scarcely maintain his self-proclaimed "good humor" when his old friend, Samuel Strudwick, was refused permission to see him. The only consolation, Burke sarcastically remarked, was the reflection that his most trifling movements were considered so threatening to the awesome power of the British Crown. Previously he was merely the "axletree of the Chariot, but never thought I made much of the surrounding dust."[60]

From Wilmington, Burke was moved to Fort Arbuthnot on Sullivan's Island near Charleston, where again he was closely confined. He appealed to the commandant at Charleston for better treatment. The reply was silent on the unusual condi-

187

tions of his incarceration but did offer him a
parole either on Sullivan's or nearby James Island.
Because of the dearth of housing where he was,
Burke agreed to the alternative, and on November 6,
almost two months after his capture, he was paroled
to James Island.[61]

At first, life was relatively agreeable.
Thomas Burke's charm, so conspicuous at other
points in his life, cushioned the mundane circumstances of his parole. While ever anxious to
leave, he did make friends with natives of the
island and was visited by old Tory friends from
pre-war days, who were residing now behind British lines.[62] He still puzzled, however, over
the unusual character of his confinement. Why
was he not paroled to his own home or exchanged
for British officers as was customary? He worried
also about his wife, who was pregnant. As early
as mid-October, he referred in pointed humor to
his fear of being neglected by his own government.[63]
By late November, the question of his detention
had become an obsession. He indulged in uncharacteristic self-questioning, worrying that the British officers had received unfavorable impressions
of him.[64] By late December, he had developed a
hard streak of cynicism, mentioning for the first
time "that oblivion which is the common fate of
the magistrates of republics."[65] As if to insult
him further, the British allowed Captain Read and
a continental officer captured at Hillsborough
to return home on parole. Hopeful of better terms,
Burke wrote to General Leslie and asked his friends
to do the same.[66]

In the meantime, a more immediate danger arose.
Tory refugees from North Carolina were relocated
on James Island near Burke, and the resentful Tories focused their hatred on the rebel Governor.
The habit of violence so firmly established on
both sides of the conflict again manifested itself.
First there were mainly threats, but then the danger
escalated. Snipers in a party of refugees fired
on a small group standing with Burke at his lodgings, killing the man at his side and wounding
another to his left. Although the intervention
of a British officer prevented further violence,

Burke strongly suspected that the next shots would be aimed at him.[67]

On the following day he wrote to General Leslie requesting a parole within the American lines, or at least a safe place in which to serve his present parole, and carefully outlined the details of his dangerous predicament. But hope quickly faded when no reply was forthcoming from the General. While this neglect continued, the situation on James Island grew more torturous. The fear of death was with him constantly. A simple walk outside became a major undertaking: since he was blind in one eye, he had to be accompanied by someone who could survey the terrain for snipers.[68]

Any lingering illusions about the quality of British mercy to state prisoners were abruptly squelched by an informal statement made by General Leslie to one of Burke's friends. The rebel governor, he confessed, was being detained at Major Craig's request as a subject for retaliation. If British adherents, particularly Fanning, fell into rebel hands, then the Governor would be a hostage for their equitable treatment or release. Burke, who recalled Craig's threats from an earlier letter to him as Governor, had no doubt that he was in earnest. He further concluded, in an unwarranted extension of Leslie's assertion, that Major Craig had planted the Tory cutthroats on James Island to perform the act of retaliation.[69]

To his legalistic mind, the terms of his parole were tantamount to a bilateral contract. Now that the terms of the contract were violated, he was relieved of his obligation. Never one to stand on niceties when action was required, Burke made plans to escape. First, he wrote a letter to a friend, Willie Jones, instructing him not to allow the state to be blackmailed into releasing Tory criminals on his behalf. Then on the night of January 16, 1782, he made his escape. By what means, he never formally revealed. James Iredell, reporting that Burke had secured a boat to get himself off the island, also speculated that the sentries were bribed to allow him to pass unchallenged.[70]

Once within American lines, Burke stopped at the headquarters of the Southern Army in South Carolina. General Nathanael Greene, ever conscious of military protocol, advised him to write a letter to General Leslie, which he did. In it, he detailed the factors leading to his escape and offered to procure a satisfactory equivalent for his exchange. Were the latter to fail, he would agree to return, but only after a pledge from Leslie guaranteeing him the same status and treatment as continental officers.[71]

After conversing with Greene and borrowing a horse, Burke left for North Carolina, expecting to find the General Assembly convened at Salem. With the legislature in session, he could consult the public on what was proper in his situation: he had always regarded the legislature as the purest expression of the *vox populi*. Unfortunately, the members were not yet assembled. On the one hand, Burke had acknowledged his status as prisoner in the letter to Leslie, which had been written at Greene's prompting. He considered the obligations of his parole, however, terminated by the British breach of contract. Customarily scrupulous about questions of honor, he later indicated that he had been reluctant to take up the public business.[72] Though anxious for the public to determine his course, he had only the Acting Governor, Alexander Martin, to advise him, and Martin urged him to resume his duties. Pointing out that the office of Speaker would expire at the next general election, he emphasized the potential harm from having a vacancy in the supreme office of state after the election. There was also the feeling that Burke's presence in the state would make it difficult for another man to govern. Besides, the expedition against the Tories, still unconsummated, might suffer from want of direction.

With so much at stake, his subtle mind found reasons to justify his resumption of office. Had not General Greene advised returning to his "government?" The note to Leslie had merely been a polite statement of self-justification with no bearing on his present status. If Burke was using legal sophistry in a matter of "honor," he was doing so

in the public interest. His immediate advantage
would have been better served by withdrawing from
public life. Instead, he conceived of himself as
wedded by obligation to his office in what was now
becoming a most unhappy marriage.[73]

Unfortunately, the public zeal exhibited by
Burke did not allay all uncertainties. The question of prisoners, especially ones of rank, was
always sensitive in such a formalistic age. Not
surprisingly, the combination of foreign war and
rebellion caused problems on both sides. Treatment of militia was particularly thorny. While
the British accorded militia prisoners second
class treatment, the Americans regarded the loyalist militia as traitors or common criminals.[74]
Major Craig for all his pitiless pursuit of his
military duties was clearly faced with a quandry.
There was no reason why he should honor his obligations to the letter when the rebels refused to do
the same. Exchanging Burke would only have brought
him unwanted Tory refugees. Yet Burke logically
expected to be placed in the same category as captured American officers. The British commander,
General Leslie, aggravated an already embroiled
situation when he shunted the Governor aside,
making him a prisoner of state contrary to common
practice and then ignoring his circumstances.

Characteristically, Burke had acted with undue
haste in resuming his duties. Preoccupied with his
own dilemma, he failed to analyze the advice he
received. He leaped at Alexander Martin's opinions
without considering their ramifications. Furthermore, he naively misconstrued Greene's advice to
return to his "government," by which the General
meant that he might take up residence once more in
North Carolina. In his haste to find a quick solution legitimized by civil and military authority,
Burke seems to have suffered one of his periodic
lapses in judgment.

Violation of paroles was a serious matter to
military men of the eighteenth century, and Greene
was no exception. He said as much in reply to a
letter from General Leslie requesting the captive's
return. Still, he soon heard enough from sources

other than Burke to realize that the Governor had
been in acute danger. What bothered Greene now
was his uncertain status. Apparently, it bothered
Burke too, for in late February he asked for a
military inquiry. The court, presided over by the
General Arthur St. Clair, refused to vindicate his
actions. In the words of Colonel Otho H. Williams,
Adjutant of the Southern Army, the report "by no
means justified the conduct of Governor Burke:
And I am persuaded that Gl. Greene considers Governor Burke a Prisoner of War."[75]

Perhaps unwisely, Colonel William Davie, after
talking to Williams at Salisbury, informed the Governor that the question of his parole had become
controversial. Davie, the state Commissary General,
related that Burke's departure from army headquarters
before the matter was settled as well as his decision to resume his office as Governor were condemned
both by the court and by Greene. According to Williams, it was felt that the enemy still had legal
claims on Governor Burke.[76]

This was too much for Burke. It precipitated
the onset of one of those personal vendettas which
had punctuated his political career. Before acting, he obtained from Greene a statement of the
General's opinion. A month later, with the evidence in hand, he fired off an angry letter to
Williams accusing him of misrepresentation. In
particular, he denied the charge that Greene had
objected to his departure from army headquarters
in advance of a settlement in what Williams had
suggested was a disgraceful manner.[77]

By this time, his own countrymen had replaced
the British as the subject of his contempt. Cynically, he sought relief in a furious and self-
destructive frame of mind. When it was proposed
to name a ship *The Governor Burke*, the namesake
spewed out his bitterness.

I am sorry you have determined to
give your vessel a name so unfortunate
as that you mentioned, and should be
much concerned if her fate should any
way resemble his, after whom you intend

to call her, which is to have laboured
much for the public to his own irre-
trievable disadvantage.[78]

While still in office, his cup continued to
overflow with gall. The lonely isolation and
neglect, contrary to his expectations, were particularly grating to one so sensitive. If the enemy
had realized how little he was missed at home, he
cynically observed, less effort would have been
made to keep him prisoner. To Greene, he complained that he was sacrificed to the duties of
state and spoke of his public service as a "folly."[79]
To a man who needed attention and approbation, the
experience of being stranded in limbo crystallized
into a very painful memory. Thomas Burke was
poorly equipped to cope with either failure or
isolation. The result would be a rapid erosion
of his revolutionary faith.

With Burke resuming office, North Carolina
experienced another change of leadership, the third
in seven months. Although the threat from Lord
Cornwallis had disintegrated, the state still suffered from the depravations of Loyalists and shortages of supply. Fanning, now recovered from his
wounds, roamed the lower counties at will. The
state's insolvency and the scarcity of supplies
stymied the Governor in the daily execution of
public business. In late February, he complained
that he could not make the necessary inspection
trips because he could not find any horses. Besides, the winter had been a severe one. In early
February, Eneas Reeves, a young army officer who
had dined with Burke, reported a storm of sleet
and snow that broke off branches from the trees
and stayed on the ground for three days. Reeves
worried about the lack of provisions for his men
and feared he might have to resort to impressment.[80]

Burke was also concerned about the chaotic
accounts kept by the state. William Davie informed
the Governor that it was impossible to conduct a
public audit, because the commissioners were not
accountable to anyone and in any case were not
keeping records to differentiate the supplies de-

livered to the state from those involving the
national government. This was particularly serious
because it meant that North Carolina lacked the
vouchers by which to collect the credits owed it
by Congress for supplies and services provided to
the Continental army. Wherever it was possible,
Burke attempted to establish supply and finance
on a more rational basis. Andrew Armstrong boasted in March that the Governor was "now calling our
over-grown fellows in the Public Departments to an
account with a very becoming Severity, and is
really making some surprising discoveries."[81]
Even so, the chief-of-state was importuned by
officers who often operated under both state and
continental jurisdiction and habitually confused
their dual capacities. Burke peevishly recalled
to one applicant that he was requesting state resources as a continental official and instructed
him to draw funds from the Paymaster of the Continental Army. As for specific items, here also
he refused to hand over the state's meager resources. Only General Greene was empowered to make
requisitions of transportation accessories from
the state government; even if Greene could not pay,
Burke now had "such confidence in him that I will
cause them to be supplied as far as the funds necessary in my power will admit."[82] As the Governor
pointed out, the state had no sources of supply
other than the specific tax; the money tax did
not answer its needs since there was not enough
revenue available, and the proceeds were often in
the form of certificates which had been distributed
in return for supplies.[83]

When the young officer, Eneas Reeves, applied
to him for a supply of arms for his troops, the
Governor's recent hospitality to Reeves failed to
secure him any special consideration. Burke refused his request, emphasizing that the arms were
the property of North Carolina and could not be
distributed to continental troops. Reeves grumbled
that the Governor was "Letting me and my men run
the Chance of being Captured by some Inconsiderable
party [rather] than part with a few Stand."[84]

Reeves assessed accurately the continuing
danger from small bands of Loyalists. Reports of

depredations and threatened raids reached Burke
with alarming regularity; the pleas for troops
and arms persisted. The Governor still nursed
his scheme for an expeditionary force to pacify
the countryside, and his plans were carefully
outlined in a letter to Major Hogg, the continental officer whom Burke had placed in command.
The Governor emphasized that "all acts of plunder
or inhumane violence" should be carefully avoided; the means of subsistence for the disaffected
should be preserved.[85] All males who were disaffected should be either taken prisoner or given
the opportunity to enlist in the state militia.
"Indeed, except the very mischievous and atrocious,"
he explained, "I wish to see very few submitted to
the executioner."[86]

Such a tender sprig as Burke's new policy
of conciliation faced a precarious existence in
the adverse climate of civil war. Colonel Davie,
for example, condemned the inhumane behavior of
the troops which had reoccupied Wilmington after
the British withdrew. He was shocked to learn that
the animosities of civil war had been visited on
the children of the Loyalists.

Several poor Wretches have been
here in search after their Children
which were kidnapped and carried off
by the Militia of General Rutherford's
Brigade from Bladen and other Counties
in the Neighborhood of Wilmington--This
is truly shocking to humanity and a
Stigma on our Character as a people.[87]

At the same time, the Governor was challenged
by Fanning for provocations against the Tories.
"I understand that you have three of my men," Fanning wrote, "and likewise have a Captain and six
men under the sentence of death."[88] The Tory
officer threatened to retaliate "blood for blood,
and tenfold for one" if Burke carried out the sen-
tences.[89] He was further incensed at the Governor's proclamation to the Loyalists. He denounced
the plan of exempting those guilty of murder, rob-
bery, and arson from being eligible for pardons.
The Tory partisan affirmed that "there never was

a man who has been on Arms on either side but what is guilty of some of the above mentioned crimes especially on the Rebel side."[90] He threatened instant death to any "rebels" that he captured if any more of his men were hanged.

As if internal difficulties were not enough, North Carolina became embroiled in a dispute with Virginia over the capture of a British owned vessel named the *Three Friends*. On February 13, 1782, the ship had embarked from the enemy-occupied port of Charleston, sailing under a flag of truce. Yet it was carrying a cargo of British goods worth about 8,000 pounds sterling, a trading connection that Congress had recently outlawed while calling for the capture of all British ships and goods.[91]

The *Three Friends* reached Edenton on February 19 and was immediately seized by the captain of the *Grand Turk*, a Virginia owned privateer operating in North Carolina waters. Rather than initiate proceedings in the state's courts, the captain removed the prize from Edenton to South Quay in Virginia. This was to prevent a division of the proceeds with another ship which had also boarded the British schooner by avoiding the North Carolina jurisdiction.[92]

On March 4, Burke wrote a letter to Governor Harrison of Virginia, explaining what had happened. To Harrison, his old friend from Congress, he complained that the schooner had submitted its "flag" to a North Carolina official and had been cleared before it was seized. Burke apparently hinted that a force might be sent to recover the schooner and to punish the captains of the privateers. Harrison hastily replied that restitution would be made and appealed to the North Carolinian not to take any rash actions, such as sending a force to South Quay. He promised that the offenders would be punished and the vessel delivered to the admiralty jurisdiction of North Carolina.[93]

Nevertheless, proceedings had already begun in Virginia, and Harrison's letter to the court of admiralty did not arrive in time. On March 8, the ship was condemned. After learning of the decision, Harrison sent a copy of the proceedings to Burke emphasizing that the matter was now beyond his control, since he had no power to interfere with the courts. He also promised to ask Congress to revoke the commission of the captain and pointed out that the owners of the *Three Friends* could appeal under the provisions of the Articles of Confederation. Again he cautioned Burke that the use of force would be unwise and would only work to the British advantage. "Hannibal is Knocking at our Gates," Harrison reminded his North Carolina counterpart, "let us by joint efforts repel them from our Coasts, and leave more trivial matters for a time of ease and tranquility."[94]

Sensing Harrison's dismay, Burke assumed a cooperative stance. He admitted that the *Three Friends* was a legitimate prize, confessing that his first view of the situation had been mistaken. Yet he emphasized that the seizure and removal to Virginia constituted an insult to the state's dignity. It was as if North Carolina could not protect ships in its jurisdiction and had to resort to courts in a neighboring state.[95] In his annual report to the Assembly, Burke made it clear that he had never intended any offense or provocation to Virginia. When he learned of Harrison's alarm, he had dropped his plans for an expedition to chastise the offending captains. He concluded that since the incident was scarcely "so serious as to justify a quarrel with a friendly and Confederated neighbor who had no intention to offend us, I pursued it no farther...when I perceived their Apprehensions."[96]

In the final weeks of Thomas Burke's term as Governor, his frustrations seemed contagious. Military disobedience still undermined his plans to suppress the enemy. One officer who failed to keep an appointment with the Governor, was arrested and then allowed to resign. More serious, however, was the failure of the plans for an expeditionary force as a result of military disobedience. A major in the state militia refused to march his troops because he had been superceded in command by Major Thomas Hogg of the Continental Line.

Burke's long cherished scheme was thereby con-
signed to oblivion.[97]

Yet the days of guerilla warfare were numbered. With the British surrender at Yorktown and
withdrawal from Wilmington, the rationale as well
as the support for the Loyalists had declined.
Besides, Fanning had lost interest and was anxious
to conclude a truce. He and Burke reached a tentative agreement, but it would have had little
chance of working out and was in any case rejected
by the Assembly. Soon after Burke left office,
Fanning took refuge in British-occupied Charleston
and eventually settled in Nova Scotia.[98]

Much of Burke's time was taken up with hearing petitions for pardons and applications for
safe conducts to the British lines. The Governor,
as far as he could pursued a lenient policy toward
the Loyalists. Yet he had made it clear that he
would retaliate against the British if it became
necessary. Responding to earlier threats by Major
Craig, he warned that the state government might
be forced to follow the example of their Indian
neighbors in "delivering over Prisoners to be tor-
tured at the pleasure of a fierce and vengeful
kindred...."[99] After experiencing Craig's severity as a captive, however, Burke lost any taste
for revenge. Soon after returning from James Island, he urged General Lillington, in moving the
families of Loyalists who were in arms against
the state, to treat "those unhappy people" in a
humane way.[100] Before leaving office, he requested
the General Assembly to pardon the Scotch Loyalists
who had saved his life at Hillsborough and helped
to ease the hardships of his forced march to Wilmington. He also gave temporary reprieves to several Tories who had been condemned to death.[101]

When the Assembly convened in April, Burke
could report that conditions had greatly improved
since the critical time of the last legislative
session. After the hardships of office, however,
he was weary of public service. William Davie
wrote him on April 14 expressing regrets that he
had been unable to attend Davie's recent marriage
to the daughter of General Allen Jones--"Mingling

oer' the friendly bowl--The feast of *reason* and the flow of *soul*."[102] Davie would have felt "a singular satisfaction in seeing you unlaced from the cares of State."[103] On the same day, Burke received a letter from a military friend, Major McCauley, that could only have distressed him. On a Sunday morning, McCauley had walked through the rooms where the delegates to the Assembly were congregating and had overheard discussions concerning the election of a Governor for the next annual term. The names of Samuel Johnston, William Sharpe, Alexander Martin, and Burke were mentioned, and the Major confided that "the way that you left Charleston is much Debated."[104] There was even some question that the Governor might still be bound by his parole. Burke's friends, McCauley reported, remained steadfast, and he had no doubts that if Burke lent them his assistance, he could be re-elected.

But Thomas Burke had already made up his mind to retire. Two days before, he reported that he was planning to leave his public capacity as soon as possible, especially since conditions within the state had improved so dramatically. To the Assembly, he presented a long and detailed account of his capture, which showed the criticisms of his actions still preying heavily on his mind.

> I do not expect to be so fortunate as that every one will judge candidly of an affair so circumstanced as this I have related and I am aware that some men who felt no concern for me while in captivity and who would have been very easy had I been murdered have taken some malicious liberties on the subject of my escape....[105]

After an energetic defense of his conduct, it is not surprising that Burke's name was placed before the Assembly. He wrote, however, insisting that his nomination be withdrawn; he made it clear that nothing could have pleased him less than being chosen to the office in 1781. He had only accepted to avoid jeopardizing the state's interests at such a critical juncture, and now

that the crisis had passed, there was no longer a
need to sacrifice his time and efforts which were
so necessary for his personal affairs. "My misfortunes during this year," he explained, "have
been heavy and complicated and have involved me
in debts and in private distresses which it would
be painful to particularize."[106] He further mentioned the credit advanced to him while he was a
prisoner and hoped that the state would assume
these debts. As for his other expenses, the records had been destroyed by the enemy. Yet he
insisted on payment of all these debts lest he be
classed "in the number of public defaulters."[107]
Although a committee was appointed to examine
his claims, restitution was never made.

Perhaps if the Assembly had generously reimbursed Burke and absolved him from all responsibility for parole violation, he might have considered another term. As it was, he still believed
that he had been grossly neglected and blamed the
"public" for his predicament. This outlook punctuated the account of his escape and was to haunt
him for the rest of his life. It now gave him a
personal justification for condemning himself to
political oblivion.

LEGACY OF REPUBLICANISM

His public career ended, Burke eagerly retired to Tyaquin. Arriving home, he reported that
"my own Cottage...as well as the grounds around
it, has evident marks of the master's Neglect as
much as of hostile Violence," and he vowed to make
repairs as soon as possible.[1] But the hardships
of office and captivity had strained his constitution. In assessing his "feeble powers," he noticed
"a languor to Which I have been long a stranger."[2]

Now at last, he was reunited with his family.
During the winter, a child had been born to the
Burkes. "My family Consists of Mrs. Burke and a
little daughter," the new father boasted, "who is
commander in Chief already."[3] The ex-Governor
planned to remain at Tyaquin until the circuit of
the Superior Court for the Hillsborough District
began in September. He would have preferred to
drop the practice of law to devote himself exclusively to farming. The crushing financial burdens,
however, left him no choice except to resume his
law practice. Although chronic indebtedness was
an accepted way of life in the South, the scarcity
of cash in the state made repayment of debts even
more difficult, and Burke had already overloaded
himself with obligations. Although he could have
repaid some earlier, he had chosen to wait, and
now he was faced with a disquieting array of debts,
some of them still remaining from his years in
Norfolk. In addition, he had not yet paid for
the tract of land purchased from Milner's estate
before the war and owed large sums to Scottish merchants. He was even indebted for the value of
the horse he had borrowed at General Greene's headquarters after his escape.[4]

Still restless, his mind soon returned to
thoughts of leaving North Carolina. He had written
an inquiry to his old friend, AEdanus Burke, now
a judge in South Carolina, asking about Georgia,
and the Judge had taken the liberty of acquiring
a plantation near Savannah on Burke's account.
Disconcerted by having his daydreams taken so

literally, the ex-Governor now sought more defin-
ite information concerning Georgia. Could the
Judge tell him, for example, what effect the climate might have on his health? After coming to
North Carolina, he had acquired a "robust health."[5]
Polly Burke, also "infirm" before moving there,
regarded with alarm the prospect of going with a
young child to Georgia.[6] Their accounts of the
"unhealthiness of the River Savannah, were indeed
frightening."[7]

At the same time, he also considered moving
to South Carolina. "The great number of families
who had been so long affluent or opulent," he
noted, "as to have no traces of littleness in their
manners...would probably render the Settlement of
the Country very easy."[8] Yet the provisions that
South Carolina had made for selling forfeited property made it extremely difficult to obtain labor.
Burke regarded it as impractical or even impossible to convert his landholdings into money or
Negroes without assuming further debts. He had
too few Negroes at present to undertake "a Southern Estate."[9]

On one point, Burke was insistent. Wherever
he went, he refused to be drawn into public service. He was so obsessed with this point that
one suspects that his expressions of distaste were
a thin disguise for the unresolved conflicts from
his ordeal as Governor. He made it clear that he
would settle only where he could live in dignity
without being drawn into the public arena lest his
activities might draw the envy of those who coveted
his position. Only in a society where there were
numerous men of prestige and property who would
devote themselves to governmental business could
he be certain to avoid this obligation without
appearing to turn it down. Burke sought every
opportunity to demonstrate how he had been misunderstood and misused while in public service. The
closer his friends, the more bitterness he displayed toward the republican ideal of serving the
public.

I feel no more that enthusiastic public
Spirit which diminished the greatest

dangers and difficulties in distress.
It is either dead or Sleeps in great
tranquility. It was a species of mad-
ness with which I had been long in-
fected, which was too powerful for
my reason, who saw it very clearly,
to care but to which the ingratitude
of republican Society had applied,
I hope, a radical Remedy.[10]

Initially, while in captivity and immediately
afterwards, the British had been the chief target
of this wrath. Besides his own peril, he had worried about his wife's pregnancy, and this was related to the condition of his finances. General
Leslie's refusal to allow him to return home undoubtedly struck him as a breach of humanity.
Although Burke was confined as a prisoner of state,
the officers of the continental line--with whom
he equated himself--were eligible for parole behind their own lines. That the Governor was in
danger could not be denied. A friend whom he met
on James Island later recalled that the British
had planned to place him in stricter confinement
the day after he left which presumably would have
made him a hostage for the Tories in North Carolina.[11]

But the recollection of his neglect as a
captive was to obsess Burke for the rest of his
life. Sometimes his bitterness seemed to encom-
pass all humanity and by implication anyone who
might have done more to help him. He was especially irritated that the state authorities had not
provided adequately for his wife's needs. Yet his
friends saw that care was given to Polly Burke and
helped by bringing supplies, writing and visiting
him while he was in captivity. Both Colonel William Davie and General Allen Jones wrote letters
to Nathanael Greene soliciting his release by way
of exchange.[12]

More explicitly, he blamed the government
for neglecting him. But what government was responsible? His final statements to the legislature

and his blunt retirement as chief executive indicated that he held the state culpable. The General Assembly had not been in session, however,
and the state was at the nadir of effectiveness.
Moreover, Governor Martin had written to Lord
Cornwallis as well as Major Craig concerning his
plight. When confronted with his insinuations
of the state's role in his misfortune, Burke denied
that he had the government of North Carolina specifically in mind. If anything, his words suggested
that the Confederation authorities were at fault.[13]

    Yet the Congress had passed a resolution soli-
citing his release, making the civil prisoners
taken at Yorktown available for his exchange.
Burke scornfully dismissed these as "a people who
the enemy are so far from wishing to regain that
they are already burthened [sic] with a useless
train of them."[14] Since Burke was a civilian prisoner, it was not unreasonable that Congress should
have offered a like quantity for his exchange. In
addition, Congress had earlier empowered General
Greene to negotiate for the release of prisoners
in the Southern Department. After Cornwallis' surrender, Washington had also advised working through
Greene.[15]

    Actually, Greene was closer to Burke's situa-
tion than either Congress, the state of North Carolina, or General Washington. After Burke's escape,
Greene and the North Carolina Governor established
a degree of rapport. In Greene's later correspondence with him, a compassion is evident that was
lacking in their previous dealings. Besides securing his exchange later in the year, Greene wrote
lengthy letters on topics of mutual interest and
consoled him in his agony. When Burke manifested
aversion for public service, Greene dutifully expressed hope that with so much valuable experience,
Burke would again someday make himself available.
The troubled ex-Governor seems, in turn, to have
regarded Nathanael Greene as someone who sympathized with his misfortune. Greene emerged from
this imbroglio as the single individual whose role
Burke really trusted.[16]

But what exactly was Greene's role? Colonel
Otho Williams testified to Greene's displeasure
with Burke's activities after the escape. While
Greene sympathized with the Governor's predicament on James Island, he later admitted that "I
would sooner have abided the consequences than have
left the Enemy's lines."[17] Was it possible that
Greene might have attempted to relieve Burke in
captivity?

Admittedly, the General occupied a difficult
position regarding prisoners, as he later confessed
to Burke. This was the period of savage retaliation between the British and Americans, and the
militia prisoners on both sides in South Carolina
were pawns sacrificed to the prevailing blood lust.
Most notable was Colonel Issac Haynes of the South
Carolina militia, executed by the British on August 4 at Charleston. After this atrocity, even
the "cartel" or system for exchanging prisoners
was broken off, and the matter was placed in the
hands of Congress. Thomas Burke unfortunately fell
into British hands at this moment.[18]

During Burke's captivity, Greene never inter-
ceded specifically on the Governor's behalf. Faced
with incredible problems of supply and strategy,
the General had scant time available and no personal ties to merit his special concern--though
he did point out that his firmness regarding British retaliations probably saved the Governor from
a worse fate. When Burke arrived at army headquarters after his escape, Greene apparently spoke only
briefly with him, since his terse advice led to a
critical misunderstanding on Burke's part. Still,
with Wilmington finally evacuated and Cornwallis
eliminated, North Carolina bore little relevance
to the South Carolina theater. Greene's attention
was centered there.

The former Quaker was not insensitive, however, and Burke's inner crisis eventually seemed
to bother him. Just before Burke left office,
Greene's letters became longer and less distant,
as if he now understood and trusted him. He also
persisted in seeking the Governor's exchange, even
after Burke left office, an effort which was fin-

205

ally rewarded in October 1782. The attempts to
include Burke in the exchange were resisted by the
British. At length, after many "shifts and eva-
sions," the British had conceded the point in order to get other advantages from the exchange.[19]

At first, Greene's view of Burke's actions
had been dictated by a strict consciousness of his
moral obligations in the case of a broken parole.
At length, he appears to have realized that Burke
suffered from an acute and dangerous sense of personal neglect and perhaps sensed his role in that
neglect. Once aware of Burke's demoralization,
the General sought to restore his sense of personal
and public worth. Greene was undoubtedly bothered
by Burke's sudden aversion to public service. In
a milieu in which civic responsibility was highly
valued, the loss of zeal or faith was a kind of
spiritual death. Green delicately tried to pull
him back from the brink of this eventuality--one
to which he may have contributed. His effort had
little effect, for Burke's once eloquent faith in
republican institutions and the sacred public will
had all but vanished. Like others before him,
Thomas Burke had been spiritually crippled by the
revolution that he had helped to create.

After his ordeal, it is not surprising that
Burke's political attitudes began to change. His
view of his role in the political process had been
warped by his ill-fated term as Governor. Whereas
he had once been prey to outbursts of egotism, he
was now characterized by self-deprecation. He insisted that his constituents had ascribed to him
greater talents than he possessed; his zeal for
liberty and expertness in his work had given him
a reputation that far exceeded his worth. His
talents were "not of the Inferior order but were
Certainly Surpassed by those of many others who
did not appear to equal advantage."[20] Like other
American revolutionaries, he had begun with a commitment to the "rights of mankind," and this commitment to liberty would not allow him to remain "aloof,
though he had never wished to be in the public eye.[21]

Yet his greatest disappointment had been the
lack of cooperation by the inhabitants of North

Carolina while he was trying to govern the state.
He recalled that at the time he took office, he
had found the people mired in a sloppy, apathetic
disregard for the public welfare and accustomed to
ignoring state authority. His efforts to reform
these abuses had, in turn, caused resentment, because as Governor he lacked the network of political connections necessary for gaining statewide
support.[22] Many of those who had resented his
policies were kept silent only by the correctness
and firmness of his actions, so obviously directed
toward the public good as to defy misinterpreta-
tion. Nevertheless, though a majority may have
agreed with him in principle, this had little effect. It had been his sad experience in public
life that such benevolent opinions had to be constantly rekindled lest "they die away into cold
Indifference [and] at length into oblivion, nor
is it uncommon for them to change...into malevo-
lence."[23]

Burke's ideology had been in flux before he
became Governor, as he moved from state sovereignty
toward an emphasis on nationalism. If he had remained in Congress or at the national level, he
doubtless would have followed the path leading
to the Constitutional Convention of 1787. For those
in continental service, the desire for stronger
central government gradually crystallized as the
war progressed. The Revolutionary experience, however, had numerous variations. While it did lead
many towards nationalism, it also stimulated sec-
tionalism. For some, it led away from support of
strong central government towards state and local
sovereignty. When Burke left the high road leading to Philadelphia, his career took a sharp turn.
The resulting experience re-oriented his political
thought. It proved fatal to his belief in the
infallibility of republican institutions, but it
also led him to seek a modified system that would
apply both to the society and its government. Once
again, the Revolutionary ambivalence between human
and property rights was the starting point for the
restructuring of his ideas. Burke had earlier
swung dramatically towards a sympathy with political and civil rights, but he was gradually returning
to a philosophy built upon the rights of property.

In short, Burke now advocated a society governed by a propertied nobility, and his ideal was
not so different from that which had characterized
the system of local politics in pre-war North Carolina. Within Burke's new scheme, the possession
of property was the basis of all political power.
He believed that a distinct class of property holders had historically come into being and gained
ascendancy for the purpose of providing political
leadership. The masses of humanity, according to
Burke, were incapable of acting in their enlightened
self-interest. Instead, the people were slaves to
impulses and lacked the fortitude to pursue a consistent plan of action. The forces of reason and
understanding, which he had once treated as basic
to human motivation, were now considered too weak
to bring about action in the public interest, and
he saw "Passions" as the most potent and perhaps
the sole source of political motivation. His new
view of man in society was similar to the views
of property and human motivation that characterized
many future Federalists.[24]

Burke further observed that men were endowed
with unequal talents and capacities for work. As
a result, some of them were inevitably in a position to acquire more than others. This inequity
would always occur, and in time this economic condition would be translated into a permanent status.
If some members of society were more respected or
had accumulated more land than others, these individuals "should be classed together as a Nobility,
and that a certain Portion of Landed Property Should
always entitle a Citizen to Become of that Order."[25]
According to Burke, only the "few" or the elite
possessed the wealth and leisure necessary for ob-
taining a rational and unfettered outlook. Inevitably, this group received a political and military education that enabled them to perceive the
public interest and to coordinate with "the Inferior Orders in Execution."[26]

Burke was not opting for a system of titled
nobility like that of Great Britain. He advocated
a society with a bourgeois nobility, a class whose
status accrued from the possession of property
rather than hereditary titles. Although the system

favored a privileged set of oligarchs, a balanced society would also be preserved. In a setting where property was easily acquired, it was important to keep the status of the nobility from being debased by an increase in their numbers. As a safeguard against this possibility, Burke proposed that land-holdings be limited to that land which could be cultivated. Furthermore, he urged that all classes of society should have equal representation, even those who possessed only their ability to work. But he made one essential distinction: only those who owned land could actually serve in the legislature, "for they only are interested in the Permanent Happiness of the Country."[27] Burke's plan would have omitted property requirements for voting, but instead would have limited office holding to a property owning aristocracy. In truth, his plan was analogous to the system practiced before the Revolution and was reminiscent of policies advocated by conservatives like Samuel Johnston at the time of independence. Unfortunately for Burke, the Revolution in North Carolina had gone too far to turn back to the old, pre-Revolutionary ideal of a society balanced between a nobility and the people, especially in an area where a settled, easily recognizable nobility had never truly existed.

Only one fragment exists of Burke's altered view of society, and it was apparently inspired by John Adams' *Thoughts on Government*. In it, Burke was attempting to evaluate Adams' proposals in the light of his new images of man and society. "Let me now observe," he stated, "that Mr. A's plan appears Defective because it has not provided for those distinctions which Naturally arise among men, and without which Provisions all Governments must degenerate into some Species of Tyranny."[28] Tyranny for Burke, in view of his own experiences, had a far different meaning than in 1776 when he had first read Adams' treatise. Ironically, his emphasis on property instead of civil rights occurred at a time when his own fortunes were declining. Indirectly, he blamed his predicament on the social dislocations caused by the Revolution, and his new ideas may have been designed to prevent its reoccurrence.

In other writings, Thomas Burke projected an equally cynical view of Revolutionary society. When he solicited information from AEdanus Burke about Georgia, he wanted to know how the system of government actually operated and not merely in its external forms. Where power was widely distributed, he believed, the effectiveness of government would hinge upon the society at large, or "the manners and moral principles of the people."[29] The former Governor was certain that such principles governed the tone of popular passions and in turn conditioned the practice of government. If such passions became irrational or violent, the result would make a "dead letter" of the laws.[30] Probably, from his experience in western North Carolina, he held that the frontier was conducive to irrationality and violence. He was worried that Georgia was still "a New Country" which attracted the "base" and "adventurous" as well as those who had failed to adjust in other states.[31] In such a setting, not unlike the back country of North Carolina, those who acted violently often did so with impunity. At this stage in his political thought, Burke argued that only a strong judicial authority grounded in public respect would assure freedom from oppressive laws but also from licentious crimes.

Thomas Burke feared the ungovernable, the unpredictable, the irrational and especially the potential for violence within his own society. Tyranny was no longer equated with the actions of government, but rather with the outrages from society at large. He forcefully expressed this viewpoint in his letter to AEdanus Burke: "sir, power is Tyranny in its most hideous form, for it is Cruel, unrelenting and Capricious as that Monster Multitude by whom it is Exercised."[32]

The former Governor had travelled far from his pre-Revolutionary faith in the popular will. His image of society had altered, but so also had his self-image, and it appears that the two were related. Undoubtedly, much of Burke's new conception of society resulted from his experiences with the breakdown of authority and indiscriminate civil war while he was Governor. But his altered views may also have been a mirror of the unresolved con-

flicts within himself. He had never fully integrated the eighteenth century Newtonian ideal of
reason and proportion into his own conduct. De-
plore as he might the rule of passion, it still
persisted within himself. The failure of the
Revolutionary ideal of a balanced society ordered
by rational government paralleled the inability
of Burke to govern his own emotions.

Despite his vow to avoid public service,
Burke was elected as a delegate to the House
of Commons from Hillsborough. On occasion, he was
also applied to for advice or assistance. He wrote
a letter, for example, on behalf of Andrew Miller
requesting a pardon that would allow him to acquire
citizenship.[33] Also, in May of 1783, he received
a letter from Colonel John Williams and the lawyers of the Hillsborough District regarding two
unpopular laws. The one which they could least
tolerate was for limiting the fees of attorneys in
the superior and county courts. Burke concurred,
stating his opinion that it was unconstitutional
and would set a precedent for "Subjecting all men
to Arbitrary power in the County Courts, of whose
Judges the General Assembly are for the most part
composed."[34] It was unfortunate, he continued,
that unscrupulous men had gained a foothold within
the profession. Their practices severely provoked
the public at large, yet only those who were ignorant and narrow-minded would attribute these faults
to the entire profession.[35] As for the General
Assembly--once the underpinning of his political
theories--its members were even more at fault.
Burke was making no attempt to disguise his elit-
ist predilections, so reminiscent of Samuel Johnston in 1775 and 1776.

The Superior Knowledge and abilities
of men of Eminence in our profession
always have been and always will be an
object both of Envy and Apprehension to
low minds...but that very knowledge and
those abilities form the most sure re-
source for the people against Tyranny
and oppression. We are therefore to
Expect that when low or arbitrary Char-
acters get into the Legislature, which

211

will too often happen during the In-
fancy of a Government, they will attempt to remove those objects of their
envy and apprehensions from that respectable Station in the public Eye....[36]

Burke refused to help change the laws, politely explaining that he practiced largely in the
Superior Courts and frequently in districts other
than Hillsborough. His refusal was in keeping with
his determination to avoid any service that might
distract him from his private interests. He did
concede that if the lawyers boycotted the courts,
he would not take personal advantage of their absence.[37]

The ex-Governor rarely discussed state and
local affairs without reference to his own bitter
experiences. In a letter to a friend who was thinking of settling in North Carolina, he advised agains
such a move. Alluding to "this ill-governed Country," he argued that farming was neither convenient
nor profitable.[38] Recalling perhaps a happier
time, he recommended Philadelphia as a place where
conveniences were close at hand. Even without a
landed estate, a man could live there comfortably
because he had only to support himself and his
family. Perhaps Burke himself still nursed the
distant hope of returning to Philadelphia.

This was in August of 1783 as darkness was
closing over him. His final letter to Nathanael
Greene, written eight months earlier, exhibited
his pervasive despair. Thomas Burke, whose life
and career were intertwined with the events of the
American Revolution, had suffered an estrangement
from that experience which might be described as
an alienation of the spirit or an ideological
death. The tragic epitaph was spinning wildly in
his mind.

I must ever keep the Circumstances of
my Captivity in awful remembrances;
the Neglect I experienced, the ruin
and distress which threatened my family
in my death, the peculiar difficulty
of my Dilemma when I escaped, all form

a weight upon my Mind which I cannot
Shake off.[39]

In April of 1783, when the Assembly was con-
vening, Burke decided to retire. James Iredell
reported to his wife that "Dr. Burke talks of
leaving the Assembly, but I much doubt it."[40]
When he did not attend, his friend from Wilmington, Archibald Maclaine, conceded that his disturbed finances offered some excuse--though he
still disapproved. A few weeks earlier, in criticizing Governor Martin, Maclaine fondly recalled
that Burke had displayed more integrity: "His
mind is too educated," Maclaine concluded, "to
stoop to the common arts of acquiring popularity."[41]

To Burke's tormented spirit and deranged finances were added bodily infirmities. The ordeal
of capture, captivity, and escape had weakened
his not too robust health. In the letter to AEdanus
Burke regarding Georgia, there was a hint of premature aging and perhaps a presentiment of the short
time that remained to him. He expressed a wish
for circumstances which would allow him the prospect of passing the remainder of his days in "an
elegant and tranquil enjoyment of pleasures of
Society tempered with the pleasing [beatitudes?]
of retirement."[42] At this time, he was not yet
thirty-nine.

In October of 1783, Burke fell seriously ill.
On November 9, he reported that his recent illness
"has nearly proved fatal."[43] He begged his correspondent to excuse the brevity of his response "for
my health is Still very infirm and writing very
painful to me."[44] This was written from Edenton
where he had gone, probably on business. With his
health still declining, Burke was deserted by his
wife.[45] On December 16, Archibald Maclaine sadly
conjectured: "Burke is, I am afraid, by this time
no more."[46]

Maclaine knew only too well. On December 2,
Thomas Burke died--alone, unable to sleep, in physical pain and mental anguish, and according to William Hooper, "Laboring under a Complication of

213

disorders."[47] Hooper suggested that Burke "fell,
in some measure, a sacrifice to the Obstinacy
which marked his character through life."[48] If
he had not gone to Edenton in November, he would
perhaps have still been alive. "It would, however,
be a question with his friends," Hooper observed,
"whether life upon the terms he had it would not
have been a curse in the extreme."[49] With delicate irony, Hooper described Burke's tragic demise
and offered a discerning epitaph.

> his whole mass of blood dissolved; his
> temper soured with disappointment; and,
> to sum up his misery, no domestic prop
> to lean upon--no friend or companion,
> at his own home, to soothe the anguish
> of his mind, or mitigate his pain of
> body--was not death to him 'a comforter,
> friend, and physician?'[50]

Hooper also made the apt observation that
Burke had "carried his indifference to his wife
to the grave with him."[51] He had placed nothing
in her control, but instead provided her with an
estate for life, appointing his neighbor, James
Hogg as well as Willie Jones of Halifax, executors
of the estate and guardians for his infant daughter. Hooper wryly commented: "no confidence re-
posed in the wife."[52]

Hooper had predicted in his comments on Thomas
Burke's death that the debts would probably consume
his estate. He guessed correctly. Burke still had
not paid for the land which he bought in 1774.
Willie Jones served only temporarily as executor,
and to James Hogg was left the thankless and inter-
minable task of settling, administering, and recov-
ering what was due the estate. Much labor and considerable litigation were required. In 1789, James
Hogg unsuccessfully petitioned the General Assembly
for the money owed to Burke for his expenses as
Governor. With the accounts still missing, Burke's
estate was no more successful than the deceased
himself had been.[53]

To those whom Burke left behind, fate was indifferent. "The late Widow Burke," a neighbor

reported in 1786, "very unhappily married to Majr.
Doherty...who is also unhappily married. They
live an intollerable [*sic*] life without Eating or
sleeping together although both under the same
roof."[54] Mary Williams Burke, his daughter, who
remained unmarried, founded a school for girls in
Hillsborough. In the 1830's, she moved to Marion,
Alabama, where she survived until after the Civil
War.[55]

While Burke had found repose, the concepts
associated with his public career led a stormy
existence. With the advent of the controversy
over the Constitution, Armageddon had arrived,
and the positions taken by Burke's former colleagues
in Congress presented some startling alterations.
Richard Henry Lee, once the champion of a stronger
government, vigorously opposed ratification of the
new Constitution.[56] Burke's other adversary from
1777, James Wilson of Pennsylvania, who had criticized the amendment to the Articles of Confederation, now employed Burke's concept to argue in
favor of the Constitution. Burke's clause on states'
rights was not incorporated until the Bill of Rights
was ratified in 1791; yet Wilson argued that the
presumption of state control over powers that were
not expressly delegated would "furnish an answer
to those who think the omission of a bill of rights
a defect in the proposed constitution."[57] In North
Carolina, the freeholders of Orange County, who had
started Burke on his meteoric career, strongly opposed the Constitution.[58] Perhaps with his fear
of tyranny, he too would have found objections,
despite his inclination towards nationalism and a
more stable system of government.

Burke's years in North Carolina and in public
service were closely linked with his Revolutionary
experience, and sometimes those who had worked
with him sadly recalled their departed comrade.
Yet no legend appeared to embellish the administrative and legislative patriot, no aura such as that
which surrounded the state military heroes or sign-
ers of the Declaration of Independence. Thomas
Burke's epitaph was his short and poignant life,
and those who honored him did so from life rather
than death. Such was the simple republican tribute

215

paid him by Archibald Maclaine in the weeks after
his death.

Poor Doctor Burke is no more--a
heavy loss to the public at this time,
notwithstanding his failings & pecu-
liarities--[59]

I. "HYMN TO SPRING"

[1] Burke to his Uncle, no date, Walter Clark (ed.), *State Records of North Carolina* (Winston and Golsboro: State of North Carolina, 16 volumes, numbered XI-XXVI, 1895-1914), XIX, 921-928, hereinafter referred to as *SRNC*. Burke to Mrs. Jones (Sidney Shaw), no date, *SRNC*, 917-921. The Genealogical Office at the Public Record Office in Dublin conducted a search. While nothing was found on Burke himself, it was confirmed that Sir Fielding Ould and members of the Ould family were buried in cemeteries of the Protestant Church of Ireland. The search also turned up a Ulick Burke from the early eighteenth century who was of Tyaquin, the name of Burke's estate in North Carolina, and who may possibly have been a grandfather or great-grandfather; Burke mentions that he was from a once wealthy family in a subsequent letter to John Bloomfield cited in the next footnote.

[2] Burke to John Bloomfield, April 25, 1772, Thomas Burke Papers, State Department of Archives and History, Raleigh, hereinafter referred to as Burke Papers, SDAH.

[3] Burke to his Uncle, no date, *SRNC*, XIX, 921-928. Burke to Mrs. Jones (Sidney Shaw), no date, *Ibid.*, XIX, 917-921. The search did turn up Sidney Shaw's marriage to David Jones in 1766, which took place before Burke's letter was written.

[4] Burke to his Uncle, no date, *SRNC*, XIX, 921-928.

[5] Minute Book, Northampton County, 1755-1763, December 9, 1760. Orders for drugs in the Burke Papers date from the earliest, 1763. See the Thomas Burke Papers, Southern Historical Collection, hereinafter referred to as Burke Papers, SHC.

[6] AEdanus Burke to Thomas Burke, December 2, 1769, *SRNC*, XV, 676-679. AEdanus Burke makes reference to Burke's education and Burke in his letter

to Sir Fielding Ould states that he would like to continue his education at a European university if he ever returned. See Burke to his Uncle, *SRNC*, XIX, 921-928.

[7]Burke to his Uncle, no date, *SRNC*, XIX, 921-928.

[8]Burke to Mrs. Jones (Sidney Shaw), no date, *SRNC*, XIX, 917-921.

[9]*Ibid.*

[10]Northampton County, Deed Book, No. 20, 1763-1767, August 13, 1776. Minute Book, No. 27, 1765-1771, April, 1776. Vestry Book, Hungars Parish, 1758-1782, No. 23, November 24, 1776.

[11]John Tazewell to Burke, September 28, 1766, SHC; AEdanus Burke to Thomas Burke, December 2, 1769, *SRNC*, XV, 676-679. Burke knew AEdanus Burke, the future Judge and Congressman from South Carolina, on the Eastern Shore, and though not related, AEdanus was apparently influenced by Thomas.

[12]Diary of Eneas Reeves, Duke University Library, February 7, 1781. Poems from 1767 indicate that Burke had one eye, and probably his smallpox dates from his earlier life, or there would have been a reference to it in his correspondence after 1767.

[13]Burke to Betsy Harmanson, no date, Burke Papers, SDAH; he refers to her here as Miss Betsy. Burke to young lady, no date and no name, Burke Papers, SDAH. This is undoubtedly also written to Betsy since it follows up his offer to instruct her. For Betsy as orphan, see Northampton County, Minute Book 27, 1765-1771, April, 1766.

[14]*Ibid.*

[15]"Hymn to Spring by a Physician," Burke Papers, SDAH; this poem and most of the others Burke wrote may be found in Richard Walser (ed.), *The Poems of Governor Thomas Burke of North Carolina* (Raleigh: North Carolina State Department of Archives and History, 1961), 1-8.

[16]Burke to John Bloomfield, April 25, 1772, Burke Papers, SDAH.

[17]Burke to his Uncle, no date, *SRNC*, XIX, 921-928.

[18]*Ibid.*

[19]*Ibid.*

[20]Carl Bridenbaugh, *Seat of Empire, The Political Role of Eighteenth-Century Williamsburg* (Williamsburg: Colonial Williamsburg, Inc., 1958), 67-71. The references in the newspapers to the Robinson affair are too numerous to mention. For the killing of Routledge, there are also numerous references; see Purdie and Dixon's *Virginia Gazette*, July 18, 1766. Bridenbaugh is particularly helpful because he puts the Robinson and Routledge affairs in the context of both local and imperial politics in the 1760's.

[21]Purdie and Dixon's *Virginia Gazette*, October 10, 1766, Walser (ed.), *The Poems of Governor Burke*, 34-35. Walser points out that the poem was entitled simply "From the East," and it was later referred to as the "Eastern Bard's Address to the Goddess Dullness." For the poem "Transmogrification," which pertains to Landon Carter, see Burke Papers, SDAH. According to Walser, the latter poem is mentioned though it was either unpublished or in a missing edition. Also see Walser (ed.), *The Poems of Governor Burke*, 65, for references to Landon Carter whom another called "Litigous, haughty, headstrong."

[22]Purdie and Dixon's *Virginia Gazette*, December 18, 1766. Walser (ed.), *The Poems of Governor Burke*, 5. For uncomplimentary references see Rind's *Virginia Gazette*, March 12, 1767.

[23]Purdie and Dixon's *Virginia Gazette*, January 22, 1767. Walser (ed.), *The Poems of Governor Burke*, 5-6.

[24]Rind's *Virginia Gazette*, December 24, 1767. Burke's essay is in one of the missing editions and this merely refers to it.

[25]"On the Recovery of Some Ladies in *Norfolk* from the SMALLPOX, *Addressed* to Mrs. AITCHESON," Purdie and Dixon's *Virginia Gazette*, September 29, 1768. I was able to identify this as Burke's creation as a result of a reference in Purdie and Dixon's *Virginia Gazette*, April 20, 1769, in which Joseph Calvert makes a derogatory reference in a footnote to Burke as the poet responsible for the "Address to Mrs. Aitcheson" and "The Bald Man." The latter was Burke's response to criticism of his poem.

[26]Rind's *Virginia Gazette*, February 23, 1769. "The Bald Man" was printed in one of the editions that is now missing. I could not locate the first essay criticizing Burke, but the second piece quotes from it. Joseph Calvert's knowledge of Burke's identity indicates that it was generally known.

[27]John Ingram to Burke, no date, G. Burke Johnston Collection, hereinafter referred to as the Johnston Collection. Burke to William Grant, November 20, 1769.

[28]Thomas J. Wertenbaker, *Norfolk, Historic Southern Port* (Durham: Duke University Press, 1930, 1962), 27-47. It is apparent that Burke knew Aitcheson and Parker at least by August or September of 1768, but he was not addressed in letters at Norfolk until 1769.

[29]Patrick Henderson, "Smallpox and Patriotism, The Norfolk Riots, 1768-1769," *The Virginia Magazine of History and Biography*, LXXIII (1965), 413-424.

[30]*Ibid.* Supplement, Purdie and Dixon's *Virginia Gazette*, April 20, 1769. Both Joseph Calvert and in the supplement, Lewis Hansford, gave accounts of the episode.

[31]Burke to John Blair, August 22, 1769, Burke Papers, SDAH. Burke to George Wythe, September 28, 1769, Burke Papers, SDAH; Burke to Blair, no date, Burke Papers, SDAH. Burke to John Tazewell, April, 1769, Burke Papers, SDAH.

[32]Burke to Joseph Calvert, June 6, 1769, Burke Papers, SDAH.

[33]*Ibid.*

[34]Burke to Joseph Calvert, no date, Burke Papers, SDAH.

[35]John Tazewell to Burke, August 29, 1769, Tazewell Papers, Virginia State Library, Richmond.

[36]Burke to Michael Christian, December 24, 1769, Burke Papers, SDAH. Burke to Cuyler, December 24, 1769, Burke Papers, SDAH. John Ingram to Burke, March 27, 1769, Johnston Collection.

[37]Norfolk County Marriage Bonds, 1706-1768, Reel 74A, Virginia State Library. Mary Doherty to Elizabeth Johnston, November 27, 1832. Although her birthdate is listed sometimes as 1752, her statement in 1832--"I am two months in Seventy-seven"--places it in 1755 or 1756. It is possible that she had conveniently misplaced several years of her life.

[38]Burke to _____, no date, Burke Papers, SHC. All indications are that this letter was Burke's proposal to Mary Freeman, though her name is not included in his draft.

[39]*Ibid.*

[40]Lower Norfolk Antiquary, IV, 62. In a letter to Burke while Governor, Andrew Armstrong, a friend of Burke, relates the tribulations that he suffered at the capricious hands of Polly and her sister, Frances McKerrall. See Andrew Armstrong to Burke, date uncertain, *SRNC*, XV, 613-617. The episode involving Redmond Burke also raises some questions about Polly and whether she played a role in provoking Redmond's attempted seduction.

[41]The references are too numerous to cite all of them. For a busy day in court for Burke, see Norfolk County Court Records, Order Book, 1771-1773, January 16, 1772. For his more distant clients, see Burke to Hudson and Thompson of Baltimore, October 28, 1769, Burke Papers, SDAH.

[42]Burke to John Blair, September 19, 1769, Burke Papers, SDAH.

[43]*Ibid.*

[44]*Ibid.*

[45]"Triumph America," "Hymn to Spring by a Physician," Burke Papers, SDAH, Walser (ed.), *The Poems of Governor Burke*, 17-20, 32-33.

[46]There are references in the Norfolk County Court Records and the Johnston Collection to Burke's ownership of York and America. For his sale of York, see Burke to Alex Shaw, March 27, 1771, Burke Papers, SHC. Inventory to Burke's estate, Orange County Records, SDAH.

[47]Burke to Nathaniel Walthoe, July 17, 1769, Burke Papers, SDAH.

[48]Burke to Edmund Pendelton, August 30, 1769. Burke to Richard Bland, October 19, 1771. Burke to Robert Carter Nicholas, no date, Burke Papers, SDAH.

[49]Burke to Neil Jamieson, August 26, 1770, Burke Papers, SDAH. Burke to Thomas Jefferson, September 3, 1770, August 19, 1771, Julian Boyd (ed.), *The Papers of Thomas Jefferson*, Vol. I (Princeton: Princeton University Press, 1950), 58-59, 81-82. This case should not be confused with another case that Burke handled involving the estate of Henry Tucker which he described to Jefferson, *Ibid.*, 74. Jefferson was apparently involved because one of the deceased's daughters resided in Albemarle County, and as a result Jefferson was made a referee for dividing the slaves among the heirs. See Norfolk County Court Records, Order Book, 1768-1771, July 20, 1769. Burke seems to have been representing Tucker's partner, John Taylor, or possibly some of the creditors. For a discussion of the question arising from the bill of exchange, see Burke to Reese Meredith, January 6, 1770, Burke Papers, SDAH.

[50]Burke to Jefferson, September 3, 1770, Boyd (ed.), *The Papers of Thomas Jefferson*, I, 58-59. Burke to Benjamin Waller, November 30, 1770, Burke Papers, SDAH.

[51]Burke to Jefferson, August 19, 1771, Boyd (ed.), *The Papers of Thomas Jefferson*, I, 81-82. There were other issues as important as that of the priority of the British creditors and the bills of exchange, including whether lands were subjected to debts as a result of the will; whether the assets were legal or equitable; the application of Parliamentary statutes; and the role of the executor in disposition of the real estate.

[52]Burke to Thomas Jefferson, September 21, 1771, Burke Papers, SHC. For receipts, see Burke Papers, SHC. Burke to Richard Bland, October 19, 1771, Burke Papers, SDAH. For the license to practice law, see North Carolina Manuscripts, Historical Society of Pennsylvania, II, 3.

[53]Burke to Richard Bland, October 19, 1771, Burke Papers, SDAH; Burke to James Milner, July 31, 1770, Burke Papers, SDAH. Wertenbaker, *Norfolk, Historic Southern Port*, 33. For land advertisements, see *Virginia Gazette*, both Rind's and Purdie and Dixon's, for the period.

[54]Frank Nash, *Hillsboro Colonial and Revolutionary* (Raleigh: Edwards and Broughton, 1903), 1-5, 27, 42. J.F.D. Smyth, *A Tour of the United States of America* (2 vol.; London: G. Robinson, 1784), I, 226.

[55]Nash, *Hillsboro Colonial and Revolutionary*, 7-12, 27. Samuel A'Court Ashe, *History of North Carolina* (Greensboro: Charles G. Van Noppen, Publisher, 1908), I, 326-376.

[56]Matthew Donovan to Burke, May 6, 1772, Burke Papers, SHC. Burke to Adam Bloomfield, December 29, 1772, Burke Papers, SDAH.

[57]Burke to Adam Bloomfield, December 29, 1772, Burke Papers, SDAH.

[58]Burke to _____, November 11, 1772, Burke Papers, SDAH.

[59]James Iredell to Burke, April 4, 1772, Burke Papers, SHC.

[60]Burke to John Hamilton, July 26, 1773, Burke Papers, SDAH.

[61]Edmund Caddy to Burke, July 1, 1769, Burke Papers, SHC.

[62]Burke to Nathaniel Coffin, October 24, 1769, Burke Papers, SDAH. Burke to Coffin, March 27, 1770, Burke Papers, SDAH. Burke to Coffin, June 12, 1770, Burke Papers, SHC. Some communications to Burke at the time of his move to North Carolina indicate that Redmond was with them; see Matthew Donovan to Burke, May 6, 1772, Burke Papers, SHC.

[63]Burke to Alex McCulloh, March 3, 1773, Burke Papers, SDAH.

[64]*Ibid.*

[65]*Ibid.*

[66]*Ibid.*

[67]*Ibid.*

[68]*Ibid.*

[69]*Ibid.*

[70]Redmond did turn up in London in 1782 when he wrote a letter requesting preferment to Lord Shelburne. In the letter, Redmond recounts that he had joined a Continental regiment during the Revolution as a surgeon; he resigned and went to the island of Port Royal and then to England seeking a pardon; at the time, he was apparently in bad health. There is a later record of a Redmond Burke's marriage in Dublin in 1796 and even later a Redmond Burke in the Civil War who rode with Jeb Stuart's cavalry troop. See Redmond Burke to Lord Shelburne, September 29, 1782, Shelburne Papers, Clements Library, Ann Arbor, Michigan.

II. IN THE PROVINCE OF LA MANCHA

[1]Robert Ganyard, "North Carolina During the American Revolution: the First Phase, 1744-1777" (Ph.D. dissertation, Duke University, 1962), 74-83.

[2]Governor Martin to the Earl of Dartmouth, November 28, 1772, William Saunders (ed.), *The Colonial Records of North Carolina* (Raleigh: State of North Carolina, 1886-1890), IX, 265-267, hereinafter referred to as *CRNC*. Martin to the Earl of Dartmouth, March 31, 1773, *Ibid.*, 358-359.

[3]Governor Martin to the Earl of Dartmouth, November 28, 1772. *CRNC*, 358-359.

[4]Burke to Andrew Miller, April 4, 1774, Burke Papers, SHC.

[5]*Ibid.*

[6]Ashe, *History of North Carolina*, I, 412-414.

[7]AEdanus Burke to Thomas Burke, December 2, 1769, *SRNC*, XV, 676-679.

[8]Ashe, *History of North Carolina*, I, 417-418. Ganyard, "North Carolina During the American Revolution," 87-96.

[9]Ashe, *History of North Carolina*, I, 419-423. Ganyard, "North Carolina During the American Revolution," 101-107.

[10]Andrew Miller to Burke, December 21, 1774, *CRNC*, IX, 1096-1097. See also Burke Papers, SHC.

[11]Andrew Miller to Burke, April 6, 1775, Burke Papers, SHC.

[12]Andrew Miller to Burke, March, 1775, Burke Papers, SHC.

[13]*Ibid.*

[14]Ashe, *History of North Carolina*, I, 432-434. *CRNC*, IX, 1178-1185. Ganyard, "North Carolina During the American Revolution," 122.

[15]*CRNC*, IX, 1178-1185.

[16]Henry Montfort to Burke, May 9, 1775, Burke Papers, SHC.

[17]Connecting passage in Adams' *Diary* taken from his Autobiography by the editor, Charles F. Adams, *The Life and Works of John Adams* (10 vol.; Boston: Little, Brown & Co., 1850-1856), II, 405. John S. Watterson III, "Concord and Lexington: Origins and Effects of News and Propaganda" (Unpublished Master's thesis, Western Reserve University, 1965), 65-84.

[18]Governor Martin to the Earl of Dartmouth, June 30, 1775, *CRNC*, X, 41-50.

[19]Ganyard, "North Carolina During the American Revolution," 198. *CRNC*, X, 174.

[20]Ashe, *History of North Carolina*, I, 476-477. Ganyard, "North Carolina During the American Revolution," 153-159, 200-202.

[21]Proceedings of the Third Provincial Congress, *CRNC*, X, 185-186, 192, 216.

[22]*CRNC*, X, 172, 201.

[23]"To The People of North Carolina Friends Neighbours and Constituents," no date, Burke Papers, SHC.

[24]*Ibid.*

[25]*Ibid.*

[26]Adam Ferguson, *An Essay on the History of Civil Society* (Edinburgh: Edinburgh University Press, 1966), 88.

[27]"To The People of North Carolina Friends Neighbours and Constituents," no date, Burke Papers SHC.

[28]*Ibid.*

[29]*Ibid.*

[30]*Ibid.*

[31]Samuel Johnston to James Iredell, August, 1775, Charles E. Johnston Collection, SDAH. Thomas McKnight to Samuel Johnston, September 17, 1775, *CRNC*, X, 249-250.

[32]John Penn to Thomas Person, February 14, 1776, Thomas Penn Papers, SDAH. Ganyard, "North Carolina During the American Revolution," 310-313.

[33]Ashe, *History of North Carolina*, 516-519. *CRNC*, X, 512.

[34]Thomas Jones to James Iredell, April 28, 1776, Griffith J. McRee, *The Life and Correspondence of James Iredell* (New York: D. Appleton & Co., 1857-1858), I, 277-278.

[35]*CRNC*, X, 505-507, 516, 519, 544, 567. Ganyard, "North Carolina During the American Revolution," 297.

[36]*CRNC*, X, 544. Committee of Secrecy, War and Intelligence of North Carolina to John Hancock, President of the Continental Congress, no date, *SRNC*, XI, 293-294. Committee of Secrecy, War and Intelligence to Major General Lee, May 6, 1776, *Ibid.*, XI, 296-297. See also Ganyard, "North Carolina During the American Revolution," 296-297.

[37]William Hooper to unknown correspondent, April 17, 1776, The Hayes Collection, microfilm copy of manuscripts at "Hayes" near Edenton, Folder 92.

[38]*Ibid.*

[39]James Iredell to unknown correspondent, no date, The Hayes Collection. Samuel Johnston to James Iredell, April 20, 1776, Joseph Jones, *A Defence of the Revolutionary History of the State of North Carolina from the Aspersions of Mr. Jefferson* (Raleigh: Turner and Hughs, 1834), 279-280.

[40]Samuel Johnston to James Iredell, December 9, 1776, Charles E. Johnson Collection, SDAH.

[41]Thomas Jones to James Iredell, May 7, 1776, McRee, *Life and Correspondence of James Iredell*, I, 280-281.

[42]Ganyard, "North Carolina During the American Revolution," 417. Correspondence Relating to Rediscovery of Adams' *Thoughts on Government*, David Swain Papers, SDAH. Charles Francis Adams (ed.), *The Works of John Adams*, IV, 193-200.

[43]Burke to General Charles Lee, June 11, 1776, Thomas Burke Papers, Duke University Library, Durham. Proceedings of the Fourth Provincial Congress, April 24, 1776, *CRNC*, X, 539. Proceedings of the Fifth Provincial Congress, December 23, 1776, *Ibid.*, X, 1001.

[44]Burke to Lee, June 11, 1776, Thomas Burke Papers, Duke University Library. Council of Safety of North Carolina to Delegates to the Continental Congress, June 24, 1776, *SRNC*, XI, 302.

[45]William Hooper to Samuel Johnston, September 20, 1776, *CRNC*, X, 811-820.

[46]William A. Graham to David L. Swain, September 2, 1845, David L. Swain Papers, SHC.

[47]Proceedings of the Fifth Provincial Congress, November 23, 1776, *CRNC*, X, 932. My description of the new delegates elected in October is the product of information supplied by Mrs. Alfred Engstrom of Chapel Hill, North Carolina.

[48]*Ibid.*

[49]"Creed of a Rioter," McRee, *Life and Correspondence of James Iredell*, I, 335-336. McRee is the only source for this document. Although politically conservative, McRee has never been accused of conscious distortion--unlike Joseph S. Jones; see Ganyard, "North Carolina During the American Revolution," 396-402.

[50]Samuel Johnston to Mrs. James Iredell, December 13, 1776, McRee, *Life and Correspondence of James Iredell*, I, 339. Sheldon Koesy, "Continuity and Change in North Carolina" (Unpublished Ph.D. Dissertation, Duke University, 1963), 64-69. Although Koesy's figures indicate no extraordinary influx of new personnel into the congresses, they do suggest an overall change in the complexion of North Carolina politics. Not only was there probably a higher degree of political participation, but also an introduction of new men on the local level who had not participated in government under the Crown and who were small property owners.

[51]Samuel Johnston to Burke, June 26, 1777, *SRNC*, XI, 504-505. As Robert Ganyard has observed, the tradition of radicals versus conservatives has no support in primary materials available. Most likely, Joseph "Shocco" Jones, whose reputation for veracity is questionable, distorted the context of revolutionary politics, creating a facsimile of political positions in the Jacksonian era. Ganyard accepts Willie Jones, however, as a radical. I believe that many of the distortions in revolutionary political attitudes and factionalism result as much from the conflicts surrounding the ratification of the Constitution and the party conflicts in the Early National Period. A conventionally polite relationship seems to have existed between Johnston and Jones during the Revolution—as for Burke, Johnston always displayed outward esteem and cordiality toward him. For a discussion of these problems, see Ganyard, "North Carolina During the American Revolution," 396-402.

[52]Instructions to the Delegates from Orange in the Halifax Congress to be held in November, 1776, *CRNC*, X, 870f-870h. Similar instructions were prepared for the delegates of Mecklenburg County. The first part is very similar to its Orange County counterpart. It is possible that Burke and whoever else was involved adopted a portion of the Mecklenburg Resolves. I believe, however, that it is more probable that Burke as the leading constitutional theorist and draftsman in the state would have played an important role in drawing up the Instructions. For earlier instructions in 1773, *CRNC*, IX, 699-700.

[53]*CRNC*, IX, 870f-870h.

[54]Ganyard, "North Carolina During the American Revolution," 414-415, quoted from William Hooper to the Fifth Provincial Congress, October 27, 1776, Hayes Collection Transcripts, 1748-1806, SDAH. See also William Hooper to the Fifth Provincial Congress, October 26, 1777, *CRNC*, X, 866-869.

[55]Ganyard, "North Carolina During the American Revolution," 426-437. Koesy, "Continuity and Change in North Carolina," 80-83. Proceedings of the Fifth Provincial Congress, December 6-12, 1776, *CRNC*, X, 954-967, 1006-1013.

[56]*CRNC*, X, 954-967. Samuel Johnston to James Iredell, December 7, 1776, McRee, *Life and Correspondence of James Iredell*, I, 337-338.

[57]Proceedings of the Fifth Provincial Congress, November 28, 1776, *CRNC*, X, 970-971. Mrs. Alfred Engstrom of Chapel Hill (see footnote 47) in answer to my questions regarding the social and economic background of the two sets of delegates, their place of residence, and ties with Hillsborough, supplied me with useful information; her letter is reproduced here in part: "As for the 1776 election: I would say the old established mandarins won in the second election. John Butler was General John Butler of Mt. Pleasant (to the west), a landed gentleman who had held many offices (but his brother was a Regulator!): Alexander Mebane ('Colonel Maben') was a native Irishman, one of the 1740's settlers, quite wealthy in land at least, influential, but not so bright in some ways.... Nathaniel Rochester was Col. Thomas Hart's partner, shrewd, acquisitive, bent on money-making (Rochester, N.Y., is named for him). I can't tell you anything about McCabe.... The men chosen in the first election were all farmers and/or millers, and evidently widely scattered in the country. (The men of the second election were much more tightly concentrated around the Courthouse in Hillsborough). William Saunders operated a mill up near the Virginia line; William Moore was a wainwright, I believe; Paine was a farmer; Atkinson served in the Revolution later. None had held high

office previously; and none had anything like the power or prestige of Butler, Mebane, or Rochester."

[58]Proceedings of the Fifth Provincial Congress, December 17, 21, 1776, *CRNC*, X, 973, 981-982. There is a tradition that Burke was at Halifax as an *ex officio* participant in the constitutional proceedings. Samuel Johnston referred in 1777 to the Constitution of North Carolina as "your plan," so perhaps he played a larger role. There is, however, no primary source to support this. Samuel Johnston to Burke, June 26, 1777, *SRNC*, XI, 504.

[59]Koesy, "Continuity and Change in North Carolina," 122. Proceedings of the House of Commons, December 13, 1777, *SRNC*, XII, 380. Willie Jones, William Hooper, and Thomas Person opposed the measure.

[60]Archibald Maclaine, February 21, 1783, McRee, *Life and Correspondence of James Iredell*, II, 40-41. James Iredell to Mrs. Iredell, April 1, 1783, *Ibid.*, II, 41.

III.   SENTINEL OF STATE SOVEREIGNTY

[1]*Biographical Directory of the American Congress, 1774-1927* (Washington: U.S. Government Printing Office, 1928), House Document No. 782. See also Elihu Katz and Paul Lazarfeld, *Personal Influence, The Part Played by the People in the Flow of Mass Communications* (Glencoe: Free Press of Glencoe, 1955), 130, 283-286. Jennings Sanders, *Evolution of the Executive Departments of the Continental Congress 1774-1789* (Chapel Hill: The University of North Carolina Press, 1935), 1-92.

[2]John Adams to James Warren, February 17, 1777, Edmund Burnett (ed.), *Letters of Members of the Continental Congress* (8 vols.; Washington: Carnegie Institute, 1921-1936), II, 260, hereinafter cited as *Letters of Members*.

[3]William Hooper to Robert Morris, February 1, 1777, *Letters of Members*, II, 232.

[4]Thomas Burke to Governor Richard Caswell, February 10, 1777, *SRNC*, XI, 376-379.

[5]Thomas Burke, Abstract of Debates, February 7, 1777, *SRNC*, 695-698.

[6]Burke, Abstract of Debates, February 8, 1777, *Letters of Members*, II, 240-242.

[7]Burke, Abstract of Debates, February 12, 15, 1777, *Letters of Members*, II, 240, 253-254.

[8]*Ibid.*

[9]Thomas Burke, Abstract of Debates, February 15, 1777, *Letters of Members*, II, 253-254.

[10]Samuel Von Pufendorf, *De Jure Naturae et Gentium Libri Octo*, trans. C.H. and W.A. Oldfather (Oxford: Clarendon Press, 1934); see also Emmerich de Vattel, *The Law of Nations; or Principles of the Law of Nature Applied to the Conduct and Affairs of Nations and Sovereigns* (Dublin: L. White, 1797), originally published in the French in 1773. According to the inventory of Burke's will, Pufendorf's work was contained in his library.

[11]Thomas Burke, Abstract of Debates, *Letters of Members*, II, 275-276. Worthington C. Ford, *et al.* (eds.), *Journals of the Continental Congress, 1774-1789* (34 vols.; Washington, D.C.: U.S. Government Printing Office, 1904-1937), February 25, 1777, VII, 115-117, 154-155, hereinafter cited as *Journals of Congress*. See also Merrill Jensen, *The Articles of Confederation* (Madison: University of Wisconsin Press, 1940), 171-172.

[12]Thomas Burke, Abstract of Debates, February 25, 1777, *Letters of Members*, II, 276.

[13]*Ibid.*

[14]*Ibid.*, 277.

[15]*Ibid.*, 278.

[16]*Ibid.*

[17] *Ibid.*

[18] *Ibid.*, 279.

[19] *Ibid.*, 279-280.

[20] *Ibid.*, 282-283.

[21] *Ibid.*, 283.

[22] *Ibid.*

[23] *Ibid.*

[24] *Ibid.*

[25] *Ibid.*, 285.

[26] *Ibid.*

[27] *Ibid.*

[28] Burke to Governor Richard Caswell, March 11, 1777, *Letters of Members*, II, 294-296.

[29] *Ibid.*

[30] *Ibid.*

[31] *Ibid.*

[32] *Ibid.*

[33] Burnett, *The Continental Congress*, 90-93, 213-229. Jensen, *The Articles of Confederation*, 249-253.

[34] Burke to Governor Caswell, April 29, 1777, *Letters of Members*, II, 345-346.

[35] *Ibid.*

[36] *Ibid.*

[37] *Ibid.*

[38] *Ibid.*

[39]*Journals of Congress*, V, 546-554, entry for July 12, 1776.

[40]*Journals of Congress*, IX, 907-925, entry for November 15, 1777. Jensen, *The Articles of Confederation*, 249-262.

[41]This interpretation, with its overtones of Charles Beard, is the most closely associated with Merrill Jensen. See Jensen, *The Articles of Confederation*, 137-139, 168-176.

[42]See the United States Constitution, Articles in Addition to and in Amendment of, the Constitution of the United States of America, Article X. The omission of the word "expressly," which had appeared in Burke's amendment, represents a significant change. It would leave an opening for the implied powers that have so significantly influenced the constitutional history of the United States.

[43]Thomas Burke, Notes on the Articles of Confederation [November 15, 1777], *Letters of Members*, II, 552-556.

[44]*Ibid.*

[45]*Ibid.*

[46]*Ibid.*

[47]"Remarks Concerning the Confederation," [November 15, 1777], *Letters of Members*, II, 555-558. "Journal of the Senate," December 19, 1777, *SRNC*, XII, 411-412. Burnett, *The Continental Congress*, 344.

[48]Cornelius Harnett to Burke, November 13, 1777, *SRNC*, XI, 677-678.

[49]*Ibid.*

[50]*Ibid.*

IV. PITFALLS OF PUBLIC SERVICE

[1]*Journals of Congress*, VII, 92, 172, entries for February 5, and March 12, 1777.

[2]John Adams, *The Diary and Autobiography of John Adams* (in L.H. Butterfield, ed.), *The Adams Papers* (14 vol.; Cambridge: Belknap Press, 1961-67), series I, III, 350.

[3]*Ibid.*

[4]*Ibid.*, II, 342.

[5]Robert Morris to the Commissioners in France, December 21, 1776, Peter Force (ed.), *The American Archives* (9 vol.; Washington, D.C.: prepared and published under the authority of Congress, 1853), series 5, Vol. III, 1336. *Journals of Congress*, VIII, 395, entry for May 29, 1777.

[6]Silas Deane to Mrs. Deane, July 3, 1775, *Letters of Members*, I, III.

[7]*Journals of Congress*, IV, 298, 311, entries for April 22, 26, 1775.

[8]*Ibid.*, VII, 574, entries for July 23 and 25, 1777. Helen E. Royer, "The Role of the Continental Congress in the Prosecution of the American Revolution in Pennsylvania" (Unpublished Ph.D. dissertation, Pennsylvania State University, 1960), 208.

[9]Governor Caswell to Burke, June 10, 17, 1777, *SRNC*, XI, 494-495, 500-501. Burke to Governor Caswell, July 5, 1777, *Letters of Members*, II, 287.

[10]Governor Caswell to Burke, February 16, 1777, *SRNC*, XI, 392-393. Caswell to Burke, June 17, 1777. *Ibid.*, 500-501. Burke to Caswell, *Letters of Members*, II, 287.

[11]Burke to Governor Caswell, May 23, 1777. *SRNC*, XI, 476-478. Caswell to Burke, June 17, 1777. *Ibid.*, 500-501.

[12]Burke to Governor Caswell, March 11, 1777, *Letters of Members*, II, 294-296.

[13]Burke to Governor Caswell, July 5, 1777, *Letters of Members*, II, 398-399.

[14]*Ibid.*

[15]Burke to Governor Caswell, May 11, 1777, *Letters of Members*, II, 360. Burke to Caswell, *SRNC*, XXII, 519-521.

[16]Burke to General Frank Nash, August 16, 1777, *SRNC*, XI, 562-563.

[17]*Ibid.*

[18]*Ibid.*

[19]*Ibid.*

[20]*Ibid.*

[21]Governor Caswell to Burke, May 13, 1777, *SRNC*, XI, 470-471. Abner Nash wrote: "Our Assembly have paid a compliment to our worthy Delegate, which no private man has experienced before. A new county taken from Surry is called after him."

[22]Burke to Governor Caswell, April 15, 1777, *SRNC*, XI, 448-451.

[23]*Ibid.*

[24]*Journals of Congress*, VII, 328-329, entry for May 5, 1779.

[25]Burke to Governor Caswell, May 29, 1779, *SRNC*, XI, 476-478.

[26]*Letters of Members*, II, xxii.

[27]*Ibid.*

[28]John Adams to James Warren, February 12, 1777, *The Life and Works of John Adams*, ed., Charles Francis Adams, IX, 452; cited in Herbert J. Henderson, "Political Factions in the Continental Congress, (Unpublished Ph.D. dissertation, Columbia University, 1962), 196.

[29]Burnett, *The Continental Congress*, 249. *Journals of Congress*, VIII, 497, entry for June 25, 1777.

[30]Henderson, "Political Factions in the Continental Congress," 155. Burke to Governor Caswell, January 27, 1777, *SRNC*, XI, 376-377.

[31]Henderson, "Political Factions in the Continental Congress," 158-159.

[32]*Ibid.*

[33]James Duane to Robert Livingston, June 24, 1777, *Letters of Members*, II, 387.

[34]*Ibid.*

[35]*Ibid.* William Duer to Robert Livingston, May 28, 1777, *Letters of Members*, II, 376-377. Henderson, "Political Factions in the Continental Congress," 158-159.

[36]William Duer to Phillip Schuyler, June 19, 1777, *Letters of Members*, II, 384-386.

[37]*Ibid.*

[38]*Ibid.*

[39]Burke to Governor Caswell, July 30, 1777, *SRNC*, XI, 449-450.

[40]Burke to Governor Caswell, September 2, 1777, *Letters of Members*, II, 472, 473.

[41]Royer, "The Role of the Continental Congress in the Prosecution of the American Revolution in Pennsylvania," 189. *Journals of Congress*, VIII, 665-666, entry for August 22, 1777.

[42]John Scharf and Thomas Wescott, *History of Philadelphia* (3 vol.; Philadelphia: Everts & Company, 1884), II, 343-344.

[43]*Ibid.* Burke to Caswell, *SRNC*, XI, 613, 621. Hugh F. Rankin, *The North Carolina Contin-*

entals (Chapel Hill: The University of North Carolina Press, 1971), 100-101.

[44]Burke to Governor Caswell, September 17, 1777, *SRNC*, XI, 620-623. Charles P. Whittemore, *A General of the Revolution, John Sullivan of New Hampshire* (New York: Columbia University Press, 1961), 56-64.

[45]*Ibid.*

[46]*Ibid.*

[47]Burke to John Sullivan, October 12, 1777, *Letters of Members*, II, 519-520. James Lovell to William Whipple, September 17, 1777, *Ibid.*, II, 495-496. Burke to Governor Caswell, September 17, 1777, *SRNC*, XI, 620-623.

[48]*Journals of Congress*, VIII, 749, entry for September 16, 1777.

[49]James Lovell to William Whipple, September 17, 1777, *Letters of Members*, II, 495-496.

[50]Henderson, "Political Factions in the Continental Congress," 164-165.

[51]John Sullivan to John Hancock, President of Congress, September 27, 1777, Otis G. Hammond (ed.), *The Papers of General John Sullivan*, vol. XIII-XV, *Collections of the New Hampshire Historical Society* (Concord: Published for the Society, 1824-1939), XIII, 460-470.

[52]*Ibid.*

[53]Burke to John Sullivan, October 12, 1777, *Letters of Members*, II, 519-520.

[54]*Ibid.*

[55]John Sullivan to Burke, October 27, 1777, Hammond (ed.), *The Papers of General John Sullivan*, XIII, 565.

[56]General Sullivan to General Washington,
October 6, 1777, Hammond (ed.), *The Papers of
General John Sullivan*, XIII, 547-552.

[57]Washington to Sullivan, September 20, 1777,
John O. Fitzpatrick (ed.), *The Writings of George
Washington, From the Original Manuscript Sources,
1745-1799* (39 vol.; Washington, D.C.: U.S. Government Printing Office, 1931-1944), IX, 241-242.
Whittemore, *A General of the Revolution, John Sullivan of New Hampshire*, 75-77.

[58]Whittemore, *A General of the Revolution,
John Sullivan of New Hampshire*, 62-66.

[59]General Sullivan to Burke, April 18, 1778,
Hammond (ed.), *The Papers of General John Sullivan*,
XIV, 35; Burke to General Sullivan, September 28,
1778, *SRNC*, XV, 86-89. Listed as 1780 in *State
Records*, but internal evidence indicates it was
during the Rhode Island campaign of 1778.

V. BURKE AND CONGRESS

[1]Burke to Governor Caswell, September 20,
1777, *SRNC*, XI, 631-632.

[2]*Ibid.*

[3]*Ibid.* Burke to Caswell, November 4, 1777,
Letters of Members, II, 542.

[4]Burnett, *The Continental Congress*, 248, 253,
259-261.

[5]Cornelius Harnett to Burke, December 8, 1777,
SRNC, XI, 693-694.

[6]*Ibid.*

[7]Cornelius Harnett to William Wilkinson, De-
cember 8, 1777, Cornelius Harnett Collection, SHC.
Harnett to Burke, December 16, 1777, Burke Papers,
SHC.

[8]Burnett, *The Continental Congress*, 321.

[9]*Ibid.* Cornelius Harnett to Burke, December 16, 1777, Burke Papers, SHC.

[10]Burke to Governor Caswell, March 12, 1778, *Letters of Members*, III, 128.

[11]Governor Caswell to Burke, February 15, 1781, *SRNC*, XIII, 42. Governor Caswell to John Penn and Cornelius Harnett, February 7, 1778, *Ibid.*, XIII, 31.

[12]Benjamin Harrison to Burke, March 28, 1778, Burke Papers, SHC. Burnett, *The Continental Congress*, 279-303.

[13]Burke to General Washington, March 15, 1778, Burke Papers, SHC.

[14]George Washington to John Bannister, April 21, 1778, Fitzpatrick (ed.), *The Writings of George Washington*, XI, 289-292. Henderson, "Political Factions in the Continental Congress," 170-171.

[15]Burke to Governor Caswell, April 9, 1778, *Letters of Members*, III, 160-163.

[16]Burke to the North Carolina Assembly, [April 29, 1778], *Letters of Members*, III, 200-201.

[17]Burnett, *The Continental Congress*, 303.

[18]*Ibid.* General Washington to the President of Congress, April 4, 1778, Fitzpatrick (ed.), *The Writings of George Washington*, XI, 289-292; Henderson, "Political Factions in the Continental Congress 170-171.

[19]*Journals of Congress*, X, 310, 329-333, entries for April 6, 10, 1777.

[20]Burke to Governor Caswell, April 29, 1778, *Letters of Members*, III, 203-206. For the Vermont controversy see Gouverneur Morris to the Governor of New York (George Clinton), March 4, 1778, *Letters of Members*, III, 107-108.

[21]*Letters of Members*, III, 203-206.

[22]*Ibid.*

[23]*Journals of Congress*, X, 386-387, entry for April 24, 1778.

[24]*Ibid.*, X, 334, entry for April 10, 1778.

[25]Burke to Governor Caswell, April 29, 1778, *Letters of Members*, III, 203-206.

[26]*Journals of Congress*, X, 390-391, entry for April 25, 1778.

[27]*Ibid.*, X, 336-337, entry for April 11, 1778. Burke to Governor Caswell, April 29, 1778, *Letters of Members*, III, 204.

[28]*Journals of Congress*, X, 336-337, entry for April 11, 1778.

[29]This view of Congress was inspired by Johan Huizinga, *Homo Ludens* (London: Roy Publishers, 1950).

[30]James Lovell to Joseph Trumbull, April 13, 1778, *Letters of Members*, III, 166.

[31]"Engagement of Members to Meet Punctually, Etc.," April 12, 1778, *Ibid.*, II, 165-166.

[32]Burke to Governor Caswell, April 29, 1778, *Ibid.*, II, 204.

[33]*Journals of Congress*, X, 336-337, entry for April 11, 1778. Burke to President of Congress, April 13, 1778, Burke Papers, SHC.

[34]*Ibid.*, X, 386-389, entry for April 24, 1778.

[35]*Ibid.*

[36]*Ibid.*

[37]*Ibid.*

[38]*Ibid.*, X, 390-391, entry for April 25, 1778.

[39]Burke to the President of Congress, April 28, 1778, *Letters of Members*, III, 193-195.

[40]*Journals of Congress*, X, 399, entry for April 27, 1778.

[41]"Journal of the House of Commons," August 14, 1778, *SRNC*, XII, 843-844. "Journal of the Senate," August 10, 1778, *Ibid.*, 772.

[42]Burke to Governor Caswell, April 29, 1778, *Letters of Members*, III, 203-206.

[43]John Locke, *An Essay Concerning the True Original, Extent and End of Civil Government*, in Ernest Rhys (ed.), *Two Treatises of Civil Government* (New York: E.P. Dutton, 1949), Paragraph 232.

[44]For an example of this problem see "By a Virginian," Pennsylvania Packet, September 17, 1778; "A majority must rule in all free countries and societies. A man who cannot bend his opinion to that of others should instantly depart to some other land."

[45]Untitled piece in Burke's handwriting, no date, Burke Papers, SHC; this item was evidently prepared after Burke left Congress in order to amplify his position before the General Assembly of North Carolina.

[46]*Ibid.* See also *Journals of Congress*, IX, 907-925; the clause in question is in Article 5.

[47]Untitled piece in Burke's handwriting, Burke Papers, SHC.

[48]*Ibid.*

VI. THE TURNING POINT

[1]"Journal of the Senate," entry for August 10, 1778, *SRNC*, XII, 770-771.

[2]Jack M. Sosin, *The Revolutionary Frontier 1763-1783* (New York: Holt, Rinehart and Winston, 1967), 37-38.

[3]*Ibid.*, 75-81.

[4]Richard Henderson to John Williams, 1778, John Williams Papers, SDAH.

[5]Richard Henderson to John Williams, October 29, 1778, *SRNC*, XIII, 491.

[6]Notes of Thomas Burke's Speech before the House of Delegates, [November 19, 1777], in Julian P. Boyd (ed.), *The Papers of Thomas Jefferson* (Princeton: Princeton University Press, 1950), II, 66-68. The date of November 1777 should be November, 1778, as the editors acknowledge.

[7]*Ibid.*

[8]William Johnston to Richard Bennehan, November 5, 1778, Richard Bennehan Letters, SDAH.

[9]Richard Henderson to Thomas Burke, copy in Burke's estate, SDAH. Included in the document are the endorsements of Burke drawing on the sum in question.

[10]*Journals of Congress*, XII, 1215, entry for December 14, 1778. Cornelius Harnett to Governor Caswell, November 28, 1778, *SRNC*, XII, 306.

[11]Burke to Anthony Wayne, July 19, 1779, Wayne Manuscripts, Pennsylvania Historical Society, Philadelphia.

[12]"Extracts from the Diary of Mrs. Anne Warder," *Pennsylvania Magazine of History and Biography*, XVII (1893), 447. "She is not so handsome as Becky Gurney, but has all of her sweetness of tenance with a taller and more agreeable person."

[13]J.P. Brissot de Warville, *New Travels in the United States*, ed. and trans. Durand Echeverria (Cambridge: The Belknap Press of Harvard University Press, 1964), 167.

[14]Walser (ed.), *The Poems of Governor Thomas Burke*, 41-49.

[15]Nancy Emlen to Thomas Burke, September 13, 1777, Burke Papers, SHC. The author of the letter is identified by her initials in the first sentence.

[16]*Ibid.*

[17]*Ibid.*

[18]James Fallon to Thomas Burke, April 1, 1779, Burke Papers, SHC.

[19]Scharf and Wescott, *History of Philadelphia*, I, 405.

[20]Journal of the House of Commons, January 26, 1779, *SRNC*, XII, 659-660.

[21]Thomas Burke to Anne Emlen, February 9, 1779, Emlen Collection, Letters and Documents 1715-1855, Pennsylvania Historical Society, Philadelphia.

[22]*Ibid.*

[23]*Ibid.*

[24]Thomas Burke to Governor Caswell, January 10, 1779, *Letters of Members*, IV, 22-24.

[25]James Fallon to Burke, April 1, 1779, Burke Papers, SHC.

[26]Charge Delivered to the Grand Jury of Wilmington District by Judge Samuel Ashe, August 14, 1778, *SRNC*, XIII, 441-443.

[27]Theodore Frelinghuysen to the Speaker of the New Jersey Assembly, April 29, 1779, *Letters of Members*, IV, 185-186.

[28]Burke to Governor Caswell, December 29, 1778, *Letters of Members*, III, 542-543. *Journals of Congress*, XII, 1048-1052, 1073, entries for October 22, 28, 1778.

[29]Burke to Governor Caswell, December 20, 1778, *Letters of Members*, III, 542-543.

[30]*Journals of Congress*, XIII, 11, 18-19, entries for January 1, 2, 1779.

[31]Burke to Governor Caswell, December 20, 1778, *Letters of Members*, III, 542-543. North Carolina Delegates to Governor Caswell, December 22, 1778, *Ibid.*, 547-548.

[32]*Ibid.*

[33]Burke to the North Carolina Assembly, [August, 1779], *Letters of Members*, IV, 369.

[34]*Journals of Congress*, XIII, 141-142, 185, entries for February 3, 15, 1779.

[35]*Journals of Congress*, XII, 950, entries for September 3, 25, 1778. Cornelius Harnett to Governor Caswell, October 24, 1778, *Letters of Members*, III, 461.

[36]General Allen Jones to Governor Caswell, October 21, 1778, *SRNC*, XIII, 245-246.

[37]Governor Caswell to the General Assembly, *SRNC*, XIII, 628-630. Caswell to General Benjamin Lincoln, *Ibid.*, XIV, 14. *Journals of Congress*, XIII, 100-102, entry for January 22, 1779. Diary of John Fell [January 20, 1779], *Letters of Members*, IV, 37.

[38]*Pennsylvania Packet*, September 15, 1778.

[39]Hampton L. Carson, "The Case of the Sloop 'Active,'" *The Pennsylvania Magazine of History and Biography*, XVI, 4 (1892), 386-387.

[40]*Ibid.*

[41]*Ibid.*

[42]*Ibid.*, 387-388. George Ross to Burke, January 24, 1779, Burke Papers, typescripts from the Emmet Collection, SDAH.

[43]Carl Ubbelohde, *The Vice-Admiralty Courts and the American Revolution* (Chapel Hill: Published for the Institute of Early American History and Culture, 1960), 203.

[44]Burke to Joseph Reed, January 28, 1779, *Letters of Members*, IV, 45-46.

[45]*Journals of Congress*, XIII, 134-137, entry for February 2, 1779.

[46]*Ibid.*

[47]*Ibid.*

[48]Carson, "The Case of the Sloop 'Active,'" 391-392. *Journals of Congress*, XIII, 281-284, entry for March 6, 1779. Burke to Joseph Reed, March 12, 1779, Burke Papers, SHC. Burke to Timothy Matlack, March 12, 1779, Simon Gratz Collection, Pennsylvania Historical Society, Philadelphia.

[49]*Ibid.*

[50]Ubbelohde, *The Vice-Admiralty Courts and the American Revolution*, 195-201.

[51]Burke to Joseph Reed, January 28, 1779, *Letters of Members*, IV, 45-46.

VII. BURKE AND THE SOUTHERN CHAMPION

[1]*Journals of Congress*, XIII, 93-94, entry for January 20, 1779. *Ibid* ., XIII, 436, entry for April 11, 1779. *Ibid.*, XIV, 719-720, entry for June 11, 1779. *Ibid.*, XIV, 511, entry for April 26, 1779. *Ibid.*, XIII, 307, entry for March 12, 1779. *Ibid.*, XIII, 336, entry for March 18, 1779.

[2]Burke to General Washington, March 22, 1779, *Letters of Members*, IV, 111-112. General Washington to Burke, April 5, 1779, *SRNC*, XIV, 59-60. A Committee of Congress to George Washington, March 15, 1779, *Letters of Members*, IV, 104-105 [the letter was signed by Burke and Laurens]. *Journals of Congress*, XIV, 949, entry for August 11, 1779.

[3]Cornelius Harnett to Governor Caswell, November 28, 1778, *SRNC*, XIII, 304-306. *Journals of Congress*, XIII, 388, entry for March 29, 1779. The latter is a resolution on behalf of defense of the South.

[4]Whitmill Hill to Burke, [May, 1779], *Letters of Members*, IV, 241-242.

[5]William Henry Drayton, Memorandum of Conference with the Minister of France (Conrad Alexandre Gerard), February 15, 1779, *Ibid.*, IV, 69-71. Burnett, *The Continental Congress*, 431.

[6]*Journals of Congress*, XIII, 239-244, entry for February 23, 1779. Burnett, *The Continental Congress*, 431.

[7]*Ibid.*, 369.

[8]*Journals of Congress*, XIII, 348-352, 369-371, entries for March 22, 23, 24, 1779. Burnett, *The Continental Congress*, 433.

[9]The North Carolina Delegates to the Governor of North Carolina (Richard Caswell), (No. 2), [April 2, 1779], *Letters of Members*, IV, 131.

[10]The North Carolina Delegates to the South Carolina Delegates (No. 1), no date, *Letters of Members*, IV, 129-130.

[11]The North Carolina Delegates to the Governor of North Carolina (No. 2), [April 2, 1779], *Letters of Members*, IV, 131.

[12]Henry Laurens to William Henry Drayton (No. 3), April 3, 1779, *Letters of Members*, IV, 134.

[13]Henry Laurens to William Henry Drayton (No. 5), April 4, 1779, *Letters of Members*, IV, 138, footnote 3.

[14]Henry Laurens to the Governor of North Carolina (Richard Caswell) (No. 6), April 4, 1779, *Letters of Members*, IV, 139.

[15]*Ibid.*

[16]*Ibid.*

[17]*Ibid.*, 140.

[18]The North Carolina Delegates to Henry Laurens (No. 8), [April 8, 1779], *Letters of Members*, IV, 145.

[19]*Ibid.*

[20]*Ibid.*

[21]Henry Laurens to the North Carolina Delegates (No. 9), April 8, 1779, *Letters of Members*, IV, 147-148.

[22]Notation in Henry Lauren's handwriting, April 8, 1779, *Letters of Members*, 148-149.

[23]Henry Laurens to John Laurens, April 8, 1779, *Letters of Members*, 149.

[24]*Ibid.*

[25]Whitmill Hill to Burke, [May, 1779], *Letters of Members*, IV, 241-242.

[26]*Journals of Congress*, XIV, 661, entry for May 27, 1779. Burnett, *The Continental Congress*, 434.

[27]*Journals of Congress*, XIV, 749-752, entry for June 19, 1779. Burnett, *The Continental Congress*, 434-435.

[28]*Journals of Congress*, XIV, 790-791, 765-767, 911, entries for July 1, June 24, July 31, 1779.

²⁹*Journals of Congress*, XIV, 956-957, entry for August 14, 1779.

³⁰Burke to Governor Caswell, December 20, 1778, *Letters of Members*, III, 542.

³¹*Ibid.*

³²Thomas P. Abernethy, "Commercial Activities of Silas Deane in France," *American Historical Review*, XXIX (April, 1934), 483-484. Burnett, *The Continental Congress*, 359-363. Julian P. Boyd, "Silas Deane, Death by a Kindly Teacher of Treason," *The William and Mary Quarterly*, Series 3, XVI (1959), 184-186.

³³John Fell Diary, [January 20, 1779], *Letters of Members*, IV, 37. Burke to the North Carolina Assembly, [August, 1779], *Ibid.*, 371.

³⁴*Ibid.*

³⁵Richard Henry Lee to Francis Lightfoot Lee, April 26, 1779, *Letters of Members*, IV, 179.

³⁶Burke to Henry Laurens, no date, Burke Papers, SDAH.

³⁷Charles Carroll to William Carmichael, May 31, 1779, *Letters of Members*, IV, 239.

³⁸Henry Laurens, Notes of Debates, May 6, 1779, *Letters of Members*, IV, 196-197.

³⁹*Ibid.*

⁴⁰*Ibid.* Attempts were made by Burke and Laurens to reopen the issue on June 10. The result was indecisive; motions to recall Lee and order Deane not to depart failed. See *Journals of Congress*, XIV, 711-714, entry for June 10, 1779.

⁴¹Carl Van Doren, *The Secret History of the American Revolution* (New York: Viking Press, 1941), 167-178, 191. *Journals of Congress*, XIII, 413-417, entry for April 3, 1779.

[42] *Ibid.*

[43] Burke to the North Carolina Assembly, August, 1779, *Letters of Members*, IV, 371. Van Doren, *Secret History of the American Revolution*, 182, 190. Boyd, "Silas Deane, Death by a Kindly Teacher of Treason," 324-328, 167-169. Boyd advances the provocative and slightly macabre hypothesis that Deane was executed by his friend, former pupil and evil genius, Dr. Edward Bancroft, whose many accomplishments included an expert knowledge of South American poisons. As for Arnold, Burke may have had a personal acquaintance with him. *Supra*, Chapter IX, 154.

VIII.   THE AGONY OF CONGRESS

[1] James Madison to Thomas Jefferson, May 6, 1780, *Letters of Members*, V, 128-129.

[2] Allen Jones to Governor Caswell, December 23, 1779, *Ibid.*, IV, 548-549.

[3] *Journals of Congress*, XIV, 615-616, 718-720, 730, entries for May 19, June 11, and June 14, 1779. Burke to the North Carolina Assembly, [August, 1779], *Letters of Members*, IV, 369.

[4] The North Carolina Delegates to Governor Caswell, February 29, 1780, *Ibid.*, V, 55-58. *Journals of Congress*, XVI, 45-46, entry for January 12, 1780. Hunt is the editor from 1780 to 1785.

[5] The North Carolina Delegates to Governor Caswell, February 29, 1780, *Letters of Members*, V, 57.

[6] Nathaniel Peabody to the President of New Hampshire (Meshech Weare), March 13, 1780, *Letters of Members*, V, 67-70.

[7] *Ibid.*

[8] *Journals of Congress*, XVI, 127, 146-152, entries for February 5, 9, 10, 1780.

[9]E. James Ferguson, *The Power of the Purse,
a History of American Public Finance, 1776-1790*
(Chapel Hill: Published for the Institute of
Early American History and Culture by the University of North Carolina Press, 1961), 51. *Journals of Congress*, XVI, 261-267, entry for March
18, 1780.

[10]*Journals of Congress*, XVI, 261, entry for
March 18, 1780.

[11]James Lovell to Samuel Adams, March 9,
1780, *Letters of Members*, V, 64.

[12]*Journals of Congress*, XVII, 448-453, entry
for May 23, 1780.

[13]*Ibid.*, 452-453.

[14]Burke naturally tended to vary from issue
to issue; in January, he supported the creation
of a Court of Appeals for interstate disputes appealed to by Congress. He also supported the
proposal to allow aggrieved members to be heard
by the house, which recalled his earlier concerns.
See *Journals of Congress*, XVI, 28, 184-186, entries for January 8, February 22, 1780. Burke
also proposed that no one be duly elected to the
Boards of Admiralty, Treasury, and War unless he
have votes of seven states. See *Journals of Congress*, XVI, 221, entry for March 1, 1780.

[15]*Journals of Congress*, XVI, 44-46, 188, 236,
277, XVII, 444, 477, entries for January 12, February 23, March 17, 22, May 22, June 1, 1780.

[16]Burke to Joseph Reed, December 22, 1779,
Letters of Members, IV, 547-548.

[17]*Journals of Congress*, XVII, 480, entry for
June 1, 1780.

[18]Elbridge Gerry to the President of Congress,
April 3, 1780. *Letters of Members*, V, 104. For
background, see *Journals of Congress*, XVI, 178-
180, 324-325, February 19, April 3, 1780.

[19]General Washington to the President of Congress, April 3, 1780, Fitzpatrick (ed.), *The Writings of George Washington from the Original Manuscript Sources*, XVIII, 207-211.

[20]Burnett, *The Continental Congress*, 445-446.

[21]Burnett, *The Continental Congress*, 102, 105-110, 275,445. *Journals of Congress*, XVI, 37-38, entry for January 10, 1780.

[22]*Journals of Congress*, XVI, 357-358, entry for April 13, 1778.

[23]Burke to Cornelius Harnett, April 15, 1780, *Letters of Members*, V, 114. The controversy over the camp committee continued for several months, as the committee became a power in its own right and tried to influence the states until finally discontinued in August, 1780.

[24]*Journals of Congress*, XVI, 106-109, entry for January 28, 1780.

[25]*Ibid.*, 239-240, entry for March 8, 1780. *Journals of Congress*, 472, entry for May 30, 1780. On January 10, in a letter from the Board of War reporting great scarcity of supply in the army and no means to pay for provisions, Livingston of New York proposed dismissing the troops whose terms would expire by April 1. It was then that Gerry first proposed a committee to headquarters. See *Ibid.*, XVI, 37-38, entry for January 10, 1780.

[26]*Ibid.*, XVI, 336-337, 345-348, entries for April 7, 11, 1780.

[27]*Ibid.*

[28]Nathaniel Folsom to the President of New Hampshire (Meschech Weare), July 1, 1780, *Letters of Members*, V, 180. *Journals of Congress*, XVII, 486, 492, entries for June 5, 6, 1782. The amount was originally to be five thousand stand of arms and stores for ten thousand troops, but this amount was apparently not available.

[29]*Journals of Congress*, XVII, 508, entry for
June 13, 1780.

[30]Burke to Anthony Wayne, July 19, 1779,
Wayne Manuscripts, VII, 52, Historical Society
of Pennsylvania, Philadelphia. Henry Lee's cavalry troop had performed invaluable services in
capturing supplies for Washington on his light-
ning raids. His raid against Paulus Hook in 1779
was a particularly brilliant maneuver. Burke to
Wayne, June 6, 1780, Wayne Manuscripts, X, 28.

[31]*Ibid.*

[32]*Ibid.* I have been unable to find the exact
nature of Lee's concern.

[33]*Ibid.*

[34]*Ibid.*

[35]See also Burke to Anthony Wayne, June 6,
1780, Wayne Manuscripts, X, 25. Burke emphasized
that he had the "highest respect and most sacred
regard" for "the feelings of a man of honor."

[36]Anthony Wayne to Henry Lee, June 6, 1780,
Wayne Manuscripts, X, 27.

[37]Burke to Anthony Wayne, June 15, 1780,
Wayne Manuscripts, X, 30.

[38]Walser (ed.), *The Poems of Governor Burke*,
52.

[39]Anthony Wayne to Burke, August 1, 1779,
Wayne Papers, VII, 82. Harry Emerson Wildes,
*Anthony Wayne, Trouble Shooter of the American
Revolution* (New York: Harcourt, Brace and Co.,
1941), 179, 202, 206, 232, 233, 449-452, 463.

[40]Burke to Cornelius Harnett, April 15, 1780,
SRNC, XV, 367-368. Part of the letter is omitted
from *Letters of Members*, V, 114.

[41]*Ibid.*

[42]*Letters of Members*, X, lxi.

IX. BURKE ASCENDANT

[1]Whitmill Hill to Burke, August 20, 1780, *SRNC*, XV, 56-58.

[2]Burke to General Gates, July, 1780, *Ibid.*, XV, 769-770. William Wallace, *Appeal to Arms, A Military History of the American Revolution* (New York: Harper and Brothers, 1951), 212-213.

[3]Burke to General Gates, July, 1780, *SRNC*, XV, 769-770.

[4]Wallace, *Appeal to Arms*, 212-214. M.F. Treacy, *Prelude to Yorktown, the Southern Campaign of Nathanael Greene, 1780-1781* (Chapel Hill: University of North Carolina Press, 1963), 25-27.

[5]Burke to the President of Congress, *SRNC*, XV, 770-773.

[6]Whitmill Hill to Burke, October 9, 1780, *Letters of Members*, V, 413-414.

[7]Burke to General Gates, September 13, 1780, *SRNC*, XV, 776-779.

[8]Burke to General Gates, September 21, 1780, *SRNC*, XV, 779. This is an unfinished letter protesting impressment.

[9]*Ibid.*

[10]John Lynn to Burke, October 16, 1780, *SRNC*, XV, 120.

[11]Burke to General Gates, no date, Burke Papers, SDAH.

[12]Burke to the President of Congress, *SRNC*, XV, 770-773. *Journals of Congress*, XVII, 775, 784, entries for August 22, 24, 1780.

[13]Wallace, *Appeal to Arms*, 228-229. Treacy, *Prelude to Yorktown*, 46-51.

[14]Burke to John Adams, *Letters of Members*, V, 502, fn. See also *SRNC*, XV, 375.

254

[15]*Ibid.*

[16]Whitmill Hill to Burke, October, 1780, *SRNC*, XV, 91-94.

[17]Wallace, *Appeal to Arms*, 224-226.

[18]Whitmill Hill to Burke, December 20, 1780, *Letters of Members*, V, 413-414.

[19]*Journals of Congress*, XVI, 164, 221, 315, 326, entries for February 14, March 1, 29, April 3, 1780.

[20]Burke to William Bingham, January 30, 1781, *Letters of Members*, V, 555. Burke to Bingham, [February 6?, 1781], *Ibid.*, 562-563.

[21]Burke to William Bingham, February 6, 1781, *Letters of Members*, V, 562-563. Burke advised Bingham not to become a candidate, and he did not.

[22]*Ibid.*

[23]Jennings B. Sanders, *Evolution of the Executive Departments of the Continental Congress, 1774-1789* (Chapel Hill: The University of North Carolina Press, 1935), 109-110.

[24]Arthur Lee to Elbridge Gerry, November 26, 1780, *Letters of Members*, V, 439, fn. 4.

[25]Ferguson, *The Power of the Purse*, 113. Burke was appointed to a committee to consider the plight of Laurens, *Journals of Congress*, XVIII, 1179, entry for December 21, 1780.

[26]Burke to his Second, no date, *SRNC*, XV, 83-85. The identity of Burke's second was Dr. Hugh Shiell; Sullivan's was Alexander MacDougall.

[27]*Ibid.*

[28]Whittemore, *General of the Revolution*, 173. General Sullivan to the President of Congress, September 27, 1777, Hammond (ed.), *Collections of the New Hampshire Historical Society*, XIII, 460-470.

[29]Thomas Rodney, Diary, *Letters of Members*, VI, 19-22, entry for [March 10, 1781].

[30]*Ibid.*

[31]*Ibid.* It should be noted that Rodney was in close agreement with Burke's views, and this undoubtedly influenced his assessment of Burke.

[32]*Journals of Congress*, XIX, 152-154, entry for February 15, 1781.

[33]Thomas Rodney, Diary, *Letters of Members*, VI, 3, entry for March 2, 1781.

[34]Thomas Rodney, Diary, *Ibid.*, entry for March 5, 1781. See also *Journals of Congress*, IX, 907-925, entry for November 15, 1777.

[35]Thomas Rodney, Diary, *Letters of Members*, VI, 8, entry for March 5, 1781.

[36]*Ibid.*

[37]*Ibid.*

[38]*Journals of Congress*, XVI, 70, 221, entries for January 18, March 1, 1780.

[39]Burnett, *The Continental Congress*, 473, 510-511.

[40]Ferguson, *The Power of the Purse*, 58-66.

[41]Thomas Rodney, Diary, *Letters of Members*, VI, 16, entry for March 7, 1781.

[42]*Ibid.*, entry for March 7, 1781; *Journals of Congress*, XIX, 278-279, 308-311, entries for March 19, 24, 1781. Burke was on the committee to consider Luzerne's letter. See also Ferguson, *The Power of the Purse*, 55-56.

[43]Samuel Johnston to James Iredell, April 8, 1781, *Letters of Members*, VI, 49-50. See for discussion of the financial plight, Burnett, *The Continental Congress*, 510-514. Also, Ferguson, *The*

Power of the Purse, 65-68. Ferguson observes that the plan of March 18, 1780, represented a repudiation of much of the continental debt.

[44]Burnett, *The Continental Congress*, 381, 475-476, 480. The impost was first proposed on a financial committee report in the autumn of 1778, while Burke was in North Carolina. Burke made the first motion in Congress on March 18, 1780.

[45]*Journals of Congress*, XIX, 110-112, entry for February 3, 1781.

[46]*Ibid.*

[47]*Ibid.*, 136, entry for February 10, 1781.

[48]Robert Morris to the Committee to Secret Correspondence, December 16, 1776, *Letters of Members*, II, 178.

[49]Samuel Johnston to Burke, June 23, 1781, *SRNC*, XV, 491-492. William Hooper to Robert Morris, December 28, 1776, *Letters of Members*, II, 195. Robert Morris to Burke, April 26, 1782, *SRNC*, XVI, 303-304. Morris assumed Burke was still governor.

[50]Benjamin Harrison to Burke, March 28, 1778, Burke Papers, SDAH. Burke to Mrs. Samuel Inglis, August 5, 1781, *Ibid.* Burke to George Clymer, August 5, 1781, *Ibid.* Burke to Robert Morris, November 4, 1780, Robert Morris Papers, Correspondence, 1775-1805, Library of Congress, Washington, D.C. In 1780, with his various financial problems, Burke was drawing on Robert Morris for personal loans.

[51]Sanders, *Evolution of Executive Departments of the Continental Congress, 1774-1789*, 95-98, 109. Burnett, *The Continental Congress*, 492.

[52]*Journals of Congress*, XIX, 287-299, entry for March 20, 1781. Sanders, *Evolution of Executive Departments of the Continental Congress, 1774-1789*, 128-130.

[53]*Journals of Congress*, XIX, 290, entry for March 21, 1781. Henderson, "Political Factions in the Continental Congress," 292-297.

[54]Wallace, *Appeal to Arms*, 233-239. Treacy, *Prelude to Yorktown*, 88-111, 142-188.

[55]Treacy, *Prelude to Yorktown*, 156-157. Cornwallis arrived in Hillsborough on February 20, 1781, and left on February 24, although he remained in the general area. For Burke's loss, see Burke Papers, July 14, 1781, SDAH.

[56]Andrew Armstrong to Burke, date uncertain, *SRNC*, XV, 613-617. It is dated August 22, 1781, in the *State Records*, but internal evidence shows that it was written in February of 1781. Armstrong mentions that the British were in Virginia. There is also a reference to Burke in Congress. He was no longer there in August of 1781.

[57]*Ibid.*

[58]*Ibid.*

[59]*Ibid.*

[60]*Ibid.*

[61]Ezekiel Cornell to Governor Greene of Rhode Island, March 5, 1781, *Letters of Members*, VI, 7, fn. 2.

[62]Samuel Johnston to James Iredell, April 8, 1781, *Ibid.*, 49-50. Burke had intended to leave on April 9 but delayed his trip. Unknown correspondent to James Porterfield, November 23, 1780, *SRNC*, XV, 416-417. Burke was to receive "two thousand hard money dollars" for a mortgage on his farm of 1,226 acres. For his plans to sell land, see Andrew Armstrong to Burke, December 15, 19, 1780, *SRNC*, XV, 180, 186. Armstrong related that James Porterfield, who executed Burke's mortgage told "Colonel Henderson" of his intention, and the latter said that "your place is truly valuable, and he thinks it will be difficult, if not impossible, to Purchase another of equal value with the money you will get for it."

[63]Burke to George Clymer, August 5, 1781,
Burke Papers, SDAH. Burke observed to Clymer
that "I found another arduous public task was
assigned to me which the circumstances of my country would not allow me to decline, tho' repugnant
to my Interest and my inclination." See also
Burke to Mrs. Samuel Inglis, August 5, 1781, *Ibid.*

[64]Proceedings of the General Assembly, June
25, 1781, *SRNC*, XVIII, 892, 896.

X.   BURKE'S ORDEAL

[1]Samuel Strudwick to Burke, July, 1781, *SRNC*,
XV, 503. Proceedings of the Senate, June 25,
1781, *Ibid.*, XVII, 899.

[2]Burke to the General Assembly, June 29,
1781, *SRNC*, XXII, 1033-1036.

[3]*Ibid.*

[4]*Ibid.*

[5]*Ibid.*

[6]*Ibid.*

[7]Burke to the General Assembly, June 30, 1781,
SRNC, XVIII, 921.

[8]Burke to the General Assembly, June 29, 1781,
SRNC, XXII, 1033-1036.

[9]Governor Nelson to Burke, July 27, 1781,
SRNC, XV, 577. Burke to Nelson, July 19, 1781,
Burke Papers, SDAH. "Magnus Apollo" quoted in
Douglass, "Thomas Burke, Disillusioned Democrat,"
The North Carolina Historical Review, XXVI (April,
1949), 174-175.

[10]Abner Nash to Burke, July 5, 1781, Type-
script, North Carolina Letters from the Emmet Collection, SDAH.

[11]Burke to the General Assembly, July 13, 1781, Burke Papers, SDAH.

[12]Questions and Propositions by the Governor, Council Journal, July 25, 1781, *SRNC*, XIX, 861-865. See also Douglass, "Thomas Burke, Disillusioned Democrat," 175-176.

[13]Questions and Propositions by the Governor, Council Journal, July 25, 1781, *SRNC*, XIX, 862-865.

[14]*Ibid.*

[15]*Ibid.*

[16]The next seventeen pages are taken in part from my article, "The Ordeal of Governor Burke," *The North Carolina Historical Review*, XLVIII, No. 2 (April, 1971), 95-117.

[17]David Fanning, *The Narrative of David Fanning* (New York and Richmond: Reprinted for Joseph Sabin, 1865), 3-11, 14-18, 22-23.

[18]Robert O. DeMond, *The Loyalists in North Carolina During the Revolution* (Durham: Duke University Press, 1940), 137-140.

[19]*Ibid.*

[20]Thomas Robison to Burke, July 10, 1781, *SRNC*, XXII, 1043-1044.

[21]Robert Rowan to Burke, July 13, 1781, Burke Papers, SDAH.

[22]Prisoners to Burke, July 22, 1781, Burke Papers, SDAH. Burke to Coroner of Halifax County, July 8, 1781, *Ibid.* Burke to William Caswell, July 9, 1781, *Ibid.*

[23]General Stephen Drayton to Burke, July 6, 1781, *SRNC*, XV, 511-514.

[24]Burke to Nathanael Greene, July 30, 1781, Burke Papers, SDAH.

[25]Nathanael Greene to Burke, August 12, 1781, *SRNC*, XV, 605.

[26]Burke to General Jethro Sumner, July 20, 1781, Burke Papers, SHC.

[27]Robert Burton to Burke, August 14, 1781, *SRNC*, XXII, 560-562.

[28]Burke to Colonel Emmet, July 30, 1781, Burke Papers, SDAH.

[29]Burke to General Butler, August 15, 1781, Burke Papers, SDAH. Burke to Butler, July 2, 1781, *Ibid.*

[30]Captain Josiah Parker to General Allen Jones, June 27, 1781, Burke Papers, SDAH.

[31]Journal of the Council of North Carolina, July 25, 1781, *SRNC*, XIX, 861-862. Burke to Nathanael Greene, July 30, 1781, Burke Papers, SDAH. Burke to Anthony Wayne, July 26, 1781, Burke Papers, SHC.

[32]General Jethro Sumner to Burke, July 17, 1781, Burke Papers, SDAH.

[33]Burke to General Allen Jones, July 18, 1781, *SRNC*, XV, 547-548.

[34]Burke to General William Caswell, August 20, 1781, Burke Papers, SDAH. Burke to General Alexander Lillington, August 6, 1781, Burke Papers.

[35]Burke to George Clymer, August 5, 1781, Burke Papers, SDAH.

[36]Captain Joseph Reed to General Allen Jones, August 13, 1781, Burke Papers, SDAH.

[37]Burke to Colonel Nicholas Long, August 20, 1781, Burke Papers, SDAH. General William Caswell to Burke, August 20, 1781, *Ibid.* Colonel Hardy Sanders to Burke, August 16, 1781, *SRNC*, XV, 610.

[38]Marquis de Lafayette to Allen Jones, August 27, 1781, Burke Papers, SDAH.

[39]Burke to Colonel Robert Burton, August 31, 1781, Burke Papers, SDAH.

[40]Burke to Colonel Robert Lutrell, September 3, 1781, Burke Papers, SDAH.

[41]Burke to Nathanael Greene, September 1, 1781, Burke Papers, SDAH. William Caswell to Burke, September 4, 1781, Burke Papers, SDAH. Burke to Allen Jones, September 5, 1781, Burke Papers, SDAH.

[42]Burke to Allen Jones, September 5, 1781, Burke Papers, SDAH.

[43]*Ibid.*

[44]Anthony Wayne to Burke, September 3, 1781, Burke Papers, SDAH.

[45]James Iredell to his wife, September 11, 1781, McRee, *The Life and Correspondence of James Iredell*, I, 542.

[46]Burke to Captain Armstrong, September __, 1781, Burke Papers, SDAH.

[47]Fanning, *The Narrative of David Fanning*, 32-34.

[48]Burke to the General Assembly, April 16, 1782, *SRNC*, XV, 12-14. Fanning, *The Narrative of David Fanning*, 32-34.

[49]Burke to General John Butler, September 9, 1781, Burke Papers, SDAH.

[50]Fanning, *The Narrative of David Fanning*, 32-34. Burke to the General Assembly, April 16, 1782, *SRNC*, XVI, 12-14.

[51]Burke to the General Assembly, April 16, 1782, *SRNC*, XVI, 12-14. Fanning, *The Narrative of David Fanning*, 32-34.

[52]Fanning, *The Narrative of David Fanning*, 32-34. Burke to the General Assembly, April 16, 1782, *SRNC*, XVI, 12-14.

[53]Fanning, *The Narrative of David Fanning*, 32-34. Eli W. Carruthers, *Revolutionary Incidents and Sketches of Character* (2 vols.; Philadelphia: Hayes & Zinn, 1850 and 1856), 206-211.

[54]Carruthers, *Revolutionary Incidents and Sketches of Character*, first series, 206-211.

[55]Fanning, *The Narrative of David Fanning*, 32-34.

[56]Burke to unknown correspondent, October 17, 1781, *SRNC*, XV, 650-654.

[57]*SRNC*, XV, 650-654. Burke to Major James Craig, June 27, 1781, *SRNC*, XXII, 1043-1044. Major Craig to Alexander Martin, October 29, 1781, Burke Papers, SDAH.

[58]Burke to unknown correspondent, October 17, 1781, *SRNC*, XV, 650-654.

[59]*SRNC*, XV, 653.

[60]*Ibid.*

[61]Burke to the General Assembly, April 16, 1782, *SRNC*, XV, 13-14.

[62]Burke to Colonel Hamilton, December 22, 1781, Burke Papers, SDAH.

[63]Burke to unknown correspondent, October 17, 1781, *SRNC*, XV, 650-654.

[64]Burke to Lewis DeRossette, November 27, 1781, Burke Papers, SHC.

[65]Burke to Major Frazier, December 18, 1781, Burke Papers, SDAH.

[66]*Ibid.*

[67]Burke to the General Assembly, April 16, 1782, *SRNC*, XVI, 14-16.

[68]*Ibid.*

[69]*Ibid.*

[70]*Ibid.*, XVI, 14-18. James Iredell to his wife, February 11, 1782, McRee, *Life and Correspondence of James Iredell*, II, 8.

[71]Burke to General Leslie, January 16, 1782, Burke Papers, SDAH.

[72]Burke to the General Assembly, April 6, 1782, *SRNC*, XVI, 16-18.

[73]*Ibid.* Nathanael Greene to Burke, March 16, 1782, *SRNC*, XVI, 238-241.

[74]Burke to Nathanael Greene, May 5, 1782, *SRNC*, XVI, 312-319. David Fanning to Governor Burke, February 26, 1782, Burke Papers, SDAH.

[75]Colonel Otho H. Williams to Colonel William R. Davie, February 24, 1781, in William R. Davie Papers, SHC.

[76]William Davie to Burke, February 23, 1782, Burke Papers, SDAH.

[77]Burke to Colonel Otho Williams, March 28, 1782, *SRNC*, XVI, 251-255.

[78]Burke to William Savage, March 4, 1782, *SRNC*, XVI, 520-521.

[79]Burke to General Greene, April 12, 1782, *SRNC*, XVI, 278-283.

[80]Burke to Colonel Burton, February 25, 1782, *SRNC*, XVI, 521-522. Burke to General Butler, February 5, 1782, *SRNC*, XVI, 500. Diary of Eneas Reeves, Duke University Library, Durham, entry for February 5, 1782, *supra*, 4.

[81]Andrew Armstrong to General Rutherford, March 12, 1782, *SRNC*, XVI, 538-539. William Davie to Burke, February 10, 1782, Burke Papers, SDAH.

[82]Nicholas Long to Burke, March 8, 1782, Burke Papers, SDAH. Burke to Long, March 9, 1782,

Ibid. Long to Burke, March 10, 1781, *SRNC*, XVI, 536-537. Burke to Long, March 11, 1782, *Ibid.*

[83]Burke to Long, March 9, 1782, Burke Papers, SDAH.

[84]Diary of Eneas Reeves, Duke University Library, Durham, entry for March 20, 1782.

[85]Burke to Major Hogg, March 13, 1782, Burke Papers, SDAH.

[86]*Ibid.*

[87]William Davie to Burke, February 10, 1782, Burke Papers, SDAH.

[88]David Fanning to Burke, February 26, 1782, Burke Papers, SDAH.

[89]*Ibid.*

[90]*Ibid.*

[91]Randolph B. Campbell, "The Case of the 'Three Friends;' an Incident in Maritime Regulation during the Revolutionary War," *The Virginia Magazine of History and Biography*, LXXIV, No. 2 (April, 1966), 190-195. *Journals of Congress*, XXI, 1153-1154, entry for December 4, 1781. The act was to go into effect February 1, 1782.

[92]Campbell, "The Case of the 'Three Friends,'" 197.

[93]*Ibid.* Henry R. McIlwaine and W.L. Hall (eds.), *Journals of the Council of the State of Virginia* (Richmond: Published by the Virginia State Library, 1931-1962), III, 56.

[94]Governor Harrison to Burke, March 19, 1782, Henry R. McIlwaine (ed.), *Official Letters of the Governors of the State of Virginia* (3 vols.; Richmond: Published by the Virginia State Library, 1926-1929), III, 175-176, quoted in Campbell, "The Case of the 'Three Friends,'" 200.

[95]Burke to Harrison, March 23, 1782, *SRNC*, XVI, 556.

[96]Burke to the General Assembly, April 18, 1782, Burke Papers, SDAH. Burke to James Iredell, March 13, 1782, Charles Francis Jenkins Collection, Historical Society of Pennsylvania, Philadelphia.

[97]Burke to Baron de Gloubeck, March 26, 1782, *SRNC*, XVI, 563. Ashe, *History of North Carolina*, I, 707. Burke to Major Hogg, March 23, 1782, *SRNC*, XVI, 559-562. Ashe, *History of North Carolina*, I, 708.

[98]Ashe, *History of North Carolina*, I, 712. DeMond, *The Loyalists of North Carolina*, 151-152.

[99]Burke to Major Craig, June 27, 1781, *SRNC*, XXII, 1028, quoted in Elisha Douglass, "Thomas Burke, Disillusioned Democrat," *The North Carolina Historical Review*, XXVI (April, 1949), 179.

[100]Burke to General Lillington, February 2, 1782, *SRNC*, XVI, 181-182.

[101]Burke to Major Lewis, April 5, 1782, *Ibid.*, XVI, 269. See also Ashe, *History of North Carolina*, I, 712-713. Burke to the General Assembly, April 16, 1782, *SRNC*, XVI, 292-295.

[102]William Davie to Burke, April 14, 1782, Burke Papers, SDAH. *SRNC*, XVI, 284.

[103]Davie to Burke, April 14, 1782, Burke Papers, SDAH.

[104]Major William McCauley to Burke, April 14, 1782, *SRNC*, XVI, 593.

[105]Burke to the General Assembly, April 16, 1782, in Journal of the House of Commons, April 16 to May 18, 1782, *SRNC*, XVI, 18-19. Burke to Nathanael Greene, April 12, 1782, *SRNC*, XVI, 278-283.

[106]Burke to the General Assembly, April 22, 1782, *SRNC*, XVI, 292-295.

[107]*SRNC*, XVI, 292-295. Burke to the General Assembly, May 6, 1782, in Journal of the House of Commons, April 16 to May 12, 1782, *SRNC*, XVI, 112.

XI. LEGACY OF REPUBLICANISM

[1]Draft of letter from Burke's ledger to an unknown correspondent, no date, Burke Papers, SHC.

[2]*Ibid.*

[3]*Ibid.*

[4]Burke to John Granberry, February 2, 1783, Burke Papers, SDAH. James Hogg to unknown correspondent, no date, David Swain Papers, 1763-1785, SDAH. Draft of letter from Burke's ledger August 4, 1782, Burke Papers, SDAH. The letter is probably to Judge AEdanus Burke.

[5]Draft of letter from Burke's ledger, August 4, 1782, Burke Papers, SDAH, hereinafter referred to as Burke to AEdanus Burke [?]. Circumstantial as well as internal evidence indicates that the letter was directed to Judge AEdanus Burke, Burke's friend from the Eastern Shore of Virginia. To a mutual friend, curiously named Thomas Bourke, Burke wrote on October 12: "I am much afraid to encounter so unhealthy a Country and such an unsettled Society. I have written largely on the Subject in Several letters to our friend Judge Burke, who, I fear, had been carried too far by his regard for me." Burke to Thomas Bourke, October 12, 1782, *SRNC*, XVI, 656. Bourke had advanced sums of money to Governor Burke while he was in captivity.

[6]Burke to AEdanus Burke [?], August 4, 1782, Burke Papers, SDAH.

[7]*Ibid.*

[8]*Ibid.*

[9]*Ibid.*

[10]Draft of a letter from Burke's ledger to an unknown correspondent, no date, Burke Papers, SDAH. The next five pages are taken from my article, "The Ordeal of Governor Burke."

[11]Archie Scott to Burke, January 10, 1783, *SRNC*, XXII, 620-621. Extract from the military papers of General Jethro Sumner, *Ibid.*, XV, 451-452. These are provisions of the "Cartel."

[12]Blackwell P. Robinson, *William R. Davie* (Chapel Hill: University of North Carolina Press, 1957), 129. Burke to Charles Floyd, February 22, 1782, Burke Papers, SDAH.

[13]Burke to unknown correspondent, April 18, 1782, Thomas Burke Papers, Duke University Library, Durham. This was probably Alexander Martin, for Burke seems to exempt his correspondent from responsibility. Alexander Martin to unknown correspondent, November 17, 1781, Miscellaneous Papers, SDAH.

[14]Burke to the General Assembly, April 12, 1782, *SRNC*, XVI, 17-19.

[15]*Journals of Congress*, XXI, 1181, entry for December 20, 1781. *Ibid.*, XVIII, 996, entry for October 20, 1780.

[16]Nathanael Greene to Burke, October 29, 1782, *SRNC*, XVI, 445-446. Burke to Greene, December 7, 1782, Burke Papers, SDAH.

[17]Nathanael Greene to Burke, May 31, 1782, *SRNC*, XVI, 330-332.

[18]Nathanael Greene to Burke, April 8, 1782, *SRNC*, XVI, 273-276. *Journals of Congress*, XXI, 917, 926, 927, entries for August 29, 31, 1781.

[19]Nathanael Greene to Burke, October 29, 1782, *SRNC*, XVI, 445-446.

[20]Burke to Nathanael Greene, July 6, 1782, Burke Papers, SDAH. This is a draft of the letter from Burke's ledger.

[21]*Ibid.*

[22]*Ibid.*

[23]*Ibid.*

[24]Fragment in Burke's handwriting, no date, Burke Papers, SDAH. There is a possibility that this was written earlier, perhaps in 1776. However, the ideas and tone indicate that it was written after his experience as Governor.

[25]*Ibid.*

[26]*Ibid.*

[27]*Ibid.*

[28]*Ibid.*

[29]Burke to AEdanus Burke [?], August 4, 1782, Burke Papers, SDAH. *Supra*, fn. 8.

[30]*Ibid.*

[31]*Ibid.*

[32]*Ibid.*

[33]Burke to the Governor of South Carolina, no date, Burke Papers, SDAH; from Burke's ledger.

[34]Burke to John Williams and others, May 20, [1783], *SRNC*, XVI, 616-618. From references by Burke, it is apparent that this was a clause appended to a statute for appointing a representative to hold a treaty conference with the Cherokees; see Statutes for 1783, Chapter 24, *Ibid.*, XXIV, 510. The other act was for suspending execution due to lack of currency in the state, and Burke as a debtor did not object to that. See Chapter 7, Statutes for 1783, *Ibid.*, XXIV, 490.

[35]*Ibid.*

[36]*Ibid.*

[37]*Ibid.*

[38]Burke to unknown correspondent, August 16, 1783, Burke Papers, SHC. It was probably Thomas Hart.

[39]Burke to Nathanael Greene, December 7, 1782, Burke Papers, SDAH.

[40]James Iredell to his wife, April 1, 1783, McRee, *Life and Correspondence of James Iredell,* II, 42.

[41]Archibald Maclaine to George Hooper, March 25, 1783, George Hooper Collection, SHC. Maclaine to Hooper, April 29, 1783, *Ibid.* Maclaine also remarked concerning a [Judge?] Grimke that he had done well, but "He is not a Burke."

[42]Burke to AEdanus Burke [?], August 4, 1783, Burke Papers, SDAH.

[43]Burke to unknown correspondent, November 9, 1783, *Ibid.*, SHC. This is the last piece of correspondence from Burke.

[44]*Ibid.*

[45]William Hooper to James Iredell, January 4, 1784, McRee, *Life and Correspondence of James Iredell,* II, 83-84. Iredell also commented that Burke was "wife hungry," Iredell to his wife, November, 1783, *Ibid.*, II, 26.

[46]Archibald Maclaine to George Hooper, December 16, 1783, William Hooper Collection, SHC.

[47]William Hooper to James Iredell, January 4, 1784, McRee, *Life and Correspondence of James Iredell,* II, 82. Mary Burke to James Phillips, February 4, 1852, Burke Papers, SHC. Mary Burke said that her father "died & was interred there [Orange County] 2d December 1783."

[48]*Ibid.*

[49]*Ibid.*

[50]*Ibid.*

[51]*Ibid.*

[52]*Ibid.*

[53]James Hogg to unknown correspondent, no date, David Swain Papers, 1763-1785, SDAH. This was probably to Willie Jones. Hogg expressed fears that funds designated for payment of debts are far from sufficient. Hogg also reported that Burke owed money for several other tracts and for a house in Hillsborough which he had bought. Burke still owed for the horse he borrowed at General Greene's camp after he escaped. Guardians of Mary Burke vs. Polly and George Doherty, Court of Equity, Hillsborough District, Bar Docket for October 1792, SHC To the Honourable General Assembly, The Petition of James Hogg Executor of Thomas Burke, Esq.,decd., November 13, 1789, Burke Papers, SHC. See also Burke's Will, November 14, 1783, *Ibid.*, SHC.

[54]Jesse Benton to unknown correspondent, April 3, 1786, Thomas Clay Papers, Library of Congress, Washington, D.C.

[55]Mary Burke to James Phillips, February 4, 1852, Burke Papers, SHC. J. de Roulhac Hamilton, "Governor Thomas Burke," *North Carolina Booklet* (October, 1906), 119.

[56]Richard Henry Lee, *Letters of a Federal Farmer*, in Paul Leicester Ford (ed.), *Pamphlets on the Constitution of the United States, Published during its Discussion by the People 1787-1788* (Brooklyn: privately printed, 1888), 319-321.

[57]James Wilson, "Substance of an Address to a Meeting of the Citizens of Philadelphia," *Ibid.*, 156.

[58]Jesse Benton to unknown correspondent, June 29, 1788, Thomas Clay Papers, Library of Congress.

[59]Archibald Maclaine to George Hooper, December 23, 1783, William Hooper Collection, SHC.

BIBLIOGRAPHY

Manuscripts

Southern Historical Collection, University of North Carolina, Chapel Hill.

The Thomas Burke Papers, 1763-1789

The Thomas Burke Papers in the Southern Historical Collection, microfilm edition prepared by the SHC and the National Historical Commission, 1965-1967

William R. Davie Papers

William A. Graham Papers

Cornelius Harnett Collection

The Hayes Collection (microfilm of collection at Hayes near Edenton, North Carolina)

The James Hogg Papers

George Hooper Collection

William Hooper Collection

Charles E. Johnson Collection

David L. Swain Collection

State Department of Archives and History, Raleigh.

Thomas Burke Paper, 1763-1852

Richard Bennehan Letters

Thomas Addison Emmet Collection (transcripts of papers in the New York Public Library)

Hayes Collection (transcripts of collection at Hayes near Edenton, North Carolina)

Samuel Johnston Papers

Miscellaneous Papers, 1755-1788

Thomas Penn Papers

David Swain Papers

John Williams Papers

Duke University Library, Durham.

Thomas Burke Papers

Henry Laurens Papers

Diary of Eneas Reeves

Historical Society of Pennsylvania, Philadelphia.

Emlen Collection, Letters and Documents 1715-1855

Simon Gratz Collection

Charles Francis Jenkins Collections

North Carolina Manuscripts

Penn Papers

Wayne Manuscripts

Library of Congress, Washington, D.C.

Thomas Clay Papers

National Archives, Washington, D.C.

Papers of the Continental Congress (microfilm)

Virginia State Library, Richmond, Virginia.

Tazewell Papers

G. Burke Johnston Collection, Blacksburg, Virginia

Thomas Burke Papers

Newspapers

The Cape Fear Mercury (Wilmington).

The North Carolina Gazette (New Bern).

Paulson's *Pennsylvania Packet or General Adver-
tiser* (Philadelphia).

Pennsylvania Evening Post (Philadelphia).

The Pennsylvania Journal (Philadelphia).

Purdie and Dixon's *Virginia Gazette* (Williamsburg).

Rind's *Virginia Gazette* (Williamsburg).

Published Sources

Adams, Charles Francis (ed.). *The Works of John
Adams, Second President of the United States:
With a Life of the Author, Notes and Illus-
trations.* 10 vols. Boston: Little, Brown
& Co., 1850-1856. Vols. II and IV.

Ballagh, James Curtis (ed.). *The Letters of Richard Henry Lee.* 2 vols. New York: The Macmillan Co., 1911. Vol. I.

Boyd, Julian P. (ed.). *The Papers of Thomas Jefferson.* 17 vols. Princeton: Princeton
University Press, 1950. Vol. II.

Burnett, Edmund (ed. and comp.). *Letters of Members of the Continental Congress.* 8 vols.
Washington: Carnegie Institute, 1921-1936.

Butterfield, Lyman H. (ed.). *The Diary and Autobiography of John Adams.* Series 1 of the
Adams Papers. 14 vols. Cambridge: The
Belknap Press of the Harvard University Press,
1961, Vol. III.

Clark, Walter (ed. and comp.). *The State Records
of North Carolina.* 20 vols. Raleigh: State
of North Carolina, 1886-1907.

"Extracts from the Diary of Mrs. Anne Warder,"
Pennsylvania Magazine of History and Biography, XVII (1893), 444-461.

Fanning, David. *The Narrative of David Fanning.*
New York and Richmond: Reprinted for Joseph
Sabin, 1865.

Fitzpatrick, John O. (ed.). *The Writings of
George Washington, From the Original Manuscript Sources, 1745-1799.* 39 vols. Washington, D.C.: U.S. Government Printing
Office, 1931-1944. Vols. IX, XI, XVIII.

Force, Peter (ed.). *The American Archives.* 9
vols. Washington, D.C.: Prepared and published under the authority of Congress, 1853.

Ford, Paul Leicester (ed. and comp.). *Pamphlets
on the Constitution of the United States,
Published during its Discussion by the People
1787-88.* Brooklyn: Privately printed, 1888.

Ford, Worthington and Hunt, Gaillard *et al.* (eds.).
*The Journals of the Continental Congress,
1774-1789.* 34 vols. Washington, D.C.: U.S.
Government Printing Office, 1904-1937. Vols.
VII-XXII.

Hall, W.L. and McIlwaine, Henry R. (eds.). *Journals of the Council of the State of Virginia.*
3 vols. Richmond: Published by the Virginia
State Library, 1931-1952. Vol. III.

Hammond, Otis G. (ed.). *The Papers of General John
Sullivan.* Vols. XI and XV of *Collections of
the New Hampshire Historical Society.* Concord:
Published for the Society, 1824-1929. Vol.
XII.

Hutchinson, William T. and Rachal, William M.E.
(eds.). *The Papers of James Madison.* 6 vols.
Chicago: University of Chicago, 1962-1969.
Vol. IV.

Isham, Charles (ed.). *Deane Papers.* Vols. XIX-
XXIII. New York: Printed for the Society,
1887-1891. Vol. XXI.

McIlwaine, Henry R. (ed.). *Official Letters of the Governors of the State of Virginia.* 3 vols. Richmond: Published by the Virginia State Library, 1926-1929. Vol. III.

McRee, John G. *The Life and Correspondence of James Iredell, One of the Associate Judges of the Supreme Court of the United States.* 2 vols. New York: D. Appleton & Co., 1857-1858.

Meng, John J. (ed.). *Dispatches and Instructions of Conrad Alexandre Gerard, 1778-1780.* Baltimore: John Hopkins Press, 1939.

Saunders, William (ed. and comp.). *The Colonial Records of North Carolina.* 10 vols. Raleigh: State of North Carolina, 1886-1890. Vols. IX and X.

Smyth, J.F.D. *A Tour of the United States of America.* 2 vols. London: G. Robinson, 1784. Vol. I.

Walser, Richard (ed. and comp.). *The Poems of Governor Thomas Burke of North Carolina.* Raleigh: State Department of Archives and History, 1961.

Warville, J.P. Brissot de. *New Travels in the United States.* Edited and translated by Durand Echeverria. Cambridge: The Belknap Press of Harvard University Press, 1964.

Books

Aldridge, Alfred O. *Man of Reason, the Life of Thomas Paine.* Philadelphia: Lippincott, 1959.

Ashe, Samuel A'Court. *History of North Carolina.* 3 vols. Greensboro: Charles G. Van Noppen, Publisher, 1908.

Biographical Directory of the American Congress,
1774-1927. Washington: U.S. Government
Printing Office, 1928.

Burnett, Edmund. *The Continental Congress.* New
York: The Macmillan Co., 1941.

Cappon, Lester and Duff, Stella. *The Virginia*
Gazette Index. 2 vols. Williamsburg: Institute of Early American History and Culture, 1950.

Chitwood, Oliver P. *Richard Henry Lee, Statesman*
of the Revolution. Morgantown: West Virginia University Library, 1967.

Connor, R.D.W. *Cornelius Harnett, an Essay in*
North Carolina History. Raleigh: Edwards
and Broughton, 1909.

Corbitt, D.L. (ed. and comp.). *Calendars of Manu-*
script Collections. Vol. 14. Publications
of the North Carolina Historical Commission.
Raleigh: Edwards & Broughton Company, 1926.

Crabtree, Elizabeth G. (comp.). *Guide to Private*
Manuscript Collections in the North Carolina
State Archives. Raleigh: Published by the
State Department of Archives and History,
1964.

Crittenden, Charles C. *The Commerce of North*
Carolina, 1763-1789. New Haven: Yale University Press, 1936.

DeMond, Robert O. *The Loyalists in North Carolina*
During the Revolution. Durham: Duke University Press, 1940.

Douglass, Elisha P. *Rebels and Democrats, the*
Struggle for Equal Political Rights and
Majority Rule During the American Revolution.
Chapel Hill: University of North Carolina
Press, 1953.

Evans, Charles. *American Bibliography.* 12 vols.
New York: Peter Smith, 1941 (first published in 1909).

Ferguson, Adam. *An Essay on the History of Civil Society.* Edinburgh: Edinburgh University Press, 1966 (first published in 1767).

Ferguson, E. James. *The Power of the Purse, A History of American Public Finance, 1776-1790.* Chapel Hill: Published for the Institute of Early American History and Culture by the University of North Carolina Press, 1961.

Fleming, Thomas J. *Beat the Last Drum, The Siege of Yorktown.* New York: St. Martin's Press, 1963.

Gough, John W. *John Locke's Political Philosophy.* Oxford: Clarendon Press, 1956.

Guide to the Manuscript Collections in the Archives of the North Carolina Historical Collection. Raleigh: North Carolina Historical Records, 1942.

Handbook of Manuscripts in the Library of Congress. Washington, D.C.: Government Printing Office, 1918.

Hatch, Louis C. *The Administration of the American Revolutionary Army.* Vol. X of the Harvard Historical Studies. New York: Longmans, Green, 1904.

Huizinga, Johan. *Homo Ludens.* London: Roy Publishers, 1950.

Jensen, Merrill. *The Articles of Confederation.* Madison: University of Wisconsin Press, 1940.

Johnson, Allen and Malone, Dumas (eds.). *Dictionary of American Biography.* 20 vols. New York: Charles Scribner's Sons, 1928.

Johnson, Victor L. *The Administration of the American Commissariat during the Revolutionary War.* Philadelphia: University of Pennsylvania Press, 1941.

279

Jones, Joseph S. *A Defence of the Revolutionary History of the State of North Carolina from the Aspersions of Mr. Jefferson.* Raleigh: Turner and Hughes, 1834.

Katz, Elihu and Lazarfield, Paul. *Personal Influence, the Part Played by the People in the Flow of Mass Communications.* Glencoe: Free Press of Glencoe, 1955.

Kuhn, Thomas. *The Structure of Scientific Revolutions.* Chicago: University of Chicago Press 1962.

Lefler, Hugh and Newsome, Albert R. *North Carolina.* Chapel Hill: University of North Carolina Press, 1954.

Locke, John. *An Essay Concerning the True Original, Extent and End of Civil Government.* Ernest Rhys (ed.). *Two Treatises of Civil Government.* New York: E.P. Dutton, 1949.

Lovejoy, Arthur O. *Reflections on Human Nature.* Baltimore: John Hopkins Press, 1961.

Meier, Richard. *A Communications Theory of Urban Growth.* Cambridge: M.I.T. Press, 1962.

Merrens, Harry R. *Colonial North Carolina in the Eighteenth Century.* Chapel Hill: University of North Carolina Press, 1964.

Mooney, James P. and Reiley, Alan C. *The Principles of Organization.* New York: Harper and Brothers, Publishers, 1939.

Nash, Frank. *Hillsboro Colonial and Revolutionary.* Raleigh: Edwards and Broughton, 1903.

Palmer, William P. (ed.). *Calendar of Virginia State Papers.* 11 vols. Richmond: James E. Goode, 1881.

Rank, Hugh. *The North Carolina Continentals.* Chapel Hill: The University of North Carolina Press, 1971.

Raper, Charles L. *North Carolina, a Study in English Colonial Government.* New York: The Macmillan Co., 1904.

Robinson, Blackwell P. *William R. Davie.* Chapel Hill: University of North Carolina Press, 1957.

Russell, Phillips. *North Carolina in the Revolutionary War.* Charlotte: Heritage Printers, 1965.

Sanders, Jennings B. *Evolution of the Executive Departments of the Continental Congress.* Chapel Hill: University of North Carolina Press, 1935.

Scharf, John and Wescott, Thomas. *History of Philadelphia.* 3 vols. Philadelphia: Everts & Company, 1884. Vol. II.

Small, Albion W. *The Beginnings of American Nationality, the Constitutional Relations Between the Colonies and States from 1774-1789.* Baltimore: Johns Hopkins University, 1890.

Sosin, Jack M. *The Revolutionary Frontier 1763-1783.* New York: Holt, Rinehart and Winston, 1967.

Stark, Werner. *Montesquieu, Pioneer of the Sociology of Knowledge.* London: Routledge & Kegan Paul Ltd., 1960.

Swem, E.G. *Virginia Historical Index.* 2 vols. Roanoke: Stone Printing and Mfg. Co., 1934-1936.

Sydnor, Charles S. *Gentlemen Freeholders, Political Practices in Washington's Virginia.* Chapel Hill: Published for the Institute of Early American History and Culture by the University of North Carolina Press, 1952.

Treacy, M.F. *Prelude to Yorktown, The Southern Campaign of Nathanael Greene 1780-1781.* Chapel Hill: University of North Carolina Press, 1963.

281

Ubbelohde, Carl. *The Vice-Admiralty Courts and the American Revolution*. Chapel Hill: Published for the Institute of Early American History and Culture by the University of North Carolina Press, 1960.

Van Doren, Carl. *The Secret History of the American Revolution*. New York: The Viking Press, 1941.

Vattel, Emmerich de. *The Law of Nations; or Principles of the Law of Nature Applied to the Conduct and Affairs of Nations and Sovereigns*. Dublin: L. White, 1797. Published in the French in 1773.

Ver Steeg, Clarence L. *Robert Morris, Revolutionary Financier*. Philadelphia: University of Pennsylvania Press, 1954.

Wallace, David D. *The Life of Henry Laurens, with a Sketch of the Life of Lieutenant-Colonel John Laurens*. New York: Russell & Russell, 1915.

Wallace, Willard M. *Appeal to Arms, a Military History of the American Revolution*. New York: Harper & Brothers, 1951.

Weber, Max. *The Theory of Social and Economic Organization*. Translated by A.M. Henderson and Talcott Parsons. New York: The Free Press of Glencoe, 1964.

Whittemore, Charles P. *A General of the Revolution, John Sullivan of New Hampshire*. New York: Columbia University Press, 1961.

Wides, Harry Emerson. *Anthony Wayne, Trouble Shooter of the American Revolution*. New York: Harcourt, Brace and Co., 1941.

Wiley, Basil. *The Eighteenth Century Background*. London: Chatto and Windus, 1940.

Wood, George. *Congressional Control of Foreign Relations During the American Revolution 1774-1789*. Allentown: H.R. Haas, 1919.

Articles and Other

Thomas P. Abernethy. "Commercial Activities of Silas Deane in France." *American Historical Review*, XXIX (1934), 477-485.

Mary Carmelita Barrett. "Thomas Burke, Governor of North Carolina." Masters Thesis, Catholic University of America, 1946.

Julian P. Boyd. "Silas Deane, Death by a Kindly Teacher of Treason." *The William and Mary Quarterly*, Series 3, XVI (1959), 165-187, 319-342, 515-550.

Randolph B. Campbell. "The Case of the 'Three Friends,' an Incident in Maritime Regulation during the Revolutionary War." *The Virginia Magazine of History and Biography*, LXXIV (1966), 190-209.

Hampton L. Carson. "The Case of the Sloop 'Active.'" *The Pennsylvania Magazine of History and Biography*, XVI (1892), 385-398.

Elisha Douglass. "Thomas Burke, Disillusioned Democrat." *The North Carolina Historical Review*, XXVI (1949), 150-186.

Robert Ganyard. "North Carolina during the American Revolution, the First Phase, 1744-1777." Ph.D. Dissertation, Duke University, 1962.

J. DeRoulhac Hamilton. "Governor Thomas Burke." *The North Carolina Historical Booklet*, VI (1906-07), 103-122.

Herbert Henderson. "Political Factions in the Continental Congress." Ph.D. Dissertation, Columbia University, 1962.

Patrick Henderson. "Smallpox and Patriotism, the Norfolk Riots, 1768-1769." *The Virginia Magazine of History and Biography*, LXXIII (1965), 413-424.

Sheldon Koesy. "Continuity and Change in North
    Carolina." Ph.D. Dissertation, Duke Univer-
    sity, 1963.

Helen E. Royer. "The Role of the Continental
    Congress in the Prosecution of the American
    Revolution in Pennsylvania." Ph.D. Disser-
    tation, Pennsylvania State University, 1960.

Jennings B. Sanders. "Thomas Burke in the Contin-
    ental Congress." *The North Carolina Histori-
    cal Review*, IX (1932), 22-37.

Ruth F. Sutton. "Thomas Burke." Masters Thesis,
    University of North Carolina, 1949.

John S. Watterson III. "News and Propaganda from
    the Battles of Concord and Lexington." Mas-
    ters Thesis, Western Reserve University, 1967.

_____. "The Ordeal of Governor Burke." *The
North Carolina Historical Review*, XLVIII (1971)
95-117.

_____. "Revolutionary Nonconformist, Thomas
Burke of North Carolina." *South Dakota History*, VI (1976), 334-352.

_____. "Poetic Justice; or an Ill-fated Epic
by Governor Thomas Burke." *The North Carolina
Historical Review*, LV (1978), 339-346.

Lee, Arthur, 132-136

Lee, Charles, 91, 94

Lee, Francis Lightfoot, 57

Lee, Henry, 149

Lee, Richard Henry, 50, 53, 57, 63, 76-78, 131, 166, 215

Leslie, Alexander, 188-190, 203

Lillington, Alexander, 180, 198

Lincoln, Benjamin, 115

Livingston, Robert, 159

Locke, John, 4, 33, 102-104

Lovell, James, 85, 98, 160-161

Loyalists, 175-176, 183-185, 194-196, 198

Luzerne, Chevalier de, 164

Maclaine, Archibald, 213, 216

McCarrel, Frances, 168

McCauley, William, 199

McKean, Thomas, 163

McNeil, Hector, 181, 185-186

Madison, James, 139, 158-159, 161

Marshall, John, 120

Martin, Alexander, 190-191, 199, 204, 213

Martin, Josiah, 16, 20, 23-24, 28-30

Maryland, 52, 57, 71, 81-82, 144, 154, 167

Matthews, John, 167

Military Affairs in Congress, 54-56, 72-74, 78, 80, 84-85, 112-113

Miller, Andrew, 26-27, 30, 211

Moore's Creek Bridge, 35, 71

Morgan, Daniel, 167

Morris, Gouverneur, 131

Morris, Robert, 110, 135, 149-151, 157, 165-167, 169, ff

Nash, Abner, 170, 174, 179

National Authority, 54-56, 64-66, 75, 120-121, 139, 142-145, 164-166

New Jersey, 51, 81, 89, 157

Norfolk, Virginia, 8-21, 35, 169, 201

North Carolina, congresses, 25-46

North Carolina, Constitution, 38, 44-45

North Carolina, General Assembly, 46, 72, 74, 90, 101-102, 170, 172-176, 198-200, 211

North Carolina, military forces, 72-75, 78, 82, 112, 115, 179, 186-187, 197-198

See Hillsborough and Orange County

Notes on the Confederation, 64-66

Olmstead, Gideon, 116-117

Orange County, North Carolina, 17-18, 32, 40-46, 54, 108, 215

Ould, Fielding, 1-2, 5

Paca, William, 117, 134, 159